A DECEMBER VISION

Charles Dickens

A DECEMBER VISION

And Other Thoughtful Writings

Edited by Neil Philip and Victor Neuburg

CONTINUUM ● NEW YORK

For my brother John

NP

For my daughter Caroline

VN

A NOTE ON THE TEXTS

The journal articles are reprinted as they first appeared, though we have sparingly modernised minor features of spelling and punctuation where the unaltered originals would needlessly distract, or where there are inconsistencies of style. We have used the journals for texts of the three articles – "On Duty with Inspector Field", "Down with the Tide" and "A Walk in a Workhouse" – which were included by Dickens in *Reprinted Pieces*, though adopting one stylistic change – "thirsty" for the original "thusty" – in "A Walk in a Workhouse".

"A Visit to Newgate" was first printed in *Sketches by Boz*: unlike the journal essays, it was extensively revised by Dickens in later years. He expunged many adjectives and altered punctuation. We have followed his final text, but noted significant alterations in the margin.

1987
The Continuum Publishing Company
370 Lexington Avenue
New York, N.Y. 10017

Conceived, designed and produced
by The Albion Press Ltd
9 Stewart Street, New Hinksey, Oxford OX1 4RH

Designer: Emma Bradford
Editor: Jane Havell
Picture Researcher: Elizabeth Loving

First published in 1986 by William Collins Sons & Co. Ltd, London
© Editorial matter: Neil Philip and Victor Neuburg 1986
© Volume: The Albion Press Ltd 1986

Typeset by Dataset, Oxford
Printed and bound in Hong Kong by
South China Printing Co.

LIBRARY OF CONGRESS CATALOGING-IN-PUBLICATION DATA

Dickens, Charles, 1812–1870
A December vision, and other thoughtful writings.
  Includes index.
  Contents: Dickens as a journalist——Dickens as a social critic——A December vision——[etc.]
  1. Social problems——Literary collections. 2. London (England)——Social conditions——Literary collections.
  3. Poor——England——London——Literary collections. I. Philip, Neil. II. Neuburg, Victor E. III. Title.
PR4553.P45 1987   823'.8   87–6682
ISBN 0–8264–0392–1

TITLE-PAGE ILLUSTRATION: *tumbling crossing-sweepers exhibiting their skill, by Phiz, 1858.*

CONTENTS

DICKENS AS A JOURNALIST

Dickens the novelist needs no introduction. Dickens the journalist has been almost forgotten. Yet journalism was always important to Dickens; he was a working journalist all his life, and his social investigations – of which some of the liveliest are selected in this book – would make him an important figure had he never written a word of fiction. The sharp-eyed observation and forceful lucid prose of Dickens's best journal essays make them quintessential literature by Ezra Pound's definition: "news that STAYS news". And as well as illuminating dark corners of Victorian life, Dickens's essays feed in to our reading of his novels. Each supports the other, as they did in Dickens's own life.

Charles Dickens in 1849, when he was planning Household Words.

Charles Dickens was born at Landport near Portsmouth in 1812. His childhood was marred by the shame of his feckless father's imprisonment for debt, and the humiliation of his own degrading employment at Warren's Blacking Warehouse. In later years he drew fruitfully on this period for his novels, but kept the reality a secret from everyone but his close friend and later biographer, John Forster. In 1827 Dickens found employment as a solicitor's clerk, and shortly afterwards as a shorthand reporter at the law court, Doctor's Commons. He worked for the *Mirror of Parliament* and the *True Sun*, began to publish stories in the *Monthly Magazine*, and in 1834 became a reporter on the *Morning Chronicle*.

Charles Mackay, a colleague on the *Morning Chronicle*, recalled that as a parliamentary reporter, Dickens "had the reputation of being the most rapid, the most accurate, and the most trustworthy reporter then engaged on the London press". However, it was clear to all that Dickens, despite these skills, would not remain long in such a limiting position. In 1836 his reprinted essays *Sketches by Boz* (many of them from the *Evening Chronicle* and *Bell's Life in London*) and his first novel *Pickwick Papers* had an astonishing double success, and Dickens became at once, as he was to remain until his death in 1870, an important figure in the London literary world.

While *Pickwick* was still proceeding, Dickens took on the editorship of a new monthly literary magazine, *Bentley's Miscellany*, and began publishing in it his second novel, *Oliver Twist*. The *Miscellany* was a light-hearted hotch-potch. It, too, was a success, but the two years of Dickens's editorship were marred by constant financial wrangles with the journal's proprietor, Richard Bentley. Dickens resented Bentley's tendency to interfere, and the relationship came to an acrimonious end. Dickens wrote *Nicholas Nickleby* in monthly parts for the publishers Chapman and Hall, and in 1840 launched with them the weekly journal *Master Humphrey's*

Clock, in which he published *The Old Curiosity Shop* and *Barnaby Rudge. Master Humphrey's Clock* had been conceived as another miscellany, though this time chiefly – and, as it turned out, wholly – by Dickens. It was a disaster, and only the headlong plunge into another novel saved it. The whimsicality of Dickens's notion of "this old file in the queer house, opening the book by an account of himself, and, among his other peculiarities, of his affection for an old quaint queer-cased clock", was decidedly not to public taste, and Master Humphrey himself soon retired into the background.

The years 1841-45 were spent travelling in America and Italy, producing *American Notes* and *Pictures from Italy*, and writing *Martin Chuzzlewit, A Christmas Carol* and *The Chimes*. Throughout 1845 Dickens was involved in plans for a new liberal daily paper, of which he was to be editor. Besides the printers, Bradbury and Evans, the chief financial backer was to be Joseph Paxton, later architect of the Great Exhibition of 1851. Dickens engaged his staff at high rates, and put the fear of God into his established rivals; *The Times* responded with a savage review of his admittedly weak Christmas book, *The Cricket on the Hearth*.

The first edition of the *Daily News* was published on Wednesday 21 January 1846. An editorial announced:

> The Principles advocated by THE DAILY NEWS will be Principles of Progress and Improvement; of Education, Civil and Religious Liberty, and Equal Legislation; Principles, such as its conductors believe the advancing spirit of the time requires: the condition of the country demands: and Justice, Reason and Experience legitimately sanction.

This is ringing stuff, but the paper itself was badly produced and generally dull. It was all a terrible mistake, and Dickens, recognising this, cut his losses after just seventeen days, handing over the editorship to John Forster.

Instead of the powerful newspaper editor, the Dickens of the late 1840s was pure novelist, producing *Dombey and Son* and *David Copperfield*. But he still hankered after journalism, and all these various attempts and false starts proved invaluable when he planned a new weekly publication. Its main purpose, he wrote to Mrs. Gaskell, was to be "the raising up of those that are down, and the general improvement of our social condition". He cast about for a title, finally settling on "*Household Words*. This is a very pretty name."

The first edition of *Household Words* was published on Saturday 30 March 1850, price 2*d*. It contained the first part of Mrs. Gaskell's *Lizzie Leigh*, and miscellaneous articles and verse on such topics as "Valentine's Day at the Post Office" and "The Amusements of the People". It set the tone for what was to come. Historical and supernatural anecdotes; jocular occasional pieces; informative essays on scientific or commercial matters; some fiction; some verse: these were the staples of *Household Words*, alongside the sharper ventures into social comment or investigative reporting which now make the journal such an

Boz drawn by Phiz in 1837, for a flysheet advertising Bentley's Miscellany. *The original title for this journal was to be* Wits' Miscellany; *when the final choice was made, Dickens's friends unkindly asked why it was necessary to go to the other extreme.*

important source of evidence for historians. Crime and punishment, poverty, education, public health, public order are constant themes. *Household Words* campaigned for safety measures to protect industrial workers, for better education of the poor, for the reform of the laws of Patent, and the courts of Equity. These concerns are also the concerns of Dickens's fiction, but are dealt with very differently. One of the aims of this book is to trace the interpenetration of journalism and fiction, as each supports and enriches the other.

Although its nineteen volumes contain Dickens's *Hard Times*, Mrs. Gaskell's *North and South* and Wilkie Collins's *The Dead Secret, Household Words* was not conceived as a vehicle for Dickens's own fiction or for anyone else's. It was a radical paper, filled with Dickens's own indignant curiosity. Like him, it had no ideology, no party line. Dickens's politics were the simple politics of the child who sees an injustice and cries, "It's not fair." As Dickens writes in *Great Expectations*:

> In the little world in which children have their existence whosoever brings
> them up, there is nothing so finely perceived and so finely felt, as injustice
> .... Within myself, I had sustained, from my babyhood, a perpetual
> conflict with injustice.

This lack of a defined political creed – which had hampered Dickens's efforts to edit the *Daily News* – was to bring positive benefits to *Household Words*. Dickens was neither doctrinaire nor highbrow, and his tastes coincided neatly with those of his comfortably concerned middle-class readership. A frequent contributor to *Household Words*, George Augustus Sala, recalled:

> What he liked to talk about was the latest new piece at the theatres, the
> latest exciting trial or police case, the latest social craze or social swindle,
> and especially the latest murder and the newest thing in ghosts. . . . He
> frequently touched on political subjects – always from that which was then
> a strong Radical point of view, but which at present [1894] I imagine
> would be thought more Conservative than Democratic; but his
> conversation, I am bound to say, once for all, did not rise above the
> amusing commonplaces of a very shrewd, clever man of the world, with
> the heartiest of hatred for shams and humbugs.

"KEEP HOUSEHOLD WORDS IMAGINATIVE!" was Dickens's constant watchword, and by doing so he caught and held a large audience which was exposed, through the imagination, to a crusading social indignation which was all the more effective for its independence and wit. Its twenty-four double-columned, unillustrated pages of "instruction and entertainment" sold about 40,000 copies a week.

Dickens brought *Household Words* to a close in 1859, replacing it with an entirely new journal, *All the Year Round*, which, as far as editor, contributors and readership were concerned, was entirely familiar. The reason for the change was the predictable one of a squabble with the publishers, Bradbury and Evans, who responded with their own copycat magazine, *Once a Week*.

While *Household Words* and *All the Year Round* are very similar,

William Henry Wills (1810–80), Dickens's sub-editor and one of his closest friends in later years.

there are crucial differences. *All the Year Round* is a much more conventional, more literary affair than its predecessor. Its selling point was its serialised fiction: Wilkie Collins's *The Woman in White, No Name* and *The Moonstone*; Dickens's own *A Tale of Two Cities* and *Great Expectations*. The mixture is much as before, but the social comment is no longer so incisive nor so impassioned. The bite has gone.

Dickens achieved in his own day a considerable reputation as an editor, and a newspaper magnate of a later period, Lord Northcliffe, pronounced him the greatest magazine editor of his own or any other age. His editorial methods were autocratic. His name alone appeared: both magazines announced on every page that they were "Conducted by Charles Dickens". The stamp of his personality and views marked the contents. Not only did Dickens himself revise and repoint many contributions, but he gathered together a nucleus of young men who fell under his spell and imitated his tricks of style, his comic exaggeration, his inclination to turn individual cases into general examples.

The upshot of this was that anything good in the magazines was automatically attributed to Dickens, much to the chagrin of up-and-coming young contributors such as Sala. Nevertheless Dickens was held in particular affection and respect by those who worked for him, and was notable for his wish to encourage talent rather than reputation. Sala recalled:

> the manuscript once handed in, I seldom, if ever, saw a proof thereof. First, Mr. W. H. Wills was the carefullest of proof-readers, and did everything necessary in the way of cutting down; and next, Dickens took the revises in hand himself, and very often surprised me by the alterations – always for the better – which he made, now in the title, and now in the matter, of my "copy".

William Henry Wills, mentioned here, was Dickens's sub-editor, responsible for the day-to-day running of the journals and for much of the practical editing. Wills had contributed to *Bentley's Miscellany*, helped found *Punch*, worked on *Chambers's Journal*, and had been first Dickens's and then Forster's secretary on the *Daily News*. Dickens's letters to him give a lively picture of the two at work. Dickens is continually urging lightness of touch, and constantly bubbling with ideas for articles, with comments, complaints and encouragement. They show how much sheer hard work supported that "elegance of fancy" which Dickens prized. Sending back his revision of Wills's police article "The Metropolitan Protectives" (*Household Words*, 26 April 1851), Dickens writes, "I have done all I could – sat at it nine hours without stirring – and hope it will come out well."

An essay by Henry Morley and Dickens in *Household Words* on 16 April 1853, "H. W.", gave the journal's readers an account of office procedures, and particularly of the plague of unsolicited material: "In the last year, we read nine hundred manuscripts, of which eleven were available for this journal, after being entirely re-written. In the same period, we received and answered two

A cruel cartoon of Dickens on a wedding ring at the time of his separation from his wife, and the consequent change from Household Words *to* All the Year Round. *Forster had a hard time dissuading Dickens from calling the new magazine* Household Harmony.

thousand letters . . ." Dickens wrote in exasperation to Wills of "the nine hundred and ninety-nine thousandth Colonial ass who wanted us to print in *H. W.* some saw-dusty literature out of the *Port-Something Journal*."

The actual contributors to Dickens's weekly journals were not generally famous names, or great writers and thinkers. They were bright young men eager to make their mark but willing to submit to the Dickensian yoke. Although the 390 identified contributors to *Household Words* include ninety women, only Mrs. Gaskell and perhaps Harriet Martineau (with whom Dickens argued bitterly and publicly in 1856) vitally affected the tone of the journal. The hard core of contributors comprised Dickens himself, Wills, Henry Morley (later founder of Morley College), Richard Henry (later Hengist) Horne, George Augustus Sala, Wilkie Collins, and about a score of others. These included many people who had worked with Dickens on previous ventures. Writers such as Sidney Laman Blanchard, William Blanchard Jerrold, Dudley Costello and Frederick Knight Hunt had all worked on the *Daily News*.

Many contributors to *Household Words* and *All the Year Round* published collections of their essays. Dickens himself gathered selections of articles from *Household Words* in *Reprinted Pieces*, and from *All the Year Round* in *The Uncommercial Traveller*. Henry Morley's *Gossip* (1857), Sala's *Gaslight and Daylight* (1859), W. H. Wills's *Old Leaves* (1860), Blanchard Jerrold's *The Chronicles of the Crutch* (1860), Harriet Martineau's *Health, Husbandry and Handicraft* (1861) and Wilkie Collins's *My Miscellanies* (1863) are typical of such books.

Dickens's uncollected sole contributions to *Household Words* were printed by B. W. Matz in the two-volume *Miscellaneous Papers* published in 1908 and attached to various collected editions of his works. His collaborative contributions, mostly written with Wills but also with Morley, Horne and others, have been meticulously edited by Harry Stone in *Uncollected Writings of Charles Dickens* (2 vols., 1968). The authorship of *Household Words* articles can be ascertained from the Office Book kept by Wills, which forms the basis of Anne Lohrli's thorough guide to the journal's contents and contributors. Unfortunately a similar key does not exist for *All the Year Round*, though all Dickens's important contributions are known.

The refusal to "write *down* to any part of our audience", and the constant exhortation to beguile rather than bludgeon the reader, make the volumes of *Household Words* and *All the Year Round* surprisingly lively and compelling reading today. Dickens's own contributions, particularly those on social questions such as the essays reprinted in this book, reveal a great writer at the height of his power, supremely confident in approach, tone and achievement. They remind us that the period of these journals was also that of his most many-layered and potent fictions, *Bleak House, Little Dorrit, Our Mutual Friend*, and the unfinished *Edwin Drood*: the sombre masterpieces of his mature December vision.

N. P.

OPPOSITE: "Boys to Mend", a typical Household Words *leading article, reproduced actual size. Co-written by Dickens and Henry Morley, it describes a visit to the Philanthropic Farm School, Red Hill, East Surrey.*

" Familiar in their Mouths as HOUSEHOLD WORDS."—Shakespeare.

HOUSEHOLD WORDS.

A WEEKLY JOURNAL.

CONDUCTED BY CHARLES DICKENS.

N°. 129.]　　　　SATURDAY, SEPTEMBER 11, 1852.　　　　[Price 2*d.*

BOYS TO MEND.

Umbrellas to mend, and chairs to mend, and clocks to mend, are called in our streets daily. Who shall count up the numbers of thousands of children to mend, in and about those same streets, whose voice of ignorance cries aloud as the voice of wisdom once did, and is as little regarded ; who go to pieces for the want of mending, and die unrepaired !

People are naturally glad to catch at any plea, in mitigation of a great national wickedness. Many good persons will urge, now-a-days, as to this neglected business of boy-mending, "O ! but there are the Ragged Schools !" Admitting the full merit of the ragged schools ; rendering the highest praise to those disinterested and devoted teachers, of both sexes, who labour in them ; urging the consideration of their claims on all who pass through the streets of great towns with eyes in their heads, and awakened hearts in their breasts ; we still must not disguise the plain fact that they are, at best, a slight and ineffectual palliative of an enormous evil. They want system, power, means, authority, experienced and thoroughly trained teachers. If the instruction of ordinary children be an art requiring such a peculiar combination of qualities and such sound discretion, that but few skilled persons arrive at perfection in it, how much more difficult is the instruction of those who, even if they be children in years, have more to unlearn than they have to learn ; whose ignorance has been coupled with constant evil education ; and among whose intellects there is no such thing as virgin soil to be found ! Good intentions alone, will never be a sufficient qualification for such a labour, while this world lasts. We have seen something of ragged schools from their first establishment, and have rarely seen one, free from very injudicious and mistaken teaching. And what they *can* do, is so little, relatively to the gigantic proportions of the monster with which they have to grapple, that if their existence were to be accepted as a sufficient excuse for leaving ill alone, we should hold it far better that they had never been.

Where, in England, is the public institution for the prevention of crime among that neglected class of youth to whom it is not second but first Nature ; who are born to nothing else, and bred to nothing else ? Where, for these, are the bolts and bars, *outside* the prison-door, which is so heavily fastened within ? Nowhere, to our knowledge. The next best thing—though there is a broad, deep gulf between the two—is an institution for the reformation of such young offenders. And to that, we made a visit on one of these last hot summer days.

A dull mist of heat had taken possession of the streets. Through the warm mist we roll in a warm omnibus. Over the parapet of London Bridge we see London in a heavy lump with the hot mist about it, and almost expect that St. Paul's presently will throw out a spark, and the whole town, like a firework, begin to fizz and crackle. There is nothing that we might not be permitted to expect as a result of heat, upon the hottest morning of the hottest dog-days within the memory of the oldest dog.

People who sit with us in the carriages of the Brighton train, wonder (and really not without occasion, as we ignorantly think) why a terminus must be built with a cover in the shape of an oven, and why it must bake batches of passengers in railway trains like cakes in tins. Now we are off, and it is cooler. We pass over the red, underdone surface of London, upon which the blacks are falling cruelly ; if London be now frying, it will make a dirty dish, we fancy. Here are market gardens, fields, hills, stations, woods, villages, and wayside inns. Here is Red Hill, where the train stops, and we get out.

There is a cluster of inns outside the station, and certain freeholders of East Surrey, warm with sun and politics, seek coolness in beer outside the inns. They are a little noisy ; but, passing between hedges we begin to toil up hill. The distant song of the freeholders is drowned by the nearer song of the thrush ; and the dog roses that make a roadside garden of each hedge, put our hearts in good humour with the dog-days. Every hedge is a garden. Where did we ever see more wild flowers clustered together ? There is a very California of honeysuckle. There are clumps of mallow, blossoming on hillocks beside every gate that leads into the corn fields ; there are yellow stars of the ranunculus, and crimson poppy blossoms, and the delicate peaked fairy hats of which Bindweed is ostensibly the

DICKENS AS A SOCIAL CRITIC

*George Cruikshank's title-
page illustration for the
Chapman and Hall edition
of* Sketches by Boz.

Sketches by Boz was published in book form on 7 February 1836,
the author's twenty-fourth birthday. Charles Dickens was then a
newspaper reporter and this was his first book. Its appearance
brought a number of favourable reviews, the majority of them
emphasising his knowledge of the subjects and the closeness of his
observation – qualities which were to bring to life many of the
social themes in his novels. There is no doubt at all that Dickens
himself was delighted by the reception of the *Sketches* – so much
so, in fact, that when the publisher William Hall called upon him
in Furnival's Inn just three days after publication, he felt confident
enough to make conditions to Hall about the proposed arrange-
ment for *Pickwick*.

Eventually *Pickwick* became a spectacular success, but even
before this Dickens had been anxious to give up his post on the
Morning Chronicle. He was tired of having to fit his writing into
the odd hours left to him after reporting duties had been done,
and he was wearied, too, with travelling across England at speed
and, above all, with the House of Commons. Accordingly he
resigned from the newspaper, but not before he had accepted, in
November 1836, the editorship of *Bentley's Miscellany*. In leaving
the hurly-burly of day-to-day reporting Dickens was making the
decision to devote his life to fiction and a more leisured kind
of journalism. The metamorphosis was entirely successful and,
although the editor of the *Chronicle* was furious at his resignation,
Dickens was able to look back in a letter to John Forster upon his
newspaper days and say, 'What gentlemen they all were to serve.'

A number of pieces in *Sketches* anticipated in a striking manner
Dickens's feeling for London, his knowledge of it, and his concern
with the social problems and issues of the day, all of which recur
in different ways and at varying levels of intensity throughout his
novels and in many of the shorter pieces he wrote for publication
in *Household Words* and elsewhere. While, however, his reputation
as a serious novelist is absolutely and rightly secure, his journalism
has not, in general, been so highly regarded, or even so widely
read, by posterity (partly, perhaps, because some of it has been
very hard to get at); and it seems not unreasonable to ask how
Dickens stands as a social critic.

Three qualities characterise his approach: restless curiosity,
enthusiasm and sympathy. All three are present in the best of his
journalism and in his novels. It will be remembered that in *Oliver
Twist, Hard Times, Bleak House* and *Little Dorrit* he launched fierce
attacks upon English institutions, and in all of them his sympathy
was with the underdog and with the hapless who were most likely
to suffer at the hands of society. Yet, as George Orwell has

pointed out, his working-class characters are not his best. He tends to sentimentalise or caricature them, and the most memorable, such as Bill Sikes, Sam Weller and Mrs. Gamp – a burglar, a valet and a midwife – are hardly representative of the working class as a whole. The Plornishes in *Little Dorrit* are perhaps the nearest he came to an adequate picture of a working-class family, while poor Stephen Blackpool in *Hard Times* remains his only portrait of an industrial worker.

Dickens's approach to social problems was essentially a moral one. He saw clearly enough how ordinary folk can suffer at the hands of the law, how the education they are offered fails them, how parliamentary government is more often than not irrelevant to their needs, and how they almost always experience economic exploitation. Nowhere, however, does he suggest how society could be changed, or its institutions reformed. Indeed, it is not necessarily the business of a creative artist to propose radical and practical remedies for the evils of society, so that in this sense Dickens was apolitical. What he does superbly well is to awaken his reader's sensibilities to the awfulness of some of the things he saw, and he draws our attention to the ways in which human beings – often small children – suffer intensely while yet, in most cases, retaining their innate sense of human dignity, and often their sense of humour as well. This is no bad lesson to learn; but when Dickens comes near to suggesting palliatives for the evils that he is describing he is at his weakest, and goes some way, perhaps without realising it, towards calling into question his own generally hopeful view of humanity.

The view that he seems to be urging is that if all employers were like the twin brothers Charles and Edwin Cheeryble in *Nicholas Nickleby*, then there would be no social problems at all. Self-made men, they are charitable to all who cross their path, models of kindness and philanthropy. Boffin in *Our Mutual Friend*, Dickens's last complete novel, is very similar. A proletarian by birth, he becomes rich by inheritance, and solves other people's problems by throwing money about in all directions. All this is very much in the "hot soup and tracts for the poor" tradition of Victorian evangelicism at its most empirical. Immediate problems can be solved by such an approach, but underlying causes are neglected. Any serious criticism of a system which allows owners of property to exploit others is rendered nugatory because the recipients of charity go away with their hearts full of gratitude; and Dickens fell into the trap of thinking like this. He saw the progressive degradation of the poor that was going on around him, but did not seem to realise that it was an economic order which was producing the misery he wrote about. It was enough for him that some human beings could rise triumphantly above it.

Precisely this kind of criticism can be levelled at other Victorian novelists who explored the "condition of England" theme. George Eliot, for example, in *Felix Holt*, dissipated the effect of her novel by setting it not in an industrial city but in a remote provincial town. Disraeli's *Sybil* and Kingsley's *Alton Locke*, both of which deal with the problems of a capitalist society, are flawed in different ways. Dickens, with his enormous creative energy, sweeps the reader along with him in his novels; but if we are to understand in more detail how he saw certain social issues, then it is to his journalism that we must turn. It is shorter and less constricted by the demands of an art form so complex as the novel.

Amongst Victorian journalists Dickens was in good company, and he became, arguably, the best of them. Perhaps his contemporaries, some of them extremely good, suffer from comparison with him, but it is really the high quality of so many of them that makes Dickens appear outstanding.

His immediate predecessor was Pierce Egan, whose *Life in London*, a series of fictional episodes published in monthly parts, first appeared in September 1820. The text was illustrated in colour by George and Robert Cruikshank, and was an immediate runaway success. The printers could not keep up with the demand for copies, and a reissue in 1821 overlapped with the later numbers of the original edition; there were also stage versions, plagiarisms and imitations of all kinds. Egan was not in any real sense an innovator, for books about London life had been popular in the eighteenth century, and the provenance of such publications goes back to Elizabethan days. He has, though, a special claim upon our attention because he pioneered a kind of urban naturalism which had a great influence upon Charles Dickens. The central characters in *Life in London* are Tom, a young man about town, a "Corinthian" or a "swell", and Jerry Hawthorn, who comes up from the country to enjoy the pleasures of London life: the book is about their adventures. Egan was more interested in costermongers, coalheavers, dustmen, flower-sellers, coach-drivers, swindlers, beggars and petty crooks, all of whom were doing their best to wring a living out of a hostile environment, than he was in the more respectable inhabitants of the city. Low life fascinated him endlessly, and he made no apology for this. At the same time he did not – despite Thackeray's claim that he did – glamorise criminals, and he was always ready to show the consequences of villainy.

It seems extremely probable that Dickens, in his early days as a writer at least, was much influenced by Pierce Egan; he owned a copy of *Life in London*. There were, too, some parallels in the lives of the two men. Both came from poor families and were largely self-educated; both taught themselves shorthand, reported parliamentary debates and went on to be successful journalists; both were fascinated by the theatre and interested in crime, particularly murder; and, above all, both had a passion for London and were entranced by the life and bustle of its crowded streets and its slums, and by its unusual and eccentric characters. Having said this, the parallel ends, for Egan never became more than an observant chronicler of the London scene, while Dickens became its great imaginative poet.

OPPOSITE: *A. Henning's title-page illustration for* The Natural History of "Stuck-up" People *by Albert Smith, 1847.*

14

Dickens also stands above his contemporaries and his successors, and some of these must be mentioned. *Sketches in London* by James Grant, published in 1838, is a substantial book, illustrated by "Phiz" and running to more than four hundred pages. In twelve chapters (or separate articles) the author takes us through various aspects of London life – begging imposters, debtors' prisons, penny theatres, police offices, workhouses, lunatic asylums, fairs, gaming houses. The emphasis is upon low life, but there are notable descriptions of parliament and a law court in action. Grant, a Calvinist, was a successful journalist and author of several books, but his rather austere style lacks the liveliness of Dickens. He was not given to flights of fancy: *Sketches in London* is essentially factual and firmly based upon what he saw for himself. Although reprinted in 1861, it seems to have attracted little attention; it is now largely, and undeservedly, forgotten.

Rather more Dickensian in tone are the two volumes of *Heads of the People* which came out in 1841 and 1842. This was a collection of prose sketches of English social types, illustrated by Kenny Meadows and written by a number of distinguished men and women of letters including Douglas Jerrold, R. H. Horne, Leigh Hunt, Laman Blanchard, William Howitt, Mrs. Gore, Mrs. S. C. Hall and many others. Amongst the types delineated are the dressmaker, stockbroker, maid-of-all-work, parish beadle, common informer, pew opener, chimney-sweep, hangman, ballad singer and British soldier. There is a light-hearted touch about a good many of the pieces, and a sense of shrewd observation: the collection was successful, and reprinted. Clearly there was a public for this kind of journalistic writing – perhaps a better term is "occasional literature" – and the "Natural History" series initiated by the publisher David Bogue in the late 1840s developed a kind of writing that Dickens had done much to shape. *The Natural History of the Gent, of Bores, of Humbugs, of "Stuck-up" People,* and so on, poked gentle fun at recognisable social types besides providing, almost between the lines, a good deal of information about Victorian society. Costing a shilling a time in paper wrappers, they were designed for the pocket, and their authors Albert Smith and Angus B. Reach were, especially Smith, much influenced by Dickens.

More recognisably sub-Dickensian is a little book by a prolific Victorian author, now pretty well forgotten: James Hain Friswell. *Houses with their Fronts Off* was published in 1854 and became an immediate success. Twelve "houses" – including a public house, a police court, a workhouse, a house with a wedding and one with a funeral – tell the story of what goes on inside them. The idea was original, and the book so well received that it was followed a year later by a similar work called *Twelve Inside and One Out,* in which the passengers on a London omnibus tell their respective stories. What Friswell's work demonstrates above all is the narrow and imprecise line which divides fiction and non-fiction – social comment was common to both.

The tradition of entertaining social description continued in *Gavarni in London: Sketches of Life and Character*, which came out in a handsome gilt quarto form in 1849. Edited by Albert Smith with contributions by him, Horace Mayhew, Angus B. Reach, Shirley Brooks and others, together with a superb series of illustrations by Gavarni, it was sufficiently popular to be reprinted rather more cheaply as a "yellowback". In 1859 G. A. Sala wrote *Twice Round the Clock: or the Hours of the Day and Night in London* a remarkable *tour de force* on London life in all its variations; and later writers such as James Greenwood and George R. Sims were also preoccupied with low life. All these men were journalists and, like Dickens, social explorers, who described and commented upon what they saw.

Albert Smith (1816–60).

Although only a fragment of the mass of available writing has been touched on here, it is clear that Dickens was one of many who found social themes of absorbing interest. What sets his writing apart is the fact that he brought to his journalism a brilliant impressionism, an extraordinary talent which illuminated every theme that he touched. His method of work is neatly summarised in the opening paragraphs of "A Visit to Newgate":

> We have only to premise, that we do not intend to fatigue the reader with any statistical accounts of the prison; they will be found at length in numerous reports of numerous committees, and a variety of authorities of equal weight. We took no notes, made no memoranda, measured none of the yards, ascertained the exact number of inches in no particular room: are unable even to report of how many apartments the gaol is composed.

And on this basis he provides a chillingly authentic picture of Newgate Prison and its inhabitants. Dickens was able to penetrate a world of feeling and convey its reality to his readers, and he does this with genius time and again.

Henry Mayhew, on the other hand, had a very different approach. His massive four-volume *London Labour and the London Poor* (1861–62) is a comprehensive survey concerned with the minutiae of daily life and providing statistical tables; and wherever possible he allows the poor to speak for themselves. The result is enormously impressive, and in a very real sense the work of Mayhew and of Dickens is complementary: the latter provides imaginative insights and a synthesis that Mayhew nowhere attempts. Both approaches are necessary if we are to understand the realities of a long vanished world, and for this reason it is pointless to argue that Dickens was "better" than Mayhew. They were engaged upon different enterprises. It is, however, worth stressing that Mayhew's concern with poverty went far beyond London, even though his reputation today rests chiefly on his survey of the metropolis.

We may speculate for a moment upon the relationship between the two men. They must have known each other, for the world of Victorian journalism was too small for them not to have done so, and Mayhew married the daughter of Douglas Jerrold, who was well known to Dickens. Besides, as an avid reader of newspapers

Dickens would certainly have been familiar with Mayhew's work. Were any of Dickens's characters taken from Mayhew? There is no hard evidence that they were. As it is, the only first-hand evidence we have of contact between the two men is that they both acted together in an amateur theatrical production!

Comparison may be more fruitful in the case of Dickens and, say, Albert Smith, to whom reference was made earlier. Smith is an unregarded author today, but he had a deep passion for London and was known as "one of Mr. Dickens's young men". His novel *Christopher Tadpole* (1848) is his best work, and shows in both plot and characterisation notable signs of Dickens's influence; but then, in his lifetime of writing, Dickens dominated the literary world and his reputation was such that many younger writers were influenced by him. Indeed, it would be difficult to overestimate Dickens's influence. As one pastor told his flock: "There have been amongst us three great social agencies: the London City Mission; the novels of Mr. Dickens; the cholera." A rare tribute, and one that the writer would have relished.

Leaving aside the complex patterns of literary and social influence, it does seem appropriate to ask just how reliable a witness Dickens was. Did he, in fact, fictionalise his articles on social problems? The answer, I believe, is no. London and many of the people who lived in it remained a central interest in Dickens's life to the day he died, and there is no evidence to suggest that in his articles for *Household Words* and other publications truth was being in any way stretched or distorted. The articles reflected what he saw, and there was no need for him to transmute them into the stuff of which he made his novels. We can see a distinction between his attitudes to fiction and to non-fiction – a balance which was not always struck by other writers – and there is in his journalistic pieces a note of authenticity that springs directly from his knowledge of London and his love for its restless, many-sided life. His first employer described that knowledge as "wonderful", and a fellow clerk, in his early days, commented upon it thus: "I thought I knew something of the town, but after a little talk with Dickens I found I knew nothing. He knew it all from Bow to Brentford."

Others paid tribute to Dickens's knowledge of London, even the *Saturday Review* (not always amongst his keenest admirers); but it was Walter Bagehot who summed up the matter best: "He describes London like a special correspondent for posterity." This is the most apt of comments. In his journalism Dickens combined knowledge with wit and an unsurpassed imagination, and he created scenes and characters for his readers in the most authentic manner. This journalism (however we define it) had, of course, an immediate appeal for his contemporaries; and because of its vivacity and readability it remains still of absorbing interest to us. For the twentieth-century reader it opens a window on the world of Victorian London in a way that is both vivid and unique.

V. N.

Dickens towards the end of his life. He had literally worn himself out.

A DECEMBER VISION

Household Words 14 December 1850

"A DECEMBER Vision" provides a rhetorical overview of the specific concerns of the other essays in this collection. In it Dickens stresses the need for educational, sanitary and legal reform, without committing himself to any doctrinaire view of what shape that reform should take. Dickens's own primary characteristic was energy, and his primary target here is inaction.

In political, social and religious matters, Dickens was profoundly impatient of any sort of ideological or theoretical approach. His dismissal of the "Priests and Teachers" in this article who squabble amongst themselves and do nothing, rather than seeking a common agreement, typifies his attitude to mere sectional differences in all walks of life. His own often-quoted political creed, avowed on 27 September 1869 in a speech at the Birmingham and Midland Institute, was simple: "My faith in the people governing is, on the whole, infinitesimal; my faith in the People governed is, on the whole, illimitable."

But that faith in "the People" was threatened by what Dickens perceived as the corruption of social relations inherent in England's neglectful upper class, smug middle class and downtrodden workforce. His villagers in *The Chimes* sing:

> O let us love our occupations,
> Bless the Squire and his relations,
> Live upon our daily rations,
> And always know our proper stations.

Much of Victorian England rested on the outmoded assumption that this expressed a desirable, equitable and workable social order. Dickens knew otherwise. But he did not want a social revolution. He shared with men such as Carlyle and Arnold the fear of the undisciplined mob. It is the truculent claims of the Chartists which Dickens hears in "A December Vision": "a wild, inexplicable mutter, confused, but full of threatening, and it made all hearers' hearts to quake within them." Dickens wanted to ameliorate, not reshape, society. *Household Words* was a vehicle for what Walter Bagehot called Dickens's "sentimental radicalism", not a platform for the sort of uncompromising vehemence which characterised the pages of the Chartist journals.

The answer, Dickens thought, was improved education, which would loosen the bonds but not dissolve the structure of the class system. He felt ignorance as an ever-present violent threat. The hidden scars of shame and distress acquired in his youth – laid bare in the moving autobiographical fragment printed in Forster's *Life* – made Dickens especially sensitive to sullied childhood. Again and again he returns to the horror of a brutalising upbringing and environment which stunts and perverts "the natural affections and repulsions of mankind". For instance, in *Household Words* on 28 December 1850, in his extensive revisions to Henry Morley's article "Mr. Bendigo Buster On Our National Defences Against Education", he called a lack of educational facilities for the poor "a mighty crime and disgrace" at the heart of Empire, and wrote:

> I do not believe that any one can be well acquainted with the sights of ignorant and neglected childhood, which are hidden in the Metropolis alone, and entertain within himself the possibility of any wealth, or any power, or any spirit in a people, sustaining, for many generations longer, a State on which that wicked blight is resting.

The hypnotic rhythms of "A December Vision" give concentrated shape to many of Dickens's most deeply held beliefs. What is most interesting about this particularly forceful and arresting piece is Dickens's insistence that neglect of squalor, poverty, ignorance and injustice entails a "heavy retribution on the general guilt". He had already expressed this notion in similar terms in *Dombey and Son,* in which "moral pestilence" threatens "to blight the innocent and spread contagion among the pure". The urgency of such a threat is stressed again in a celebrated passage in his next novel, *Bleak House,* in which he describes the slum Tom-all-Alone's:

> Much mighty speech-making there has been, both in and out of Parliament, concerning Tom, and much wrathful disputation how Tom shall be got right. Whether he shall be put into the main road by constables, or by beadles, or by bellringing, or by force of figures, or by correct principles of taste, or by high church, or by low church, or by no church; whether he shall be set to splitting trusses of polemical straws with the crooked knife of his mind, or whether he shall be put to stone-breaking instead. In the midst of which dust and noise, there is but one thing perfectly clear, to wit, that Tom only may and can, or shall and will, be reclaimed according to somebody's theory but nobody's practice. And in the hopeful meantime, Tom goes to perdition head foremost in his old determined spirit.
>
> But he has his revenge. Even the winds are his messengers, and they serve him in these hours of darkness. There is not a drop of Tom's corrupted blood but propagates infection and contagion somewhere. It shall pollute, this very night, the choice stream (in which chemists on analysis would find the genuine nobility) of a Norman house, and his Grace shall not be able to say Nay to the infamous alliance. There is not an atom of Tom's slime, not a cubic inch of any pestilential gas in which he lives, not one obscenity or degradation about him, not an ignorance, not a wickedness, not a brutality of his committing, but shall work its retribution, through every order of society, up to the proudest of the proud, and to the highest of the high.

For Dickens, sanitary reform and social reform are essentially the same thing.

Dickens's contempt for the established forms of government ran deep. In the novel following *Bleak House, Little Dorrit,* Dickens invented a whole government department, "the Circumlocution Office", to exemplify bureaucracy's inexorable tendency to delay, confusion, and talk without action. But it is hard to see where such a contempt – and the despair with the legal system evidenced in *Bleak House* and often aired in *Household Words* – could lead, save to a desire to see "the People governed" defy the insolence of power, and seize control of their own destinies. Dickens came sometimes perilously close to such a view. But all his instincts were against it. He was a notoriously tidy man (he was remembered as constantly combing his hair) and ranged himself as wholeheartedly with the forces of law and order as he did against the forces of oppression.

Despite his natural optimism, Dickens's view of the world blackened as he grew older. Mr. Venus's description of his shop in *Our Mutual Friend* may be taken as a savage comic equivalent of the grand periods and noble rhetoric of "A December Vision":

> "Oh dear me, dear me!" sighs Mr. Venus, heavily, snuffing the candle, "the world that appeared so flowery has ceased to blow! You're casting your eye round the shop, Mr. Wegg. Let me show you a light. My working bench. My young man's bench. A wice. Tools. Bones, warious. Skulls, warious. Preserved Indian baby. African ditto. Bottled preparations, warious. Everything within reach of your hand, in good preservation. The mouldy ones a-top. What's in them hampers over them again, I don't quite remember. Say, human warious. Cats. Articulated English baby. Dogs. Ducks. Glass eyes, warious. Mummied bird. Dried cuticle, warious. Oh, dear me! That's the general panoramic view."

A DECEMBER VISION

I SAW a mighty Spirit, traversing the world without any rest or pause. It was omnipresent, it was all-powerful, it had no compunction, no pity, no relenting sense that any appeal from any of the race of men could reach. It was invisible to every creature born upon the earth, save once to each. It turned its shaded face on whatsoever living thing, one time; and straight the end of that thing was come. It passed through the forest, and the vigorous tree it looked on shrunk away; through the garden, and the leaves perished and the flowers withered; through the air, and the eagles flagged upon the wing and dropped; through the sea, and the monsters of the deep floated, great wrecks, upon the waters. It met the eyes of lions in their lairs, and they were dust; its shadow darkened the faces of young children lying asleep, and they awoke no more.

It had its work appointed; it inexorably did what was appointed to it to do; and neither sped nor slackened. Called to, it went on unmoved, and did not come. Besought, by some who felt that it was drawing near, to change its course, it turned its shaded face upon them, even while they cried, and they were dumb. It passed into the midst of palace chambers, where there were lights and music, pictures, diamonds, gold and silver; crossed the wrinkled and the grey, regardless of them; looked into the eyes of a bright bride; and vanished. It revealed itself to the baby on the old crone's knee, and left the old crone wailing by the fire. But, whether the beholder of its face were, now a King, or now a labourer, now a Queen, or now a seamstress; let the hand it palsied, be on the sceptre, or the plough, or yet too small and nerveless to grasp anything; the Spirit never paused in its appointed work, and, sooner or later, turned its impartial face on all.

A street beggar in the late 1840s, drawn by Gavarni (Guillaume Sulpice Chevallier). Chalked on the pavement is the legend, "I am starving."

I saw a Minister of State, sitting in his Closet; and, round about him, rising from the country which he governed, up to the Eternal Heavens, was a low dull howl of Ignorance. It was a wild, inexplicable mutter, confused, but full of threatening, and it made all hearers' hearts to quake within them. But, few heard. In the single city where this Minister of State was seated, I saw Thirty Thousand children, hunted, flogged, imprisoned, but not taught – who might have been nurtured by the wolf or bear, so little of humanity had they, within them or without – all joining in this doleful cry. And, ever among them, as among all ranks and grades of mortals, in all parts of the globe, the Spirit went; and ever by thousands, in their brutish state, with all the gifts of God perverted in their breasts or trampled out, they died.

The Minister of State, whose heart was pierced by even the little he could hear of these terrible voices, day and night rising to Heaven, went among the Priests and Teachers of all denominations, and faintly said:

"Harken to this dreadful cry! What shall we do to stay it?"

20

One body of respondents answered, "Teach this!"

Another said, "Teach that!"

Another said, "Teach neither this nor that, but t'other!"

Another quarrelled with all the three; twenty others quarrelled with all the four, and quarrelled no less bitterly among themselves. The voices, not stayed by this, cried out day and night; and still, among those many thousands, as among all mankind, went the Spirit who never rested from its labour; and still, in brutish sort, they died.

Then, a whisper murmured to the Minister of State:

"Correct this for thyself. Be bold! Silence those voices, or virtuously lose thy power in the attempt to do it. Thou cans't not sow a grain of good seed in vain. Thou knowest it well. Be bold, and do thy duty!"

The Minister shrugged his shoulders, and replied, "It is a great wrong – BUT IT WILL LAST MY TIME." And so he put it from him.

Then, the whisper went among the Priests and Teachers, saying to each, "In thy soul thou knowest it is a truth, O man, that there are good things to be taught, on which all men may agree. Teach those, and stay this cry."

To which, each answered in like manner, "It is a great wrong – BUT IT WILL LAST MY TIME." And so *he* put it from him.

I saw a poisoned air, in which Life drooped. I saw Disease, arrayed in all its store of hideous aspects and appalling shapes, triumphant in every alley, bye-way, court, back-street, and poor abode, in every place where human beings congregated – in the proudest and most boastful places, most of all. I saw innumerable hosts, fore-doomed to darkness, dirt, pestilence, obscenity, misery, and early death. I saw, wheresoever I looked, cunning preparations made for defacing the Creator's Image, from the moment of its appearance here on earth, and stamping over it the image of the Devil. I saw, from those reeking and pernicious stews, the avenging consequences of such Sin issuing forth, and penetrating to the highest places. I saw the rich struck down in their strength, their darling children weakened and withered, their marriageable sons and daughters perish in their prime. I saw that not one miserable wretch breathed out his poisoned life in the deepest cellar of the most neglected town, but, from the surrounding atmosphere, some particles of his infection were borne away, charged with heavy retribution on the general guilt.

There were many attentive and alarmed persons looking on, who saw these things too. They were well clothed, and had purses in their pockets; they were educated, full of kindness, and loved mercy. They said to one another, "This is horrible, and shall not be!" and there was a stir among them to set it right. But, opposed to these, came a small multitude of noisy fools and greedy knaves, whose harvest was in such horrors; and they, with impudence and turmoil, and with scurrilous jests at misery and death, repelled the better lookers-on, who soon fell back and stood aloof.

Then, the whisper went among those better lookers-on, saying,

ADVICE GRATIS TO THE POOR.

Doctor: "Yes, Mrs. Brown! You must give her plenty of nice puddings, some calves' foot jelly – a little wine – a fowl or two – take her to the seaside, and, if possible, go with her to Baden-Baden." Punch 1846.

"Over the bodies of those fellows, to the remedy!"

But, each of them moodily shrugged his shoulders, and replied, "It is a great wrong – BUT IT WILL LAST MY TIME!" And so they put it from them.

I saw a great library of laws and law-proceedings, so complicated, costly, and unintelligible, that, although numbers of lawyers united in a public fiction that these were wonderfully just and equal, there was scarcely an honest man among them, but who said to his friend, privately consulting him, "Better put up with a fraud or other injury than grope for redress through the manifold blind turnings and strange chances of this system."

I saw a portion of the system, called (of all things) EQUITY, which was ruin to suitors, ruin to property, a shield for wrong-doers having money, a rack for right-doers having none: a by-word for delay, slow agony of mind, despair, impoverishment, trickery, confusion, insupportable injustice. A main part of it, I saw prisoners wasting in jail; mad people babbling in hospitals; suicides chronicled in the yearly records; orphans robbed of their inheritance; infants righted (perhaps) when they were grey.

Certain lawyers and laymen came together, and said to one another, "In only one of these our Courts of Equity, there are years of this dark perspective before us at the present moment. We must change this."

Uprose, immediately, a throng of others, Secretaries, Petty

"Reform [Mr. Punch] Removing the Bandage from the Eyes of Justice", 1851. Punch*'s social satire at this time had a radical edge; Dickens was very friendly with the* Punch *circle, especially Douglas Jerrold and Mark Lemon.*

Bags, Hanapers, Chaffwaxes, and what not, singing (in answer) "Rule Britannia", and "God save the Queen"; making flourishing speeches, pronouncing hard names, demanding committees, commissions, commissioners, and other scarecrows, and terrifying the little band of innovators out of their five wits.

Then, the whisper went among the latter, as they shrunk back, saying, "If there is any wrong within the universal knowledge, this wrong is. Go on! Set it right!"

Whereon, each of them sorrowfully thrust his hands in his pockets, and replied, "It is indeed a great wrong; – BUT IT WILL LAST MY TIME!" – and so *they* put it from them.

The Spirit, with its face concealed, summoned all the people who had used this phrase about their Time, into its presence. Then, it said, beginning with the Minister of State:

"Of what duration is *your* Time?"

The Minister of State replied, "My ancient family has always been long-lived. My father died at eighty-four; my grandfather, at ninety-two. We have the gout, but bear it (like our honours) many years."

"And you," said the Spirit to the Priests and Teachers, "What may *your* time be?"

Some believed they were so strong, as that they should number many more years than threescore and ten; others were the sons of old incumbents who had long outlived youthful expectants. Others, for any means they had of calculating, might be long-lived or short-lived – generally (they had a strong persuasion) long. So, among the well-clothed lookers-on. So, among the lawyers and laymen.

"But, every man, as I understand you, one and all," said the Spirit, "has his time?"

"Yes!" they exclaimed together.

"Yes," said the Spirit; "and it is – ETERNITY! Whosoever is a consenting party to a wrong, comforting himself with the base reflection that it will last his time, shall bear his portion of the wrong throughout ALL TIME. And, in the hour when he and I stand face to face, he shall surely know it, as my name is Death!"

It departed, turning its shaded face hither and thither as it passed along upon its ceaseless work, and blighting all on whom it looked.

Then went among many trembling hearers the whisper, saying, "See, each of you, before you take your ease, O wicked, selfish, men, that what will 'last your time', be Just enough to last for ever!"

Nemesis comes to a rich man. A. Henning, 1847.

From **Little Dorrit** *book I chapter 10*

THE Circumlocution Office was (as everybody knows without being told) the most important Department under Government. No public business of any kind could possibly be done at any time without the acquiescence of the Circumlocution Office. Its finger was in the largest public pie, and in the smallest public tart. It was equally impossible to do the plainest right and to undo the plainest wrong without the express authority of the Circumlocution Office. If another Gunpowder Plot had been discovered half an hour before the lighting of the match, nobody would have been justified in saving the parliament until there had been half a score of boards, half a bushel of minutes, several sacks of official memoranda, and a family-vault full of ungrammatical correspondence, on the part of the Circumlocution Office.

This glorious establishment had been early in the field, when the one sublime principle involving the difficult art of governing a country, was first distinctly revealed to statesmen. It had been foremost to study that bright revelation and to carry its shining influence through the whole of the official proceedings. Whatever was required to be done, the Circumlocution Office was beforehand with all the public departments in the art of perceiving – HOW NOT TO DO IT.

Through this delicate perception, through the tact with which it invariably seized it, and through the genius with which it always acted on it, the Circumlocution Office had risen to over-top all the public departments; and the public condition had risen to be – what it was.

It is true that How not to do it was the great study and object of all public departments and professional politicians all round the Circumlocution Office. It is true that every new premier and every new government, coming in because they had upheld a certain thing as necessary to be done, were no sooner come in than they applied their utmost faculties to discovering How not to do it. It is true that from the moment when a general election was over, every returned man who had been raving on hustings because it hadn't been done, and who had been asking the friends of the honourable gentleman in the opposite interest on pain of impeachment to tell him why it hadn't been done, and who had been asserting that it must be done, and who had been pledging himself that it should be done, began to devise, How it was not to be done. It is true that the debates of both Houses of Parliament the whole session through, uniformly tended to the protracted deliberation, How not to do it. It is true that the royal speech at the opening of such session virtually said, My lords and gentlemen, you have a considerable stroke of work to do, and you will please retire to your respective chambers, and discuss, How not to do it. It is true that the royal speech, at the close of such session, virtually said, My lords and gentlemen, you have through several laborious months been considering with great loyalty and patriotism, How not to do it, and you have found out; and with the blessing of Providence upon the harvest (natural, not political), I now dismiss you. All this is true, but the Circumlocution Office went beyond it.

Because the Circumlocution Office went on mechanically, every day, keeping this wonderful, all-sufficient wheel of statesmanship, How not to do it, in motion. Because the Circumlocution Office was down upon any ill-advised public servant who was going to do it, or who appeared to be by any surprising accident in remote danger of doing it, with a minute, and a memorandum, and a letter of instructions that extinguished him. It was this spirit of national efficiency in the Circumlocution Office that had gradually led to its having something to do with everything. Mechanicians, natural philosophers, soldiers, sailors, petitioners, memorialists, people with grievances, people who wanted to prevent grievances, people who wanted to redress grievances, jobbing people, jobbed people, people who couldn't get rewarded for merit, and people who couldn't get punished for demerit, were all indiscriminately tucked up under the foolscap paper of the Circumlocution Office.

Numbers of people were lost in the Circumlocution Office. Unfortunates with wrongs, or with projects for the general welfare (and they had better have had wrongs at first, than have taken that bitter English recipe for certainly getting them), who in slow lapse of time and agony had passed safely through other public departments; who, according to rule, had been bullied in this, over-reached by that, and evaded by the other; got referred at last to the Circumlocution Office, and never reappeared in the light of day. Boards sat upon them, secretaries minuted upon them, commissioners gabbled about them, clerks registered, entered, checked, and ticked them off, and they melted away. In short, all the business of the country went through the Circumlocution Office, except the business that never came out of it; and *its* name was Legion.

Sometimes, angry spirits attacked the Circumlocution Office. Sometimes, parliamentary questions were asked about it, and even parliamentary motions made or threatened about it by demagogues so low and ignorant as to hold that the real recipe of government was, How to do it. Then would the noble lord, or right honourable gentleman, in whose department it was to defend the Circumlocution Office, put an orange in his pocket, and make a regular field-day of the occasion. Then would he come down to that house with a slap upon the table, and meet the honourable gentleman foot to foot. Then would he be there to tell that honourable gentleman that the Circumlocution Office not only was blameless in this matter, but was commendable in this matter, was extollable to the skies in this matter. Then would he be there to tell that honourable gentleman that, although the Circumlocution Office was invariably right and wholly right, it never was so right as in this matter. Then would he be there to tell that honourable gentleman that it would have been more to his honour, more to his credit, more to his good taste, more to his good sense, more to half the dictionary of commonplaces, if he had left the Circumlocution Office alone, and never approached this matter. Then would he keep one eye upon a coach or crammer from the Circumlocution Office sitting below the bar, and smash the honourable gentleman with the Circumlocution Office account of this matter. And although one of two things always happened; namely, either that the Circumlocution Office had nothing to say and said it, or that it had something to say of which the noble lord, or right honourable gentleman, blundered one half and forgot the other; the Circumlocution Office was always voted immaculate by an accommodating majority.

ON DUTY WITH INSPECTOR FIELD

Household Words 14 June 1851

"ON Duty with Inspector Field" is an admirable example of the lively, expressive qualities of Dickens's journalism, and of the relationship of that journalism to his fiction. Indeed, from the attention-grabbing "How goes the night?" with which it opens, it is constructed like a piece of fiction, with a gallery of Dickensian grotesques – Bully Bark, Blackey, Mr. Click and so on. There is no reason to doubt the essential truthfulness of the account; equally, we can recognise this narrative as of a piece with the vivid extravagance of Dickens's fiction.

Inspector Field himself is certainly real. His name was Charles Frederick Field, and in first writing about him Dickens lightly disguised him as "Inspector Wield" in "A Detective Police Party" (*Household Words* 27 July and 10 August 1850) and "Three 'Detective' Anecdotes" (*Household Words* 14 September 1850). Field was born in 1805, and joined the Metropolitan Police as a sergeant in September 1829, transferring to "L" Division (Lambeth) as inspector in 1833. He became Chief of the Detective Department at Scotland Yard in 1846, four years after its formation. At this period the department consisted of a staff of two inspectors and six sergeants, with thirty-four constables attached in pairs to each police division.

Public suspicion of plain-clothes policemen ran high, and it seems likely that Dickens's enthusiasm for their work provided Field with a longed-for public relations coup. Dickens admired Field and his detectives as a vast improvement on the old incompetent and corrupt Bow Street Police. A letter of 1862 shows that Dickens then believed that Field had been in his youth a Bow Street runner; the truth of this is uncertain. But George Augustus Sala, a *Household Words* journalist, noted that Field "reminded me forcibly of one of the old Bow Street runners, with more than one of whom I was on friendly terms in my harum-scarum youth". Sala disapproved of Dickens's "curious and almost morbid partiality for communing with and entertaining police officers", and thought Field – "a clean-shaven, farmer-like, elderly individual" – considerably less impressive than his fictional counterpart, Mr. Bucket in *Bleak House*.

That Field was the model for Bucket is beyond question, despite Dickens's denial. Field had many of Bucket's characteristics, particularly a theatrical love of disguise and subterfuge, and a disconcertingly affable manner of making his arrests. Like Bucket, too, he made eloquent use of his "fat forefinger". In "The Detective Police" Dickens describes him as "a middle-aged man of a portly presence, with a large, moist, knowing eye, a husky voice, and a habit of emphasising his conversation by the aid of a corpulent forefinger, which is constantly in juxtaposition with his eyes or nose".

Dickens was writing *Bleak House* between November 1851 and August 1853. Bucket – English literature's first detective – is introduced in chapter 22 as "a stoutly built, steady-looking, sharp-eyed man in black, of about the middle-age". We soon follow him into the fever-haunted slum Tom-all-Alone's, in search of the crossing-sweeper Jo. Bucket is as at home in the "lairs" and foul streets as Field, and talks with down-and-outs and ruffians with the same bantering authority.

Dickens's intimate acquaintance with London's low life was largely acquired on trips such as the one described here. He did venture to such places alone – a man employed in his youth to take dictation at the offices of *All the Year Round* remembered, rather improbably, that Dickens would "go down to the Seven Dials, about the worst place in London, and sleep and eat there. He roasted his herring where the rest did, and slept with the poorest. He loved low society." On one occasion Dickens had to be rescued from a criminal rookery by police. In 1867 he gave his own account of such trips to an American, the Rev. Dr. G. D. Carrow:

> In my visits to the dens of thieves and other haunts of infamy, I deemed it prudent to associate myself with a brace of policemen who were well versed in the ways of the localities I wished to examine, and who introduced me to the professionals as an old friend who was making the accustomed round with them merely for the opportunity of a talk about old times. These were what I called my field-days.

Another American report, by Dickens's friend J. T. Fields, editor of the *Atlantic Monthly*, gives a clearer insight into these "field-days". On two nights in May 1869, Dickens and Fields ventured under police protection into "lock-ups, watch-houses, and opium-eating establishments". Inspector Field had retired on a pension in 1852, and started a detective agency, the Secret Enquiry Office, but he was still game for such ventures. J. T. Fields recalls:

> We were standing in a room half filled with people of both sexes, whom the police accompanying us knew to be thieves. Many of these abandoned persons had served out their terms in jail or prison, and would probably again be sentenced under the law. They were all silent and sullen as we entered the room, until an old woman spoke up with a strong, beery voice: "Good evening, gentlemen. We are all very poor, but strictly honest." At which cheerful apocryphal statement, all the inmates of the room burst into boisterous laughter, and began pelting the imaginative female with epithets uncomplimentary and unsavoury.

Dickens was not alone in making such excursions, though he was both sharper-eyed and more serious of purpose than many who enjoyed such fashionable guided tours of the slums. The Hon. Frederick Wellesley, for instance, recalled a similar trip in the 1860s under the guidance of "a little weazened man called Field". Like Dickens, Wellesley was immensely impressed by Field's demeanour.

The chief source of parallel information, however, is the fourth volume of Henry Mayhew's *London Labour and the London Poor*, in which John Binny describes a number of similar expeditions, and also records the life stories and working methods of the various criminals, notably the "stock-buzzers" or stealers of handkerchiefs. The "Narrative of a London Sneak, or Common Thief", for instance, yields many telling insights into the hierarchy of crime in the lodging-houses, and also the odd innocence of their "degraded", "worthless", "abandoned" occupants: "We spend our evenings telling tales and conversing to each other on our wanderings, and playing at games, such as 'hunt the slipper'."

While the Victorian social observers generally emphasise the wretched and vicious state of the criminal poor, their reporting also rings with a stubborn wit and resilience. The "thieves, prostitutes and cadgers" who populated areas such as St. Giles could turn a mocking eye on their betters. In 1849 a teenager called Cornelius Hearne tried to pick the pocket of Mark Lemon, who had co-edited *Punch* with Henry Mayhew. Dickens gave evidence in court that he had previously seen the accused in the House of Correction; Hearne, seizing his chance, gave the court this devastating account of the witness:

> Now, your worship, he must have been in quod there himself or he couldn't have seen me. I know these two gentlemen well; they're no better than swell mobsmen, and get their living by buying stolen goods. That one [pointing to Mr. Dickens] keeps a "fence" and I recollect him [to Mr. Lemon] at the prison, where he was put in for six months, while I was there for only two.

ON DUTY WITH INSPECTOR FIELD

How goes the night? St. Giles's clock is striking nine. The weather is dull and wet, and the long lines of street-lamps are blurred, as if we saw them through tears. A damp wind blows, and rakes the pieman's fire out, when he opens the door of his little furnace, carrying away an eddy of sparks.

St. Giles's clock strikes nine. We are punctual. Where is Inspector Field? Assistant Commissioner of Police is already here, enwrapped in oil-skin cloak, and standing in the shadow of St. Giles's steeple. Detective Serjeant, weary of speaking French all day to foreigners unpacking at the Great Exhibition, is already here. Where is Inspector Field?

Inspector Field is, to-night, the guardian genius of the British Museum. He is bringing his shrewd eye to bear on every corner of its solitary galleries, before he reports "all right". Suspicious of the Elgin marbles, and not to be done by cat-faced Egyptian giants, with their hands upon their knees, Inspector Field, sagacious, vigilant, lamp in hand, throwing monstrous shadows on the walls and ceiling, passes through the spacious rooms. If a mummy trembled in an atom of its dusty covering, Inspector Field would say, "Come out of that, Tom Green. I know you!" If the smallest "Gonoph" about town were crouching at the bottom of a classic bath, Inspector Field would nose him with a finer scent than the ogre's, when adventurous Jack lay trembling in his kitchen copper. But all is quiet, and Inspector Field goes warily on, making little outward show of attending to anything in particular, just recognising the Ichthyosaurus as a familiar acquaintance, and wondering, perhaps, how the detectives did it in the days before the Flood.

Will Inspector Field be long about this work? He may be half-an-hour longer. He sends his compliments by Police Constable, and proposes that we meet at St. Giles's Station House, across the road. Good. It were as well to stand by the fire, there, as in the shadow of St. Giles's steeple.

Anything doing here to-night? Not much. We are very quiet. A lost boy, extremely calm and small, sitting by the fire, whom we now confide to a constable to take home, for the child says that if you show him Newgate Street, he can show you where he lives – a raving drunken woman in the cells, who has screeched her voice away, and has hardly power enough left to declare, even with the passionate help of her feet and arms, that she is the daughter of a British officer, and strike her blind and dead, but she'll write a letter to the Queen! but who is soothed with a drink of water – in another cell, a quiet woman with a child at her breast, for begging – in another, her husband in a smock-frock, with a basket of watercresses – in another, a pickpocket – in another, a meek tremulous old pauper man who has been out for a holiday "and has took but a little drop, but it has overcome him arter so many

gonoph: a young thief

Inspector Charles Field. Dickens admired his "horrible sharpness".

months in the house" – and that's all, as yet. Presently, a sensation at the Station House door. Mr. Field, gentlemen!

Inspector Field comes in, wiping his forehead, for he is of a burly figure, and has come fast from the ores and metals of the deep mines of the earth, and from the Parrot Gods of the South Sea Islands, and from the birds and beetles of the tropics, and from the Arts of Greece and Rome, and from the Sculptures of Nineveh, and from the traces of an elder world, when these were not. Is Rogers ready? Rogers is ready, strapped and great-coated, with a flaming eye in the middle of his waist, like a deformed Cyclops. Lead on, Rogers, to Rats' Castle!

How many people may there be in London, who, if we had brought them deviously and blindfold, to this street, fifty paces from the Station House, and within call of St. Giles's church, would know it for a not remote part of the city in which their lives are passed? How many, who amidst this compound of sickening smells, these heaps of filth, these tumbling houses, with all their vile contents, animate and inanimate, slimily overflowing into the black road, would believe that they breathe *this* air? How much Red Tape may there be, that could look round on the faces which now hem us in – for our appearance here has caused a rush from all points to a common centre – the lowering foreheads, the sallow cheeks, the brutal eyes, the matted hair, the infected, vermin-haunted heaps of rags – and say "I have thought of this. I have not dismissed the thing. I have neither blustered it away, nor frozen it away, nor tied it up and put it away, nor smoothly said pooh, pooh! to it, when it has been shown to me"?

This is not what Rogers wants to know, however. What Rogers wants to know, is whether you *will* clear the way here, some of you, or whether you won't; because if you don't do it right on end, he'll lock you up! What! *You* are there, are you, Bob Miles? You haven't had enough of it yet, haven't you? You want three months more, do you? Come away from that gentleman! What are you creeping round there for?

"What am I a doing, thinn, Mr. Rogers?" says Bob Miles, appearing, villainous, at the end of a lane of light, made by the lantern.

"I'll let you know pretty quick, if you don't hook it. WILL you hook it?"

A sycophantic murmur rises from the crowd. "Hook it, Bob, when Mr. Rogers and Mr. Field tells you! Why don't you hook it, when you are told to?"

The most importunate of the voices strikes familiarly on Mr. Rogers's ear. He suddenly turns his lantern on the owner.

"What! *You* are there, are you, Mister Click? You hook it too – come?"

"What for?" says Mr. Click, discomfited.

"You hook it, will you!" says Mr. Rogers with stern emphasis.

Both Click and Miles *do* "hook it", without another word, or, in plainer English, sneak away.

Two Metropolitan Police constables, late 1860s

"Close up there, my men!" says Inspector Field to two constables on duty who have followed. "Keep together gentlemen; we are going down here. Heads!"

St. Giles's church strikes half-past ten. We stoop low, and creep down a precipitous flight of steps into a dark close cellar. There is a fire. There is a long deal table. There are benches. The cellar is full of company, chiefy very young men in various conditions of dirt and raggedness. Some are eating supper. There are no girls or women present. Welcome to Rats' Castle, gentlemen, and to this company of noted thieves!

"Well, my lads! How are you my lads? What have you been doing to-day? Here's some company come to see you, my lads! *There's* a plate of beefsteak, Sir, for the supper of a fine young man! And there's a mouth for a steak, Sir! Why, I should be too proud of such a mouth as that, if I had it myself! Stand up and show it, Sir! Take off your cap. There's a fine young man for a nice little party, Sir! An't he?"

Inspector Field is the bustling speaker. Inspector Field's eye is the roving eye that searches every corner of the cellar as he talks. Inspector Field's hand is the well-known hand that has collared half the people here, and motioned their brothers, sisters, fathers, mothers, male and female friends, inexorably, to New South Wales. Yet Inspector Field stands in the den, the Sultan of the place. Every thief here cowers before him like a schoolboy before his schoolmaster. All watch him, all answer when addressed, all laugh at his jokes, all seek to propitiate him. This cellar-company alone – to say nothing of the crowd surrounding the entrance from the street above, and making the steps shine with eyes – is strong enough to murder us all, and willing enough to do it; but, let Inspector Field have a mind to pick out one thief here, and take him; let him produce that ghostly truncheon from his pocket, and say, with his business-air, "My lad, I want you!" and all Rats' Castle shall be stricken with paralysis, and not a finger move against him, as he fits the handcuffs on!

"A Dinner at a Cheap Lodging-House", 1850s. Of such a place Henry Mayhew writes, "Four frequenters of that room had been transported, and yet the house had been open only as many years, and of the associates and companions of those present, no less than forty had left the country in the same manner. The names of some of these were curious. I subjoin a few of them. The Banger, The Slasher, White-coat Mushe, Lankey Thompson, Tom Sales (he was hung), and Jack Sheppard". In 1839 the police calculated that the metropolis contained 221 "low lodging-houses", giving shelter to 2,431 vagrants, pickpockets and prostitutes. Thomas Beames offers a guide to them in The Rookeries of London *(1850).*

Where's the Earl of Warwick? – Here he is, Mr. Field! Here's the Earl of Warwick, Mr. Field! – O there you are, my Lord, Come for'ard. There's a chest, Sir, not to have a clean shirt on. An't it? Take your hat off, my Lord. Why, I should be ashamed if I was you – and an Earl, too – to show myself to a gentleman with my hat on! – The Earl of Warwick laughs, and uncovers. All the company laugh. One pickpocket, especially, laughs with great enthusiasm. O what a jolly game it is, when Mr. Field comes down – and don't want nobody!

So, *you* are here, too, are you, you tall, grey, soldierly-looking, grave man, standing by the fire? – Yes, Sir. Good evening, Mr. Field! – Let us see. You lived servant to a nobleman once? – Yes, Mr. Field. – And what is it you do now; I forget? – Well, Mr. Field, I job about as well as I can. I left my employment on account of delicate health. The family is still kind to me. Mr. Wix of Piccadilly is also very kind to me when I am hard up. Likewise Mr. Nix of Oxford Street. I get a trifle from them occasionally, and rub on as well as I can, Mr. Field. Mr. Field's eye rolls enjoyingly, for this man is a notorious begging-letter writer. – Good night, my lads! – Good night, Mr. Field, and thank'ee, Sir!

Clear the street here, half a thousand of you! Cut it, Mrs. Stalker – none of that – we don't want you! Rogers of the flaming eye, lead on to the tramps' lodging-house!

A dream of baleful faces attends to the door. Now, stand back all of you! In the rear, Detective Serjeant plants himself, composedly whistling, with his strong right arm across the narrow passage. Mrs. Stalker, I am something'd that need not be written here, if you won't get yourself into trouble, in about half a minute, if I see that face of yours again!

St. Giles's church clock, striking eleven, hums through our hand from the dilapidated door of a dark outhouse as we open it, and are stricken back by the pestilent breath that issues from within. Rogers, to the front with the light, and let us look!

Ten, twenty, thirty – who can count them! Men, women, children, for the most part naked, heaped upon the floor like maggots in a cheese! Ho! In that dark corner yonder! Does any body lie there? Me Sir, Irish me, a widder, with six children. And yonder? Me Sir, Irish me, with me wife and eight poor babes. And to the left there? Me Sir, Irish me, along with two more Irish boys as is me friends. And to the right there? Me Sir and the Murphy fam'ly, numbering five blessed souls. And what's this, coiling, now, about my foot? Another Irish me, pitifully in want of shaving, whom I have awakened from sleep – and across my other foot lies his wife – and by the shoes of Inspector Field lie their three eldest – and their three youngest are at present squeezed between the open door and the wall. And why is there no one on that little mat before the sullen fire? Because O'Donovan, with wife and daughter, is not come in yet from selling Lucifers! Nor on the bit of sacking in the nearest corner? Bad luck! Because that Irish family is late to-night, a-cadging in the streets!

"The Lucifer Match Girl", from a daguerrotype by Beard, 1850s. "Lucifer" was originally a brand name, but came to be used for any match. The phosphorus used in the manufacture of matches gave the women who made them a painful disease known as phossyjaw.

31

They are all awake now, the children excepted, and most of them sit up, to stare. Wheresoever Mr. Rogers turns the flaming eye, there is a spectral figure rising, unshrouded, from a grave of rags. Who is the landlord here? – I am, Mr. Field! says a bundle of ribs and parchment against the wall, scratching itself. – Will you spend this money fairly, in the morning, to buy coffee for 'em all? – Yes Sir, I will! – O he'll do it Sir, he'll do it fair. He's honest! cry the spectres. And with thanks and Good Night sink into their graves again.

Thus, we make our New Oxford Streets, and our other new streets, never heeding, never asking, where the wretches whom we clear out, crowd. With such scenes at our doors, with all the plagues of Egypt tied up with bits of cobweb in kennels so near our homes, we timorously make our Nuisance Bills and Boards of Health, nonentities, and think to keep away the Wolves of Crime and Filth, by our electioneering ducking to little vestry-men, and our gentlemanly handling of Red Tape!

Intelligence of the coffee money has got abroad. The yard is full, and Rogers of the flaming eye is beleaguered with entreaties to show other Lodging Houses. Mine next! Mine! Mine! Rogers, military, obdurate, stiff-necked, immovable, replies not, but leads away; all falling back before him. Inspector Field follows. Detective Serjeant, with his barrier of arm across the little passage, deliberately waits to close the procession. He sees behind him, without any effort, and exceedingly disturbs one individual far in the rear by coolly calling out, "It won't do Mr. Michael! Don't try it!"

After council holden in the street, we enter other lodging houses, public-houses, many lairs and holes; all noisome and offensive; none so filthy and so crowded as where Irish are. In one, the Ethiopian party are expected home presently – were in Oxford Street when last heard of – shall be fetched, for our delight, within ten minutes. In another, one of the two or three Professors who draw Napoleon Buonaparte and a couple of mackerel, on the pavement, and then let the work of art out to a speculator, is refreshing after his labours. In another, the vested interest of the profitable nuisance has been in one family for a hundred years, and the landlord drives in comfortably from the country to his snug little stew in town. In all, Inspector Field is received with warmth. Coiners and smashers droop before him; pickpockets defer to him; the gentle sex (not very gentle here) smile upon him. Half-drunken hags check themselves in the midst of pots of beer, or pints of gin, to drink to Mr. Field, and pressingly to ask the honour of his finishing the draught. One beldame in rusty black has such admiration for him, that she runs a whole street's length to shake him by the hand; tumbling into a heap of mud by the way, and still pressing her attentions when her very form has ceased to be distinguishable through it. Before the power of the law, the power of superior sense – for common thieves are fools beside these men – and the power of a perfect mastery of their character, the garrison of Rats' Castle and the adjacent Fortresses make but a skulking show indeed when reviewed by Inspector Field.

St. Giles's clock says it will be midnight in half-an-hour, and Inspector Field says we must hurry to the Old Mint in the Borough. The cab-driver is low-spirited, and has a solemn sense of his responsibility. Now, what's your fare, my lad? – O *you* know, Inspector Field, what's the good of asking *me*!

Say, Parker, strapped and great-coated, and waiting in dim Borough doorway by appointment, to replace the trusty Rogers whom we left deep in St. Giles's, are you ready? Ready, Inspector Field, and at a motion of my wrist behold my flaming eye.

The narrow street, sir, is the chief part of the Old Mint, full of low lodging-houses, as you see by the transparent canvas-lamps and blinds, announcing beds for travellers! But it is greatly changed, friend Field, from my former knowledge of it; it is infinitely quieter and more subdued than when I was here last, some seven years ago? O yes! Inspector Haynes, a first-rate man,

English Ethiopians: blacked-up street minstrels, a familiar sight in Victorian London. Henry Mayhew interviewed two of them, recording their patter and their musical repertoire – "Going Ober de Mountain", "Buffalo Gals", "Dandy Jim of Carolina". About fifty men of various nationalities – including one genuine African – plied this trade. One of their number noted that his fellows "drink as hard as they can, and a good many of them live with women of the town". Drawn by Watts Phillips in 1851.

is on this station now, and plays the Devil with them!

Well, my lads! How are you to-night, my lads! Playing cards here, eh? Who wins? – Why, Mr. Field, I, the sulky gentlemen with the damp flat side-curls, rubbing my bleared eye with the end of my neck-kerchief which is like a dirty eel-skin, am losing just at present, but I suppose I must take my pipe out of my mouth, and be submissive to *you* – I hope I see you well, Mr. Field? – Aye, all right, my lad. Deputy, who have you got up-stairs? Be pleased to show the rooms!

Why Deputy, Inspector Field can't say. He only knows that the man who takes care of the beds and lodgers is always called so. Steady, O Deputy, with the flaring candle in the blacking bottle, for this is a slushy back-yard, and the wooden staircase outside the house creaks and has holes in it.

Again, in these confined intolerable rooms, burrowed out like the holes of rats or the nests of insect vermin, but fuller of intolerable smells, are crowds of sleepers, each on his foul truckle-bed coiled up beneath a rug. Halloa here! Come! Let us see you! Shew your face! Pilot Parker goes from bed to bed and turns their slumbering heads towards us, as a salesman might turn sheep. Some wake up with an execration and a threat. – What! who spoke? O! If it's the accursed glaring eye that fixes me, go where I will, I am helpless. Here! I sit up to be looked at. Is it me you want? – Not you, lie down again! – and I lie down, with a woeful growl.

Wherever the turning lane of light becomes stationary for a moment, some sleeper appears at the end of it, submits himself to be scrutinized, and fades away into the darkness.

There should be strange dreams here, Deputy. They sleep sound enough, says Deputy, taking the candle out of the blacking

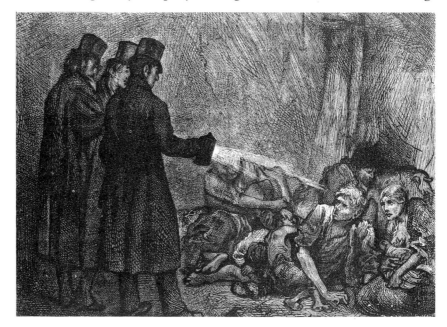

34

bottle, snuffing it with his fingers, throwing the snuff into the bottle, and corking it up with the candle; that's all *I* know. What is the inscription, Deputy, on all the discoloured sheets? A precaution against loss of linen. Deputy turns down the rug of an unoccupied bed and discloses it. STOP THIEF!

To lie at night, wrapped in the legend of my slinking life; to take the cry that pursues me, waking, to my breast in sleep; to have it staring at me, and clamouring for me, as soon as consciousness returns; to have it for my first-foot on New Year's day, my Valentine, my Birthday salute, my Christmas greeting, my parting with the old year. STOP THIEF!

And to know that I *must* be stopped, come what will. To know that I am no match for this individual energy and keenness, or this organised and steady system! Come across the street, here, and, entering by a little shop, and yard, examine these intricate passages and doors contrived for escape, flapping and counter-flapping, like the lids of the conjuror's boxes. But what avail they? Who gets in by a nod, and shews their secret working to us? Inspector Field.

Don't forget the old Farm House, Parker! Parker is not the man to forget it. We are going there, now. It is the old Manor House of these parts, and stood in the country once. Then, perhaps, there was something, which was not the beastly street, to see from the shattered low fronts of the overhanging wooden houses we are passing under – shut up now, pasted over with bills about the literature and drama of the Mint, and mouldering away. This long paved yard was a paddock or a garden once, or a court in front of the Farm House. Perchance, with a dovecot in the centre, and fowls pecking about – with fair elm trees, then, where discoloured chimney-stacks and gables are now – noisy, then, with rooks which have yielded to a different sort of rookery. It's likelier than not, Inspector Field thinks, as we turn into the common kitchen, which is in the yard, and many paces from the house.

Well, my lads and lasses, how are you all! Where's Blackey, who has stood near London Bridge these five-and-twenty years, with a painted skin to represent disease? – Here he is, Mr. Field! – How are you, Blackey? – Jolly, sa! – Not playing the fiddle to-night, Blackey? – Not a night, sa! – A sharp, smiling youth, the wit of the kitchen, interposes. He an't musical to-night, sir. I've been giving him a moral lecture; I've been a talking to him about his latter end, you see. A good many of these are my pupils, sir. This here young man (smoothing down the hair of one near him, reading a Sunday paper) is a pupil of mine. I'm a teaching of him to read, sir. He's a promising cove, sir. He's a smith, he is, and gets his living by the sweat of the brow, sir. So do I, myself, sir. This young woman is my sister, Mr. Field. *She's* a getting on very well too. I've a deal of trouble with 'em, sir, but I'm richly rewarded, now I see 'em all a doing so well, and growing up so creditable. That's a great comfort, that is, an't it, sir? – In the midst of the kitchen (the whole kitchen is in ecstacies with this

"I was born a cripple" reads the notice round the neck of this street seller of nutmeg-graters in the 1850s. His knees are shod.

impromptu "chaff") sits a young, modest, gentle-looking creature, with a beautiful child in her lap. She seems to belong to the company, but is so strangely unlike it. She has such a pretty, quiet face and voice, and is so proud to hear the child admired – thinks you would hardly believe that he is only nine months old! Is she as bad as the rest, I wonder? Inspectorial experience does not engender a belief contrariwise, but prompts the answer, Not a ha'porth of difference!

There is a piano going in the old Farm House as we approach. It stops. Landlady appears. Has no objections, Mr. Field, to gentlemen being brought, but wishes it were at earlier hours, the lodgers complaining of ill-conwenience. Inspector Field is polite and soothing – knows his woman and the sex. Deputy (a girl in this case) shows the way up a heavy broad old staircase, kept very clean, into clean rooms where many sleepers are, and where painted panels of an older time look strangely on the truckle beds. The sight of whitewash and the smell of soap – two things we seem by this time to have parted from in infancy – make the old Farm House a phenomenon, and connect themselves with the so curiously misplaced picture of the pretty mother and child long after we have left it, – long after we have left, besides, the neighbouring nook with something of a rustic flavour in it yet, where once, beneath a low wooden colonnade still standing as of yore, the eminent Jack Sheppard condescended to regale himself, and where, now, two old bachelor brothers in broad hats (who are whispered in the Mint to have made a compact long ago that if either should ever marry, he must forfeit his share of the joint property) still keep a sequestered tavern, and sit o'nights smoking pipes in the bar, among ancient bottles and glasses, as our eyes behold them.

How goes the night now? St. George of Southwark answers with twelve blows upon his bell. Parker, good night, for Williams is already waiting over in the region of Ratcliffe Highway, to show the houses where the sailors dance.

I should like to know where Inspector Field was born. In Ratcliffe Highway, I would have answered with confidence, but for his being equally at home wherever we go. *He* does not trouble his head as I do, about the river at night. *He* does not care for its creeping, black and silent, on our right there, rushing through sluice gates, lapping at piles and posts and iron rings, hiding strange things in its mud, running away with suicides and accidentally drowned bodies faster than midnight funeral should, and acquiring such various experience between its cradle and its grave. It has no mystery for *him*. Is there not the Thames Police!

Accordingly, Williams lead the way. We are a little late, for some of the houses are already closing. No matter. You show us plenty. All the landlords know Inspector Field. All pass him, freely and good-humouredly, wheresoever he wants to go. So thoroughly are all these houses open to him and our local guide, that, granting that sailors must be entertained in their own way –

A family down on its luck, drawn by Watts Phillips in 1851. Singing in the street was illegal as a form of begging; it was the last resort of many destitute families before going into the workhouse.

as I suppose they must, and have a right to be – I hardly know how such places could be better regulated. Not that I call the company very select, or the dancing very graceful – even so graceful as that of the German Sugar Bakers, whose assembly, by the Minories, we stopped to visit – but there is watchful maintenance of order in every house, and swift expulsion where need is. Even in the midst of drunkenness, both of the lethargic kind and the lively, there is sharp landlord supervision, and pockets are in less peril than out of doors. These houses show, singularly, how much of the picturesque and romantic there truly is in the sailor, requiring to be especially addressed. All the songs (sung in a hailstorm of halfpence, which are pitched at the singer without the least tenderness for the time or tune – mostly from great rolls of copper carried for the purpose – and which he occasionally dodges like shot as they fly near his head) are of the sentimental sea sort. All the rooms are decorated with nautical subjects. Wrecks, engagements, ships on fire, ships passing lighthouses on iron-bound coasts, ships blowing up, ships going down, ships running ashore, men lying out upon the main yard in a gale of wind, sailors and ships in every variety of peril, constitute the illustrations of fact. Nothing can be done in the fanciful way, without a thumping boy upon a scaly dolphin.

How goes the night now? Past one. Black and Green are waiting in Whitechapel to unveil the mysteries of Wentworth Street. Williams, the best of friends must part. Adieu!

Are not Black and Green ready at the appointed place? O yes! They glide out of shadow as we stop. Imperturbable Black opens the cab-door; Imperturbable Green takes a mental note of the driver. Both Green and Black then open each his flaming eye, and marshal us the way that we are going.

The lodging-house we want is hidden in a maze of streets and courts. It is fast shut. We knock at the door, and stand hushed looking up for a light at one or other of the begrimed old lattice windows in its ugly front when another constable comes up – supposes that we want "to see the school". Detective Serjeant meanwhile has got over a rail, opened a gate, dropped down an area, overcome some other little obstacles, and tapped at a window. Now returns. The landlord will send a deputy immediately.

Deputy is heard to stumble out of bed. Deputy lights a candle, draws back a bolt or two, and appears at the door. Deputy is a shivering shirt and trousers by no means clean, a yawning face, a shock head much confused externally and internally. We want to look for some one. You may go up with the light, and take 'em all, if you like, says Deputy, resigning it, and sitting down upon a bench in the kitchen with his ten fingers sleepily twisting in his hair.

Halloa here! Now then! Show yourselves. That'll do. It's not you. Don't disturb yourself any more! So on, through a labyrinth of airless rooms, each man responding, like a wild beast, to the keeper who has tamed him, and who goes into his cage. What, you haven't found him, then? says Deputy, when we came down. A woman mysteriously sitting up all night in the dark by the smouldering ashes of the kitchen fire, says it's only tramps and cadgers here; it's gonophs over the way. A man, mysteriously walking about the kitchen all night in the dark, bids her hold her tongue. We come out. Deputy fastens the door and goes to bed again.

Black and Green, you know Bark, lodging-house keeper and receiver of stolen goods? – O yes, Inspector Field. – Go to Bark's next.

Bark sleeps in an inner wooden hutch, near his street-door. As we parley on the step with Bark's Deputy, Bark growls in his bed. We enter, and Bark flies out of bed. Bark is a red villain and a wrathful, with a sanguine throat that looks very much as if it were expressly made for hanging, as he stretches it out, in pale defiance, over the half-door of his hutch. Bark's parts of speech are of an awful sort – principally adjectives. I won't, says Bark, have no adjective police and adjective strangers in my adjective premises! I won't, by adjective and substantive! Give me my trousers, and I'll send the whole adjective police to adjective and substantive! Give me, says Bark, my adjective trousers! I'll put an adjective knife in the whole bileing of 'em. I'll punch their adjective heads. I'll rip up their adjective substantives. Give me my adjective trousers! says Bark, and I'll spile the bileing of 'em!

Now, Bark, what's the use of this? Here's Black and Green,

"Vagrant from the Refuge in Playhouse Yard, Cripplegate". Engraved from a photograph, 1850s.

Detective Serjeant, and Inspector Field. You know we will come in. – I know you won't! says Bark. Somebody give me my adjective trousers! Bark's trousers seem difficult to find. He calls for them, as Hercules might for his club. Give me my adjective trousers! says Bark, and I'll spile the bileing of 'em!

Inspector Field holds that it's all one whether Bark likes the visit or don't like it. He, Inspector Field, is an Inspector of the Detective Police, Detective Serjeant *is* Detective Serjeant, Black and Green are constables in uniform. Don't you be a fool, Bark, or you know it will be the worse for you. – I don't care, says Bark. Give me my adjective trousers!

At two o'clock in the morning, we descend into Bark's low kitchen, leaving Bark to foam at the mouth above, and Imperturbable Black and Green to look at him. Bark's kitchen is crammed full of thieves, holding a *conversazione* there by lamplight. It is by far the most dangerous assembly we have seen yet. Stimulated by the ravings of Bark, above, their looks are sullen, but not a man speaks. We ascend again. Bark has got his trousers, and is in a state of madness in the passage with his back against a door that shuts off the upper staircase. We observe, in other respects, a ferocious individuality in Bark. Instead of "Stop Thief!" on his linen, he prints "Stolen from Bark's!"

Now Bark, we are going up stairs! – No, you an't! – You refuse admission to the Police, do you, Bark? – Yes, I do! I refuse it to all the adjective police, and to all the adjective substantives. If the adjective coves in the kitchen was men they'd come up now, and do for you! Shut me that there door! says Bark, and suddenly we are enclosed in the passage. They'd come up and do for you! cries Bark, and waits. Not a sound in the kitchen! They'd come up and do for you! cries Bark again, and waits. Not a sound in the kitchen! We are shut up, half-a-dozen of us, in Bark's house, in the innermost recesses of the worst part of London, in the dead of the night – the house is crammed with notorious robbers and ruffians – and not a man stirs. No, Bark. They know the weight of the law, and they know Inspector Field and Co. too well.

We leave Bully Bark to subside at leisure out of his passion and his trousers, and, I dare say, to be inconveniently reminded of this little brush before long. Black and Green do ordinary duty here, and look serious.

As to White, who waits on Holborn Hill to show the courts that are eaten out of rotten Gray's Inn Lane, where other lodging-houses are, and where (in one blind alley) the Thieves' Kitchen and Seminary for the teaching of the art to children, is, the night has so worn away, being now "almost at odds with morning, which is which," that they are quiet, and no light shines through the chinks in the shutters. As undistinctive Death will come here, one day, sleep comes now. The wicked cease from troubling sometimes, even in this life.

A policeman drawn by Kenny Meadows in 1840. The top hat was the earliest uniform headgear for the Metropolitan Police in London. He bears a number on his collar, a tradition of identification which persists in the police force to this day.

From **Bleak House** *chapter 22*

As they walk along, Mr. Snagsby observes, as a novelty, that however quick their pace may be, his companion still seems in some undefinable manner to lurk and lounge; also, that whenever he is going to turn to the right or left, he pretends to have a fixed purpose in his mind of going straight ahead, and wheels off, sharply, at the very last moment. Now and then, when they pass a police constable on his beat, Mr. Snagsby notices that both the constable and his guide fall into a deep abstraction as they come towards each other, and appear entirely to overlook each other, and to gaze into space. In a few instances, Mr. Bucket, coming behind some undersized young man with a shining hat on, and his sleek hair twisted into one flat curl on each side of his head, almost without glancing at him touches him with his stick; upon which the young man, looking round, instantly evaporates. For the most part Mr. Bucket notices things in general, with a face as unchanging as the great mourning ring on his little finger, or the brooch, composed of not much diamond and a good deal of setting, which he wears in his shirt.

When they come at last to Tom-all-Alone's, Mr. Bucket stops for a moment at the corner, and takes a lighted bull's-eye from the constable on duty there, who then accompanies him with his own particular bull's-eye at his waist. Between his two conductors, Mr. Snagsby passes along the middle of a villainous street, undrained, unventilated, deep in black mud and corrupt water – though the roads are dry elsewhere – and reeking with such smells and sights that he, who has lived in London all his life, can scarce believe his senses. Branching from this street and its heaps of ruins, are other streets and courts so infamous that Mr. Snagsby sickens in body and mind, and feels as if he were going, every moment deeper down, into the infernal gulf.

"Draw off a bit here, Mr. Snagsby," says Bucket, as a kind of shabby palanquin is borne towards them, surrounded by a noisy crowd. "Here's the fever coming up the street!"

As the unseen wretch goes by, the crowd, leaving that object of attraction, hovers round the three visitors like a dream of horrible faces, and fades away up alleys and into ruins, and behind walls; and with occasional cries and shrill whistles of warning, thenceforth flits about them until they leave the place.

"Are those the fever-houses, Darby?" Mr. Bucket coolly asks, as he turns his bull's-eye on a line of stinking ruins.

Darby replies that "all them are", and further that in all, for months and months, the people "have been down by dozens", and have been carried out, dead and dying "like sheep with the rot". Bucket observing to Mr. Snagsby as they go on again, that he looks a little poorly, Mr. Snagsby answers that he feels as if he couldn't breathe the dreadful air.

There is enquiry made, at various houses, for a boy named Jo. As few people are known in Tom-all-Alone's by any Christian sign, there is much reference to Mr. Snagsby whether he means Carrots, or the Colonel, or Gallows, or Young Chisel, or Terrier Tip, or Lanky, or the Brick. Mr. Snagsby describes over and over again. There are conflicting opinions respecting the original of his picture. Some think it must be Carrots; some say the Brick. The Colonel is produced, but is not at all near the thing. Whenever Mr. Snagsby and his conductors are stationary, the crowd flows round, and from its squalid depths obsequious advice heaves up to Mr. Bucket. Whenever they move, and the angry bull's-eyes glare, it fades away, and flits about them up the alleys, and in the ruins, and behind the walls, as before.

At last there is a lair found out where Toughy, or the Tough Subject, lays him down at night; and it is thought that the Tough Subject may be Jo. Comparison of notes between Mr. Snagsby and the proprietress of the house – a drunken face tied up in a black bundle, and flaring out of a heap of rags on the floor of a dog-hutch which is her private apartment – leads to the establishment of this conclusion. Toughy has gone to the Doctor's to get a bottle of stuff for a sick woman, but will be here anon.

"And who have we got here tonight?" says Mr. Bucket, opening another door and glaring in with his bull's-eye. "Two drunken men, eh? And two women? The men are sound enough," turning back each sleeper's arm from his face to look at him. "Are these your good men, my dears?"

"Yes, sir," returns one of the women. "They are our husbands."

"Brickmakers, eh?"

"Yes, sir."

"What are you doing here? You don't belong to London."

"No, sir. We belong to Hertfordshire."

"Whereabouts in Hertfordshire?"

"Saint Albans."

"Come up on the tramp?"

"We walked up yesterday. There's no work down with us at present, but we have done no good by coming here, and shall do none, I expect."

"That's not the way to do much good," says Mr. Bucket, turning his head in the direction of the unconscious figures on the ground.

"It an't indeed," replies the woman with a sigh. "Jenny and me knows it full well."

The room, though two or three feet higher than the door, is so low that the head of the tallest of the visitors would touch the blackened ceiling if he stood upright. It is offensive to every sense; even the gross candle burns pale and sickly in the polluted air. There are a couple of benches, and a higher bench by way of table. The men lie asleep where they stumbled down, but the women sit by the candle. Lying in the arms of the woman who has spoken, is a very young child.

"Why, what age do you call that little creature?" says Bucket. "It looks as if it was born yesterday." He is not at all rough about it; and as he turns his light gently on the infant, Mr. Snagsby is strangely reminded of another infant, encircled with light, that he has seen in pictures.

"He is not three weeks old yet, sir," says the woman.

"Is he your child?"

"Mine."

The other woman, who was bending over it when they came in, stoops down again, and kisses it as it lies asleep.

"You seem as fond of it as if you were the mother yourself," says Mr. Bucket.

"I was the mother of one like it, master, and it died."

"Ah Jenny, Jenny!" says the other woman to her; "better so. Much better to think of dead than alive, Jenny! Much better!"

"Why, you an't such an unnatural woman, I hope," returns Bucket, sternly, "as to wish your own child dead?" . . . .

As Mr. Snagsby blows his nose, and coughs his cough of sympathy, a step is heard without. Mr. Bucket throws his light into the doorway, and says to Mr. Snagsby, "Now, what do you say to Toughy? Will *he* do?"

"That's Jo," says Mr. Snagsby.

DOWN WITH THE TIDE

Household Words 5 February 1853

DICKENS's fertile imagination was constantly at work. *Household Words* made a point of its arresting and intriguing titles, and the question of what to call an article would summon from Dickens a stream of amusing and varyingly apt suggestions. His letters to W. H. Wills are full of ideas for articles, conjured out of nothing as he writes. "Down with the Tide" – Dickens's account of a night jaunt with the river police, and a lengthy interview with the toll-collector on Waterloo Bridge – started in this way. Writing to Wills on 7 October 1852, Dickens observes:

> "The Shot Tower of Waterloo Bridge" ought to make a good article. The Bridge itself – bridges of London in general – would be a fine subject for Sala, in another article. If the Waterloo Bridge people would give us a little information about the change in their affairs since the Railroad – and would let us lay hold of one of their *Night Toll-takers,* a very fine thing might perhaps be made of it. I wish you would look into the subject, and see whether it will do for me, before you lay Sala on.

Sala did visit Waterloo and describe the night toll-taker for his survey of London by day and night, *Twice Round the Clock,* but this was too good an idea for Dickens to delegate, especially when he realised it could be turned into another police article to follow Wills's "The Modern Science of Thief-Taking" and "The Metropolitan Protectives" (*Household Words* 13 July 1850 and 26 April 1851) and his own "A Detective Police Party", "Three 'Detective' Anecdotes" and "On Duty with Inspector Field" (*Household Words* 27 July, 10 August and 14 September 1850 and 14 June 1851).

Waterloo Bridge exercised a strong imaginative pull on Dickens. In Italy he wistfully yearned for it; in his essay "Night Walks" in *The Uncommercial Traveller* he moodily surveys it:

> Drip, drip, drip, from ledge and coping, splash from pipes and water-spouts, and by-and-bye the houseless shadow would fall upon the stones that pave the way to Waterloo Bridge; it being in the houseless mind to have a halfpenny worth of excuse for saying "Good-night" to the toll-keeper, and catching a glimpse of his fire. A good fire and a good great-coat and a good woollen neck-shawl, were comfortable things to see in conjunction with the toll-keeper; also his brisk wakefulness was excellent company when he rattled the change of halfpence down upon that metal table of his, like a man who defied the night, with all its sorrowful thoughts, and didn't care for the coming of dawn. There was need of encouragement on the threshold of the bridge, for the bridge was dreary . . . the river had an awful look, the buildings on the banks were muffled in black shrouds, and the reflected lights seemed to originate deep in the water, as if the spectres of suicides were holding them to show where they went down.

Lying behind this seemingly morbid preoccupation with Waterloo's suicides is Thomas Hood's poem "The Bridge of Sighs". This was inspired by the attempted suicide of Mary Furley, with her child, in March 1844. The child died, and – with a lack of feeling that appalled both Hood and Dickens – Mary was prosecuted and sentenced to death (though later reprieved). Dickens glanced sardonically at the case in his mock "Threatening Letter to Thomas Hood, from an ancient gentleman", which appeared in *Hood's Magazine,* May 1844. Hood's poem – which takes some liberties with the facts of this particular case – immediately followed Dickens's letter, and may indeed have been prompted by it.

Hood's poetry is not highly regarded now, but "The Bridge of Sighs" is, for all its pat rhymes and heightened sentiment, powered by genuine feeling and shaped with discreet skill. Dickens was most moved by it, and deeply affected when he heard it sung: "My God, how sorrowful and pitiful it is!" It is worth quoting the whole of its best-known stanza:

> The bleak wind of March
> Made her tremble and shiver;
> But not the dark arch,
> Or the black flowing river:
> Mad from life's history,
> Glad to death's mystery,
> Swift to be hurl'd –
> Anywhere, anywhere
> Out of the world!

The potency of Hood's plea for pity and understanding for a fellow creature driven to despair, coupled with the imagery of stained purity, has outlasted the Victorian fascination with the fallen woman. But its special appeal to Dickens is clear. It is present in his mind throughout the first part of "Down with the Tide", and also in his depiction of Martha Endell in *David Copperfield* and in the nightmarish scene in which Little Dorrit and her backward friend Maggy meet the desperate prostitute on London Bridge.

As in "On Duty with Inspector Field", we learn in "Down with the Tide" both about the methods and organisation of a branch of the police, and about the atmosphere in which they work and the characters with whom they deal. Dickens put his knowledge of both to use in his fiction. At the climax of *Great Expectations,* Pip and Magwitch are apprehended by a police galley such as the one described here; Dickens seems to have drawn on the police officer he calls "Peacoat" for the character of Mr. Inspector in *Our Mutual Friend.*

When Pip asks Wemmick in *Great Expectations* if he is well acquainted with London, Wemmick allows, "I know the moves of it." Nowhere in Dickens's work is it brought home more thoroughly how well *he* knew the moves of it than in his minute depiction in *Our Mutual Friend* of the strange, lean pickings to be had on and by the Thames, some of which are enumerated in this article.

In all his police articles, Dickens shows particular respect for their methodical approach to crime: prevention, detection and administration. His pleasure here in the "charge books so admirably kept" recurs again in *Our Mutual Friend*. Dickens's enthusiasm for the police may seem to contradict the popular picture of him as the champion of the poor and oppressed. But although in his novels from *Oliver Twist* to *Edwin Drood* Dickens entered criminal mentalities with consummate skill, and brilliantly exposed the social roots of crime, he was not inclined to excuse or champion criminals. Society's guilt did not mean their innocence.

Dickens's compassion for victims and young miscreants was quick and practical; his thirst for retribution against hardened criminals was relentless. He genuinely believed that, as he wrote of Sikes in the preface to *Oliver Twist,* "there are in the world some insensible and callous natures, that do become utterly and incurably bad". The only defence against such natures was vigilant and strict policing and punishment. They could not be reclaimed.

It is for this reason – and because of his innate love of order – that Dickens identified, in the battle of wits between society and its outcasts, with authority. His immense imaginative sympathy with criminals was matched by an equally immense emotional antipathy.

DOWN WITH THE TIDE

A VERY dark night it was, and bitter cold; the east wind blowing bleak, and bringing with it stinging particles from marsh, and moor, and fen – from the Great Desert and Old Egypt, maybe. Some of the component parts of the sharp-edged vapour that came flying up the Thames at London might be mummy-dust, dry atoms from the Temple at Jerusalem, camels' foot-prints, crocodiles' hatching places, loosened grains of expression from the visages of blunt-nosed sphynxes, waifs and strays from caravans of turbaned merchants, vegetation from jungles, frozen snow from the Himalayas. O! It was very very dark upon the Thames, and it was bitter bitter cold.

"And yet," said the voice within the great pea-coat at my side, "you'll have seen a good many rivers too, I dare say?"

"Truly," said I, "when I come to think of it, not a few. From the Niagara, downward to the mountain rivers of Italy, which are like the national spirit – very tame, or chafing suddenly and bursting bounds, only to dwindle away again. The Moselle, and the Rhine, and the Rhone; and the Seine, and the Saône; and the St. Lawrence, Mississippi, and Ohio; and the Tiber, the Po, and the Arno; and the – "

Peacoat coughing as if he had had enough of that, I said no more. I could have carried the catalogue on to a teasing length, though, if I had been in the cruel mind.

"And after all," said he, "this looks so dismal?"

"So awful," I returned, "at night. The Seine at Paris is very gloomy too, at such a time, and is probably the scene of far more crime and greater wickedness; but this river looks so broad and vast, so murky and silent, seems such an image of death in the midst of the great city's life, that –"

That Peacoat coughed again. He *could not* stand my holding forth.

We were in a four-oared Thames Police Galley, lying on our oars in the deep shadow of Southwark Bridge – under the corner arch of the Surrey side – having come down with the tide from Vauxhall. We were fain to hold on pretty tight, though close in shore, for the river was swollen and the tide running down very strong. We were watching certain water-rats of human growth, and lay in the deep shade as quiet as mice; our light hidden and our scraps of conversation carried on in whispers. Above us, the massive iron girders of the arch were faintly visible, and below us its ponderous shadow seemed to sink down to the bottom of the stream.

We had been lying here some half an hour. With our backs to the wind, it is true; but the wind being in a determined temper blew straight through us, and would not take the trouble to go round. I would have boarded a fireship to get into action, and mildly suggested as much to my friend Pea.

"No doubt," says he as patiently as possible; "but shore-going tactics wouldn't do with us. River thieves can always get rid of stolen property in a moment by dropping it overboard. We want to take them *with* the property, so we lurk about and come out upon 'em sharp. If they see us or hear us, over it goes."

Pea's wisdom being indisputable, there was nothing for it but to sit there and be blown through, for another half hour. The water-rats thinking it wise to abscond at the end of that time without commission of felony, we shot out, disappointed, with the tide.

"Grim they look, don't they?" said Pea, seeing me glance over my shoulder at the lights upon the bridge, and downward at their long crooked reflections in the river.

"Very," said I, "and make one think with a shudder of Suicides. What a night for a dreadful leap from that parapet!"

"Aye, but Waterloo's the favourite bridge for making holes in the water from," returned Pea. "By the bye – avast pulling lads! – would you like to speak to Waterloo on the subject?"

My face confessing to a surprised desire to have some friendly conversation with Waterloo Bridge, and my friend Pea being the most obliging of men, we put about, pulled out of the force of the stream, and in place of going at great speed with the tide, began to strive against it, close in shore again. Every colour but black seemed to have departed from the world. The air was black, the water was black, the barges and hulks were black, the piles were black, the buildings were black, the shadows were only a deeper shade of black upon a black ground. Here and there, a coal fire in an iron cresset blazed upon a wharf; but, one knew that it too had been black a little while ago, and would be black again soon. Uncomfortable rushes of water suggestive of gurgling and drowning, ghostly rattling of iron chains, dismal clankings of discordant engines, formed the music that accompanied the dip of our oars and their rattling in the rullocks. Even the noises had a black sound to me – as the trumpet sounded red to the blind man.

Our dexterous boat's crew made nothing of the tide, and pulled us gallantly up to Waterloo Bridge. Here Pea and I disembarked, passed under the black stone archway, and climbed the steep stone steps. Within a few feet of their summit, Pea presented me to Waterloo (or an eminent toll-taker representing that structure), muffled up to the eyes in a thick shawl, and amply great-coated and fur-capped.

Waterloo received us with cordiality, and observed of the night that it was "a Searcher". He had been originally called the Strand Bridge, he informed us, but had received his present name at the suggestion of the proprietors, when Parliament had resolved to vote three hundred thousand pound for the erection of a monument in honour of the victory. Parliament took the hint (said Waterloo, with the least flavour of misanthropy), and saved the money. Of course the late Duke of Wellington was the first passenger, and of course he paid his penny, and of course a noble lord preserved it evermore. The treadle and index at the toll-house

An Inspector of the Thames Police, 1891.

45

"The Bridge of Sighs", by Gustave Doré. This illustrates Thomas Hood's influential poem, but it might just as easily be Martha Endell in David Copperfield*: "I can't keep away from it. I can't forget it. It haunts me day and night. It's the only thing in all the world that I am fit for, or that's fit for me. Oh, the dreadful river!"*

(a most ingenious contrivance for rendering fraud impossible), were invented by Mr. Lethbridge, then property-man at Drury Lane Theatre.

Was it suicide, we wanted to know about? said Waterloo. Ha? Well, he had seen a good deal of that work, he did assure us. He had prevented some. Why, one day a woman, poorish looking, came in between the hatch, slapped down a penny, and wanted to go on without the change! Waterloo suspected this, and says to his mate, "give an eye to the gate," and bolted after her. She had got to the third seat between the piers, and was on the parapet just a–going over, when he caught her and gave her in charge. At the police office next morning, she said it was along of trouble and a bad husband.

"Likely enough," observed Waterloo to Pea and myself, as he

adjusted his chin in his shawl. "There's a deal of trouble about, you see – and bad husbands too!"

Another time, a young woman at twelve o'clock in the open day got through, darted along; and, before Waterloo could come near her, jumped upon the parapet, and shot herself over sideways. Alarm given, watermen put off, lucky escape – clothes buoyed her up.

"This is where it is," said Waterloo. "If people jump off straight forards from the middle of the parapet of the bays of the bridge, they are seldom killed by drowning, but are smashed, poor things; that's what *they* are; they dash themselves upon the buttress of the bridge. But you jump off," said Waterloo to me, putting his forefinger in a button hole of my great coat; "you jump off from the side of the bay, and you'll tumble, true, into the stream under the arch. What you have got to do, is to mind how you jump in! There was poor Tom Steele from Dublin. Didn't dive! Bless you, didn't dive at all! Fell down so flat into the water, that he broke his breast-bone, and lived two days!"

I asked Waterloo if there were a favourite side of his bridge for this dreadful purpose? He reflected, and thought yes, there was. He should say the Surrey side.

Three decent looking men went through one day, soberly and quietly, and went on abreast for about a dozen yards: when the middle one, he sung out, all of a sudden. "Here goes, Jack!" and was over in a minute.

Body found? Well. Waterloo didn't rightly recollect about that. They were compositors, *they* were.

He considered it astonishing how quick people were! Why, there was a cab came up one Boxing-night, with a young woman in it, who looked, according to Waterloo's opinion of her, a little the worse for liquor; very handsome she was too – very handsome. She stopped the cab at the gate, and said she'd pay the cabman then: which she did, though there was a little hankering about the fare, because at first she didn't seem quite to know where she wanted to be drove to. However she paid the man, and the toll too, and looking Waterloo in the face (he thought she knew him, don't you see!) said, "I'll finish it somehow!" Well, the cab went off, leaving Waterloo a little doubtful in his mind, and while it was going on at full speed the young woman jumped out, never fell, hardly staggered, ran along the bridge pavement a little way passing several people, and jumped over from the second opening. At the inquest it was giv' in evidence that she had been quarrelling at the Hero of Waterloo, and it was brought in jealousy. (One of the results of Waterloo's experience was, that there was a deal of jealousy about.)

"Do we ever get madmen?" said Waterloo, in answer to an inquiry of mine. "Well, we *do* get madmen. Yes, we have had one or two; escaped from 'Sylums, I suppose. One hadn't a halfpenny; and because I wouldn't let him through, he went back a little way, stooped down, took a run, and butted at the hatch like a ram. He smashed his hat rarely, but his head didn't seem no worse – in my opinion on account of his being wrong in it afore. Sometimes people haven't got a halfpenny. If they are really tired and poor we give 'em one and let 'em through. Other people will leave things – pocket-handkerchiefs mostly. I *have* taken cravats and gloves, pocket knives, toothpicks, studs, shirt pins, rings (generally from young gents, early in the morning), but handkerchiefs is the general thing.

"Regular customers?" said Waterloo. "Lord, yes! We have regular customers. One, such a worn out used-up old file as you can scarcely picter, comes from the Surrey side as regular as ten o'clock at night comes; and goes over, *I* think, to some flash house on the Middlesex side. He comes back, he does, as reg'lar as the clock strikes three in the morning, and then can hardly drag one of his old legs after the other. He always turns down the water-stairs, comes up again, and then goes on down the Waterloo Road. He always does the same thing, and never varies a minute. Does it every night – even Sundays."

I asked Waterloo if he had given his mind to the possibility of this particular customer going down the water-stairs at three o'clock some morning, and never coming up again? He didn't think *that* of him, he replied. In fact, it was Waterloo's opinion,

Two o'clock in the morning at the tollgate of Waterloo Bridge, drawn by William M'Connell in 1859. Revellers and night walkers mix with a carter bringing goods into town from the south.

founded on his observation of that file, that he know'd a trick worth two of it.

"There's another queer old customer," said Waterloo, "comes over, as punctual as the almanack, at eleven o'clock on the sixth of January, at eleven o'clock on the fifth of April, at eleven o'clock on the sixth of July, at eleven o'clock on the tenth of October. Drives a shaggy little rough pony, in a sort of a rattle-trap arm-chair sort of a thing. White hair he has, and white whiskers, and muffles himself up with all manner of shawls. He comes back again the same afternoon, and we never see more of him for three months. He is a captain in the navy – retired – wery old – wery odd – and served with Lord Nelson. He is particular about drawing his pension at Somerset House afore the clock strikes twelve every quarter. I *have* heerd say that he thinks it wouldn't be according to the Act of Parliament, if he didn't draw it afore twelve."

Having related these anecdotes in a natural manner, which was the best warranty in the world for their genuine nature, our friend Waterloo was sinking deep into his shawl again, as having exhausted his communicative powers and taken in enough east wind, when my other friend Pea in a moment brought him to the surface by asking whether he had not been occasionally the subject of assault and battery in the execution of his duty? Waterloo recovering his spirits, instantly dashed into a new branch of his subject. We learnt how "both these teeth" – here he pointed to the places where two front teeth were not – were knocked out by an ugly customer who one night made a dash at him (Waterloo) while his (the ugly customer's) pal and coadjutor made a dash at the toll-taking apron where the money-pockets were; how Waterloo, letting the teeth go (to Blazes, he observed indefinitely) grappled with the apron-seizer, permitting the ugly one to run away; and how he saved the bank, and captured his man, and consigned him to fine and imprisonment. Also how, on another night, "a Cove" laid hold of Waterloo, then presiding at the horse gate of his bridge, and threw him unceremoniously over his knee, having first cut his head open with his whip. How Waterloo "got right", and started after the Cove all down the Waterloo Road, through Stamford Street, and round to the foot of Blackfriars Bridge, where the Cove "cut into" a public house. How Waterloo cut in too; but how an aider and abettor of the Cove's who happened to be taking a promiscuous drain at the bar, stopped Waterloo; and the Cove cut out again, ran across the road down Holland Street, and where not, and into a beershop. How Waterloo breaking away from his detainer was close upon the Cove's heels, attended by no end of people who, seeing him running with the blood streaming down his face, thought something worse was "up" and roared Fire! and Murder! on the hopeful chance of the matter in hand being one or both. How the Cove was ignominiously taken, in a shed where he had run to hide, and how at the Police Court they at first wanted to make a

Captain Bobadil: from Ben Jonson's *Every Man in his Humour*. Dickens acted this role in 1845, and there is a painting of him in character by Charles Leslie

sessions job of it; but eventually Waterloo was allowed to be "spoke to", and the Cove made it square with Waterloo by paying his doctor's bill (W. was laid up for a week) and giving him "Three, ten." Likewise we learnt what we had faintly suspected before, that your sporting amateur on the Derby day, albeit a captain, can be – "if he be", as Captain Bobadil observes, "so generously minded" – anything but a man of honour and a gentleman; not sufficiently gratifying his nice sense of humour by the witty scattering of flour and rotten eggs on obtuse civilians, but requiring the further excitement of "bilking the toll", and "pitching into" Waterloo, and "cutting him about the head with his whip", finally being, when called upon to answer for the assault, what Waterloo described as "Minus", or, as I humbly conceived it, not to be found. Likewise did Waterloo inform us, in reply to my inquiries, admiringly and deferentially preferred through my friend Pea, that the takings at the Bridge had more than doubled in amount, since the reduction of the toll one half. And being asked if the aforesaid takings included much bad money, Waterloo responded, with a look far deeper than the deepest part of the river, *he* should think not! – and so retired into his shawl for the rest of the night.

Then did Pea and I once more embark in our four-oared galley, and glide swiftly down the river with the tide. And while the shrewd East rasped and notched us, as with jagged razors, did my friend Pea impart to me confidences of interest relating to the Thames Police; we betweenwhiles finding "duty boats" hanging in dark corners under banks, like weeds – our own was a "super-vision boat" – and they, as they reported "all right!" flashing their hidden light on us, and we flashing ours on them. These duty boats had one sitter in each, an Inspector, and were rowed "Ran-dan", which – for the information of those who never graduated, as I was once proud to do, under a fireman-waterman and winner of Kean's Prize Wherry; who, in the course of his tuition, took hundreds of gallons of rum and egg (at my expense) at the various houses of note above and below bridge; not by any means because he liked it, but to cure a weakness in his liver, for which the faculty had particularly recommended it – may be explained as rowed by three men, two pulling an oar each, and one a pair of sculls.

Thus, floating down our black highway, sullenly frowned upon by the knitted brows of Blackfriars, Southwark, and London, each in his lowering turn, I was shown by my friend Pea that there are, in the Thames Police Force whose district extends from Battersea to Barking Creek, ninety-eight men, eight duty boats, and two supervision boats; and that these go about so silently, and lie in wait in such dark places, and so seem to be nowhere, and so may be anywhere, that they have gradually become a police of prevention, keeping the river almost clear of any great crimes, even while the increased vigilance on shore has made it much harder than of yore to live by "thieving" in the streets. And as to

the various kinds of water thieves, said my friend Pea, there were the Tier-rangers, who silently dropped alongside the tiers of shipping in the Pool, by night, and who, going to the companion-head, listened for two snores – snore number one, the skipper's; snore number two, the mate's – mates and skippers always snoring great guns, and being dead sure to be hard at it if they had turned in and were asleep. Hearing the double fire, down went the Rangers into the skippers' cabins; groped for the skippers' inexpressibles, which it was the custom of those gentlemen to shake off, watch, money, braces, boots, and all together, on the floor; and therewith made off as silently as might be. Then there were the Lumpers, or labourers employed to unload vessels. They wore loose canvas jackets with a broad hem in the bottom, turned inside, so as to form a large circular pocket in which they could conceal, like clowns in pantomimes, packages of surprising sizes. A great deal of property was stolen in this manner (Pea confided to me) from steamers; first, because steamers carry a larger number of small packages than other ships; next, because of the extreme rapidity with which they are obliged to be unladen for their return voyages. The Lumpers dispose of their booty, easily, to marine store dealers, and the only remedy to be suggested is that marine store shops should be licensed, and thus brought under the eye of the police as rigidly as public-houses. Lumpers also smuggle goods ashore for the crews of vessels. The smuggling of tobacco is so considerable, that it is well worth the while of the sellers of smuggled tobacco to use hydraulic presses, to squeeze a single pound into a package small enough to be contained in an ordinary pocket. Next, said my friend Pea, there were the Truckers – less thieves than smugglers, whose business it was to land more considerable parcels of goods than the Lumpers could manage. They sometimes sold articles of grocery, and so forth, to the crews, in order to cloak their real calling, and get aboard without suspicion. Many of them had boats of their own, and made money. Besides these, there were the Dredgermen, who, under pretence of dredging up coals and such like from the bottom of the river, hung about barges and other undecked craft, and when they saw an opportunity, threw any property they could lay their hands on over board: in order slyly to dredge it up when the vessel was gone. Sometimes, they dexterously used their dredges to whip away anything that might lie within reach. Some of them were mighty neat at this, and the accomplishment was called dry dredging. Then there was a vast deal of property, such as copper nails, sheathing, hardwood, etc., habitually brought away by shipwrights and other workmen from their employers' yards, and disposed of to marine store dealers, many of whom escaped detection through hard swearing, and their extraordinary artful ways of accounting for the possession of stolen property. Likewise, there were special-pleading practitioners, for whom barges "drifted away of their own selves" – they having no hand in it, except first cutting them loose, and afterwards plundering them – innocents, meaning no harm, who had the misfortune to observe those foundlings wandering about the Thames.

We were now going in and out, with little noise and great nicety, among the tiers of shipping, whose many hulls, lying close together, rose out of the water like black streets. Here and there, a Scotch, an Irish, or a foreign steamer, getting up her steam as the tide made, looked, with her great chimney and high sides, like a quiet factory among the common buildings. Now the streets opened into clearer spaces, now contracted into alleys; but the tiers were so like houses, in the dark, that I could almost have believed myself in the narrower byeways of Venice. Everything was wonderfully still; for it wanted full three hours of flood, and nothing seemed awake but a dog here and there.

So we took no Tier-rangers captive, nor any Lumpers, nor Truckers, nor Dredgermen, nor other evil disposed person or persons; but went ashore at Wapping where the old Thames Police office is now a station house, and where the old Court, with its cabin windows looking on the river, is a quaint charge room; with nothing worse in it usually than a stuffed cat in a glass case, and a portrait, pleasant to behold, of a rare old Thames Police officer, Mr. Superintendent Evans, now succeeded by his son. We looked over the charge books, admirably kept, and found the prevention so good, that there were not five hundred entries (including drunken and disorderly) in a whole year. Then we looked into the store-room; where there was an oakum smell, and a nautical seasoning of dreadnought clothing, rope yarn, boat hooks, sculls and oars, spare stretchers, rudders, pistols, cutlasses, and the like. Then, into the cell, aired high up in the wooden wall through an opening like a kitchen plate-rack: wherein there was a drunken man, not at all warm, and very wishful to know if it were morning yet. Then, into a better sort of watch and ward room, where there was a squadron of stone bottles drawn up, ready to be filled with hot water and applied to any unfortunate creature who might be brought in apparently drowned. Finally we shook hands with our worthy friend Pea, and ran all the way to Tower Hill, under strong Police suspicion occasionally, before we got warm.

The Thames Police headquarters at Wapping, 1891.

From **Little Dorrit** *book I chapter 14*

THREE o'clock, and half-past three, and they had passed over London Bridge. They had heard the rush of the tide against obstacles; and looked down, awed, through the dark vapour on the river; had seen little spots of lighted water where the bridge lamps were reflected, shining like demon eyes, with a terrible fascination in them for guilt and misery. They had shrunk past homeless people, lying coiled up in nooks. They had run from drunkards. They had started from slinking men, whistling and signing to one another at bye corners, or running away at full speed. Though everywhere the leader and the guide, Little Dorrit, happy for once in her youthful appearance, feigned to cling to and rely upon Maggy. And more than once some voice, from among a knot of brawling or prowling figures in their path, had called out to the rest to "let the woman and the child go by!"

So, the woman and the child had gone by, and gone on, and five had sounded from the steeples. They were walking slowly towards the east, already looking for the first pale streak of day, when a woman came after them.

"What are you doing with the child?" she said to Maggy.

She was young – far too young to be there, Heaven knows! – and neither ugly nor wicked-looking. She spoke coarsely, but with no naturally coarse voice; there was even something musical in its sound.

"What are you doing with yourself?" retorted Maggy, for want of a better answer.

"Can't you see, without my telling you?"

"I don't know as I can," said Maggy.

"Killing myself. Now I have answered you, answer me. What are you doing with the child?"

The supposed child kept her head drooped down, and kept her form close at Maggy's side.

"Poor thing!" said the woman. "Have you no feeling, that you keep her out in the cruel streets at such a time as this? Have you no eyes, that you don't see how delicate and slender she is? Have you no sense (you don't look as if you had much) that you don't take more pity on this cold and trembling little hand?"

She had stepped across to that side, and held the hand between her own two, chafing it. "Kiss a poor lost creature, dear," she said, bending her face, "and tell me where's she taking you."

Little Dorrit turned towards her.

"Why, my God!" she said, recoiling, "you're a woman!"

"Don't mind that!" said Little Dorrit, clasping one of her hands that had suddenly released hers. "I am not afraid of you."

"Then you had better be," she answered. "Have you no mother?"

"No."

"No father?"

"Yes, a very dear one."

"Go home to him, and be afraid of me. Let me go. Good night!"

"I must thank you first; let me speak to you as if I really were a child."

"You can't do it," said the woman. "You are kind and innocent; but you can't look at me out of a child's eyes. I never should have touched you, but I thought that you were a child."

And with a strange, wild cry, she went away.

A VISIT TO NEWGATE

Sketches by Boz, 1836

NEWGATE Prison, wrote W. Hepworth Dixon in 1850, "is massive, dark and solemn, arrests the eye and holds it . . . for it is one of the half dozen buildings in this wilderness of bricks and mortar, which have a character." The prison had a long history. It was built, according to London's first historian, John Stow, "about the raigne of Henry II or Richard I"; after some reconstruction, that building was destroyed during the Gordon Riots of 1780 (its burning was graphically described by Dickens in several chapters of *Barnaby Rudge*). After its rebuilding in 1782, public executions took place outside it until 1868 (Fagin was hanged there); the building was finally demolished in 1903-4 when the Central Criminal Court was erected on its site. The very name of the prison became part of the language, and phrases like "Newgate fashion" and "black as Newgate's knocker" seem to have outlasted its physical existence. When the reformer John Howard visited it towards the end of the eighteenth century he was told that "criminals who had affected an air of boldness during their trial, and appeared quite unconcerned at the pronouncing sentence upon them, were struck with horror, and shed tears" when they were taken to the cells.

The conditions under which prisoners of both sexes were held in Newgate remained, until 1817, appalling. After this date some reforms were carried out and there was a good deal of rebuilding within its walls. When, therefore, "Boz" visited Newgate in 1835 conditions in the prison were not as bad as they had been earlier in the century. "I have", he explained to his publisher, "long projected sketching its Interior and I think it would tell extremely well." Three weeks later the piece was written. A corrected proof was highly praised by two experienced journalists, and "A Visit to Newgate" proved to be extremely popular. More than forty years later, in about 1880, it was reprinted with a rather sensational appendix in C. H. Ross's Penny Library as *Newgate by Charles Dickens; to which are added some Curious Facts relating to the Prison and its Prisoners.*

Dickens's next major work was *Pickwick,* and here the overall humorous tone, despite some sombre moments, precluded any serious social comment. The scenes which take place in a civil prison, however, are presented with a harsh reality, so that even Mr. Pickwick's normal ebullience of spirit is dampened: "I have seen enough . . . My head aches with these scenes, and my heart too."

Newgate continued to fascinate Dickens. By 1836 he was already planning a novel called *Gabriel Vardon, the Locksmith of London,* in which Newgate was to play a central part. In the event, for various reasons, the novel did not come out until 1841 under a rather different title, *Barnaby Rudge.* In the meantime, between 1837 and 1839, *Oliver Twist* was published, with the shadow of Newgate looming over the criminal world described in it, and with the grim culmination to the novel of Oliver Twist's visit to Fagin in the condemned cell of the prison. Dickens's last, and unfinished, novel *Edwin Drood* was also to have ended in a condemned cell, and he was planning to take Luke Fildes, his illustrator, to see the one at Maidstone Gaol, the nearest prison to Gad's Hill where the novel was being written.

As Philip Collins's excellent study *Dickens and Crime* shows, Dickens had a deep and abiding interest in prisons, but an ambivalent attitude to them as institutions, to their effectiveness, and to the effect they had upon their inmates. In chapter 67 of

Barnaby Rudge he relates how, although prisoners in Newgate made a dash for freedom when the building was attacked by rioters and destroyed, a number of them returned and were found hanging about the ruins in the following days.

In *Great Expectations,* Wemmick, clerk to Jaggers the attorney, takes Pip into the prison with him. "Would you like to have a look at Newgate?" he asks, "Have you time to spare?" Pip has – but he finds the prison scene "frouzy, ugly, disorderly, depressing". Wemmick, on the other hand, is used to visiting Jaggers's clients there and moves confidently among the prisoners with a kind of friendly detachment which is most evident when he stops to pass a few words with the "Colonel", a man convicted of making counterfeit coins who is to be hanged in a few days:

> "Colonel to you!" said Wemmick; "how are you, Colonel?"
> "All right, Mr. Wemmick."
> "Everything was done that could be done, but the evidence was too strong for us, Colonel."
> "Yes, it was too strong, sir – but *I* don't care."
> "No, no," said Wemmick coolly, "*you* don't care." Then turning to me, "Served his Majesty this man. Was a soldier in the line and bought his discharge."

The kind of authenticity that Dickens brought to his descriptions of the prison was echoed in an autobiographical essay, "Lodged in Newgate", which appeared in *Household Words* on 3 September 1853. Although published anonymously, the article was written by T. H. Wilson, and prepared for publication by Henry Morley, then on the staff of the magazine. The details of the prisoner's reception and the subsequent two weeks are extremely well written, with a sharp eye to unexpected detail which has the ring of truth about it. There is the summons to exercise:

> A stentorian voice shouted from the yard, "All – down!" I heard the cell doors being opened in the corridor; and, in due turn mine was flung open, and the jailer looked in. The impression my body had left on the rugs enraged him dreadfully. "What," he cried, almost in a scream, "you've been a lying on that 'ere bed have you! You just let me catch you on it again till night, that's all!"

Beds in prison, like those in army recruitment camps, have a very special place in the daily routine. Each morning they have to be "made up", that is, with the blankets neatly and uniformly folded at the bed-head. The following morning is too real for anyone to have imagined it:

> Hearing my neighbours who had made up their beds clumsily sharply admonished, I packed mine up in a military style before the jailer came to me. He looked surprised and gratified. The order being "Go below and wash!", I obeyed it.

On his return, the prisoner was taken by the jailer into a nearby cell and ordered to instruct its occupant in the art of prison bed-making.

So the days passed. There are some fascinating sketches of fellow prisoners, with a visit by the narrator's wife and some comments on the occasional acts of kindness shown by jailers. Another prisoner is visited by a very sanctimonious brother who, on being told that prison meals are unappetising, says to the jailer present, "Prison fare is good enough for him, too good for him", and refuses to pay for extra food.

The way in which such detail is presented to the reader speaks well for Morley's intervention in the text – and for Dickens's influence on him. The author disclaims any literary aspirations: "I have", he wrote, "told my story simply as so much experience and have no desire or talent for constructing any theories upon it."

Dickens himself wrote on 1 January 1853, also in *Household Words:* "We have never outgrown the rugged walls of Newgate. . . . All within, is the same blank of remorse and misery." For the remaining years of his life he retained this view.

A VISIT TO NEWGATE

"THE force of habit" is a trite phrase in everybody's mouth; and it is not a little remarkable that those who use it most as applied to others, unconsciously afford in their own persons singular examples of the power which habit and custom exercise over the minds of men, and of the little reflection they are apt to bestow on subjects with which every day's experience has rendered them familiar. If Bedlam could be suddenly removed like another Aladdin's palace, and set down on the space now occupied by Newgate, scarcely one man out of a hundred, whose road to business every morning lies through Newgate Street, or the Old Bailey, would pass the building without bestowing a hasty glance on its small, grated windows, and a transient thought upon the condition of the unhappy beings immured in its dismal cells; and yet these same men, day by day, and hour by hour, pass and repass this gloomy depository of the guilt and misery of London, in one perpetual stream of life and bustle, utterly unmindful of the throng of wretched creatures pent up within it – nay, not even knowing, or if they do, not heeding, the fact, that as they pass one particular angle of the massive wall with a light laugh or a merry whistle, they stand within one yard of a fellow-creature, bound and helpless, whose hours are numbered, from whom the last feeble ray of hope has fled for ever, and whose miserable career will shortly terminate in a violent and shameful death. Contact with death even in its least terrible shape, is solemn and appalling. How much more awful is it to reflect on this near vicinity to the dying – to men in full health and vigour, in the flower of youth or the prime of life, with all their faculties and perceptions as acute and perfect as your own; but dying, nevertheless – dying as surely – with the hand of death imprinted upon them as indelibly – as if mortal disease had wasted their frames to shadows, and corruption had already begun!

It was with some such thoughts as these that we determined, not many weeks since, to visit the interior of Newgate – in an amateur capacity, of course; and, having carried our intention into effect, we proceed to lay its results before our readers, in the hope – founded more upon the nature of the subject, than on any presumptuous confidence in our own descriptive powers – that this paper may not be found wholly devoid of interest. We have only to premise, that we do not intend to fatigue the reader with any statistical accounts of the prison; they will be found at length in numerous reports of numerous committees, and a variety of authorities of equal weight. We took no notes, made no memoranda, measured none of the yards, ascertained the exact number of inches in no particular room: are unable even to report of how many apartments the gaol is composed.

We saw the prison, and saw the prisoners; and what we did see, and what we thought, we will tell at once in our own way.

Having delivered our credentials to the servant who answered our knock at the door of the governor's house, we were ushered into the "office"; a little room, on the right-hand side as you enter, with two windows looking into the Old Bailey: fitted up like an ordinary attorney's office, or merchant's counting-house, with the usual fixtures – a wainscoted partition, a shelf or two, a desk, a couple of stools, a pair of clerks, an almanack, a clock, and a few maps. After a little delay, occasioned by sending into the interior of the prison for the officer whose duty it was to conduct us, that functionary arrived; a respectable-looking man of about two or three and fifty, in a broad-brimmed hat, and full suit of black, who, but for his keys, would have looked quite as much like a clergyman as a turnkey. We were disappointed; he had not even top-boots on. Following our conductor by a door opposite to that at which we had entered, we arrived at a small room, without any other furniture than a little desk, with a book for visitors' autographs, and a shelf, on which were a few boxes for papers, and casts of the heads and faces of the two notorious murderers, Bishop and Williams; the former, in particular, exhibiting a style of head and set of features, which might have afforded sufficient moral grounds for his instant execution at any time, even had there been no other evidence against him. Leaving this room also, by an opposite door, we found ourself in the lodge which opens on the Old Bailey; one side of which is plentifully garnished with a choice collection of heavy sets of irons, including those worn by the redoubtable Jack Sheppard – genuine; and those *said* to have been graced by the sturdy limbs of the no less celebrated Dick Turpin – doubtful. From this lodge, a heavy oaken gate, bound with iron, studded with nails of the same material, and guarded by another turnkey, opens on a few steps, if we remember right, which terminate in a narrow and dismal stone passage, running parallel with the Old Bailey, and leading to the different yards, through a number of tortuous and intricate windings, guarded in

Bishop and Williams: body-snatchers, hung in 1831

Jack Sheppard and Dick Turpin: highwaymen, and heroes of popular novels by Dickens's friend Harrison Ainsworth

The exterior of Newgate, 1862. This is the scene passed by Nicholas and Ralph Nickleby on their way to the Saracen's Head: "There, at the very core of London, in the heart of its business and animation, in the midst of a whirl of noise and motion: stemming as it were the giant currents of life that flow ceaselessly on from different quarters, and meet beneath its walls, stands Newgate."

57

their turn by huge gates and gratings, whose appearance is sufficient to dispel at once the slightest hope of escape that any newcomer may have entertained; and the very recollection of which, on eventually traversing the place again, involves one in a maze of confusion.

It is necessary to explain here, that the buildings in the prison — or in other words the different wards — form a square, of which the four sides abut respectively on the Old Bailey, the old College of Physicians (now forming a part of Newgate market), the Sessions-house, and Newgate Street. The intermediate space is divided into several paved yards, in which the prisoners take such air and exercise as can be had in such a place. These yards, with the exception of that in which prisoners under sentence of death are confined (of which we shall presently give a more detailed description), run parallel with Newgate Street, and consequently from the Old Bailey, as it were, to Newgate market. The women's side is in the right wing of the prison nearest the Sessions-house. As we were introduced into this part of the building first, we will adopt the same order, and introduce our readers to it also.

Turning to the right, then, down the passage to which we just now adverted, omitting any mention of intervening gates — for if we noticed every gate that was unlocked for us to pass through, and locked again as soon as we had passed, we should require a gate at every comma — we came to a door composed of thick bars of wood, through which were discernible, passing to and fro in a narrow yard, some twenty women: the majority of whom, however, as soon as they were aware of the presence of strangers, retreated to their wards. One side of this yard is railed off at a considerable distance, and formed into a kind of iron cage, about five feet ten inches in height, roofed at the top, and defended in front by iron bars, from which the friends of the female prisoners communicate with them. In one corner of this singular-looking den, was a yellow, haggard, decrepit old woman, in a tattered gown that had once been black, and the remains of an old straw bonnet, with faded ribbon of the same hue, in earnest conversation with a young girl — a prisoner, of course — of about two-and-twenty. It is impossible to imagine a more poverty-stricken object, or a creature so borne down in soul and body, by excess of misery and destitution, as the old woman. The girl was a good-looking, robust female, with a profusion of hair streaming about in the wind — for she had no bonnet on — and a man's silk pocket-handkerchief loosely thrown over a most ample pair of shoulders. The old woman was talking in that low, stifled tone of voice which tells so forcibly of mental anguish; and every now and then burst into an irrepressible sharp, abrupt cry of grief, the most distressing sound that ears can hear. The girl was perfectly unmoved. Hardened beyond all hope of redemption, she listened doggedly to her mother's entreaties, whatever they were: and, beyond inquiring after "Jem", and eagerly catching at the few

The visitors' enclosure at Clerkenwell House of Correction. A watercolour by T. H. Shepherd, about 1850.

halfpence her miserable parent had brought her, took no more apparent interest in the conversation than the most unconcerned spectators. Heaven knows there were enough of them, in the persons of the other prisoners in the yard, who were no more concerned by what was passing before their eyes, and within their hearing, than if they were blind and deaf. Why should they be? Inside the prison, and out, such scenes were too familiar to them, to excite even a passing thought, unless of ridicule or contempt for feelings which they had long since forgotten.

A little farther on, a squalid-looking woman in a slovenly, thick-bordered cap, with her arms muffled in a large red shawl, the fringed ends of which straggled nearly to the bottom of a dirty white apron, was communicating some instructions to *her* visitor – her daughter evidently. The girl was thinly clad, and shaking with the cold. Some ordinary word of recognition passed between her and her mother when she appeared at the grating, but neither hope, condolence, regret, nor affection was expressed on either side. The mother whispered her instructions, and the girl received them with her pinched-up, half-starved features twisted into an expression of careful cunning. It was some scheme for the woman's defence that she was disclosing, perhaps; and a sullen smile came over the girl's face for an instant, as if she were pleased: not so much at the probability of her mother's liberation, as at the chance of her "getting off" in spite of her prosecutors. The dialogue was soon concluded; and with the same careless indifference with which they had approached each other, the mother turned towards the inner end of the yard, and the girl to the gate at which she had entered.

The girl belonged to a class – unhappily but too extensive – the very existence of which should make men's hearts bleed. Barely past her childhood, it required but a glance to discover that she was one of those children, born and bred in neglect and vice, who have never known what childhood is: who have never been taught to love and court a parent's smile, or to dread a parent's frown. The thousand nameless endearments of childhood, its gaiety and its innocence, are alike unknown to them. They have entered at once upon the stern realities and miseries of life, and to their better nature it is almost hopeless to appeal in after-times, by any of the references which will awaken, if it be only for a moment, some good feeling in ordinary bosoms, however corrupt they may have become. Talk to *them* of parental solicitude, the happy days of childhood, and the merry games of infancy! Tell them of hunger and the streets, beggary and stripes, the gin-shop, the station-house, and the pawnbroker's, and they will understand you.

Two or three women were standing at different parts of the grating, conversing with their friends, but a very large proportion of the prisoners appeared to have no friends at all, beyond such of their old companions as might happen to be within the walls. So, passing hastily down the yard, and pausing only for an instant to notice the little incidents we have just recorded, we were

neglect: "poverty" in first edition

almost hopeless: "hopeless" in first edition

The chief warder of Newgate, with an assistant, at the prison's massive inner door, sometime in the mid-century. He holds himself like an ex-soldier.

conducted up a clean and well-lighted flight of stone stairs to one of the wards. There are several in this part of the building, but a description of one is a description of the whole.

It was a spacious, bare, whitewashed apartment, lighted, of course, by windows looking into the interior of the prison, but far more light and airy than one could reasonably expect to find in such a situation. There was a large fire with a deal table before it, round which ten or a dozen women were seated on wooden forms at dinner. Along both sides of the room ran a shelf; below it, at regular intervals, a row of large hooks were fixed in the wall, on each of which was hung the sleeping mat of a prisoner: her rug and blanket being folded up, and placed on the shelf above. At night, these mats are placed on the floor, each beneath the hook on which it hangs during the day; and the ward is thus made to answer the purposes both of a day-room and sleeping apartment. Over the fireplace was a large sheet of pasteboard, on which were displayed a variety of texts from Scripture, which were also scattered about the room in scraps about the size and shape of the copy-slips which are used in schools. On the table was a sufficient provision of a kind of stewed beef and brown bread, in pewter dishes, which are kept perfectly bright, and displayed on shelves in great order and regularity when they are not in use.

The women rose hastily, on our entrance, and retired in a hurried manner to either side of the fireplace. They were all cleanly – many of them decently – attired, and there was nothing peculiar, either in their appearance or demeanour. One or two resumed the needlework which they had probably laid aside at the commencement of their meal; others gazed at the visitors with listless curiosity; and a few retired behind their companions to the very end of the room, as if desirous to avoid even the casual observation of the strangers. Some old Irish women, both in this and other wards, to whom the thing was no novelty, appeared perfectly indifferent to our presence, and remained standing close to the seats from which they had just risen; but the general feeling among the females seemed to be one of uneasiness during the period of our stay among them: which was very brief. Not a word was uttered during the time of our remaining, unless, indeed, by the wardswoman in reply to some question which we put to the turnkey who accompanied us. In every ward on the female side, a wardswoman is appointed to preserve order, and a similar regulation is adopted among the males. The wardsmen and wardswomen are all prisoners, selected for good conduct. They alone are allowed the privilege of sleeping on bedsteads; a small stump bedstead being placed in every ward for that purpose. On both sides of the gaol is a small receiving-room, to which prisoners are conducted on their first reception, and whence they cannot be removed until they have been examined by the surgeon of the prison.

Retracing our steps to the dismal passage in which we found ourselves at first (and which, by-the-bye, contains three or four dark cells for the accommodation of refractory prisoners), we were led through a narrow yard to the "school" – a portion of the prison set apart for boys under fourteen years of age. In a tolerable-sized room in which were writing-materials and some copy-books, was the schoolmaster, with a couple of his pupils; the remainder having been fetched from an adjoining apartment, the whole were drawn up in line for our inspection. There were fourteen of them in all, some with shoes, some without; some in pinafores without jackets, others in jackets without pinafores, and one in scarce anything at all. The whole number, without an exception we believe, had been committed for trial on charges of pocket-picking; and fourteen such terrible little faces we never beheld. – There was not one redeeming feature among them – not a glance of honesty – not a wink expressive of anything but the gallows and the hulks, in the whole collection. As to anything like shame or contrition, that was entirely out of the question. They were evidently quite gratified at being thought worth the trouble of looking at; their idea appeared to be that we had come to see Newgate as a grand affair, and that they were an indispensable part of the show; and every boy as he "fell in" to the line, actually seemed as pleased and important as if he had done something excessively meritorious in getting there at all. We never looked upon a more disagreeable sight, because we never saw fourteen such hopeless creatures of neglect, before.

hopeless creatures of neglect: "hopeless and irreclaimable wretches" in first edition

On either side of the school-yard is a yard for men, in one of which – that towards Newgate Street – prisoners of the more respectable class are confined. Of the other, we have little description to offer, as the different wards necessarily partake of the same character. They are provided, like the wards on the women's side, with mats and rugs, which are disposed of in the same manner during the day; the only very striking difference between their appearance and that of the wards inhabited by the females, is the utter absence of any employment. Huddled together on two opposite forms, by the fireside, sit twenty men perhaps; here, a boy in livery; there, a man in a rough great-coat and top-boots; farther on, a desperate-looking fellow in his shirt-sleeves, with an old Scotch cap upon his shaggy head; near him again, a tall ruffian, in a smock-frock; next to him, a miserable being of distressed appearance, with his head resting on his hand: – all alike in one respect, all idle and listless. When they do leave the fire, sauntering moodily about, lounging in the window, or leaning against the wall, vacantly swinging their bodies to and fro. With the exception of a man reading an old newspaper, in two or three instances, this was the case in every ward we entered.

The only communication these men have with their friends, is through two close iron gratings, with an intermediate space of about a yard in width between the two, so that nothing can be handed across, nor can the prisoner have any communication by touch with the person who visits him. The married men have a separate grating, at which to see their wives, but its construction is the same.

The prison chapel is situated at the back of the governor's house: the latter having no windows looking into the interior of the prison. Whether the associations connected with the place – the knowledge that here a portion of the burial service is, on some dreadful occasions, performed over the quick and not upon the dead – cast over it a still more gloomy and sombre air than art has imparted to it, we know not, but its appearance is very striking. There is something in a silent and deserted place of worship, solemn and impressive at any time; and the very dissimilarity of this one from any we have been accustomed to, only enhances the impression. The meanness of its appointments – the bare and scanty pulpit, with the paltry painted pillars on either side – the women's gallery with its great heavy curtain – the men's with its unpainted benches and dingy front – the tottering little table at the altar, with the commandments on the wall above it, scarcely legible through lack of paint, and dust and damp – so unlike the velvet and gilding, the marble and wood, of a modern church – are strange and striking. There is one object, too, which rivets the attention and fascinates the gaze, and from which we may turn horror-stricken in vain, for the recollection of it will haunt us, waking and sleeping, for a long time afterwards. Immediately below the reading-desk, on the floor of the chapel, and forming the most conspicuous object in its little area, is *the condemned pew*; a huge black pen, in which the wretched people, who are singled out for death, are placed on the Sunday preceding their execution, in sight of all their fellow-prisoners, from many of whom they may have been separated but a week before, to hear prayers for their own souls, to join in the responses of their own burial service, and to listen to an address, warning their recent companions to take example by their fate, and urging themselves, while there is yet time – nearly four-and-twenty hours – to "turn, and flee from the wrath to come!" Imagine what have been the feelings of the men whom that fearful pew has enclosed, and of whom, between the gallows and the knife, no mortal remnant may now remain! Think of the hopeless clinging to life to the last, and the wild despair, far exceeding in anguish the felon's death itself, by which they have heard the certainty of their speedy transmission to another world, with all their crimes upon their heads, rung into their ears by the officiating clergyman!

At one time – and at no distant period either – the coffins of the men about to be executed, were placed in that pew, upon the seat by their side, during the whole service. It may seem incredible, but it is true. Let us hope that the increased spirit of civilisation and humanity which abolished this frightful and degrading custom, may extend itself to other usages equally barbarous; usages which have not even the plea of utility in their defence, as every year's experience has shown them to be more and more inefficacious.

Leaving the chapel, descending to the passage so frequently alluded to, and crossing the yard before noticed as being allotted to prisoners of a more respectable description than the generality of men confined here, the visitor arrives at a thick iron gate of great size and strength. Having been admitted through it by the turnkey on duty, he turns sharp round to the left, and pauses before another gate; and, having passed this last barrier, he stands in the most terrible part of this gloomy building – the condemned ward.

The press-yard, well known by name to newspaper readers, from its frequent mention in accounts of executions, is at the corner of the building, and next to the ordinary's house, in Newgate Street: running from Newgate Street, towards the centre of the prison, parallel with Newgate market. It is a long, narrow court, of which a portion of the wall in Newgate Street forms one end, and the gate the other. At the upper end, on the left hand – that is, adjoining the wall in Newgate Street – is a cistern of water,

Gustave Doré: a Newgate warder.

The Exercise Yard, Newgate, by Gustave Doré, 1869. Blanchard Jerrold recalled that Doré did not use his pencil at this scene, but merely looked. "'I will tell you', he said, 'what most of these men are.' He pointed to a common thief, a forger, a highway robber, an embezzler; and the gaoler was astonished. His guesses were, mostly, quite correct. The next day when we met, he laid before me his circle of prisoners. It was a chain of portraits from the poor frightened little postman, who had succumbed to temptation in his poverty, to the tall officer who had cheated a widow out of her last mite."

chevaux de frise: spikes

and at the bottom a double grating (of which the gate itself forms a part) similar to that before described. Through these grates the prisoners are allowed to see their friends; a turnkey always remaining in the vacant space between, during the whole interview. Immediately on the right as you enter, is a building containing the press-room, day-room, and cells; the yard is on every side surrounded by lofty walls guarded by *chevaux de frise;* and the whole is under the constant inspection of vigilant and experienced turnkeys.

In the first apartment into which we were conducted – which was at the top of a staircase, and immediately over the press-room – were five-and-twenty or thirty prisoners, all under sentence of death, awaiting the result of the recorder's report – men of all ages and appearances, from a hardened old offender with swarthy face and grizzly beard of three days' growth, to a handsome boy, not fourteen years old, and of singularly youthful appearance even for that age, who had been condemned for burglary. There was nothing remarkable in the appearance of these prisoners. One or two decently-dressed men were brooding with a dejected air over the fire; several little groups of two or three had been engaged in conversation at the upper end of the room, or in the windows; and the remainder were crowded round a young man seated at a table, who appeared to be engaged in teaching the younger ones to write. The room was large, airy, and clean. There was very little anxiety or mental suffering depicted in the countenance of any of the men; – they had all been sentenced to death, it is true, and the recorder's report had not yet been made; but, we question whether there was a man among them, notwithstanding, who did not *know* that although he had undergone the ceremony, it never was intended that his life should be sacrificed. On the table lay a Testament, but there were no tokens of its having been in recent use.

In the press-room below, were three men, the nature of whose offence rendered it necessary to separate them, even from their companions in guilt. It is a long, sombre room, with two windows sunk into the stone wall, and here the wretched men are pinioned on the morning of their execution, before moving towards the scaffold. The fate of one of these prisoners was uncertain, some mitigatory circumstances having come to light since his trial, which had been humanely represented in the proper quarter. The other two had nothing to expect from the mercy of the crown; their doom was sealed; no plea could be urged in extenuation of their crime, and they well knew that for them there was no hope in this world. "The two short ones", the turnkey whispered, "were dead men."

The man to whom we have alluded as entertaining some hopes of escape, was lounging, at the greatest distance he could place between himself and his companions, in the window nearest to the door. He was probably aware of our approach, and had assumed an air of courageous indifference; his face was purposely averted towards the window, and he stirred not an inch while we were present. The other two men were at the upper end of the room. One of them, who was imperfectly seen in the dim light, had his back towards us, and was stooping over the fire, with his right arm on the mantel-piece, and his head sunk upon it. The other was leaning on the sill of the farthest window. The light fell full upon him, and communicated to his pale, haggard face, and disordered hair, an appearance which, at that distance, was ghastly. His cheek rested upon his hand; and, with his face a little raised, and his eyes wildly staring before him, he seemed to be unconsciously intent on counting the chinks in the opposite wall. We passed this room again afterwards. The first man was pacing up and down the court with a firm military step – he had been a soldier in the foot-guards – and a cloth cap jauntily thrown on one side of his head. He bowed respectfully to our conductor, and the salute was returned. The other two still remained in the positions we have described, and were as motionless as statues.

A few paces up the yard, and forming a continuation of the building, in which are the two rooms we have just quitted, lie the

Dickens's footnote: "These two men were executed shortly afterwards. The other was respited during his Majesty's pleasure."

condemned cells. The entrance is by a narrow and obscure staircase leading to a dark passage, in which a charcoal stove casts a lurid tint over the objects in its immediate vicinity, and diffuses something like warmth around. From the left-hand side of this passage, the massive door of every cell on the storey opens; and from it alone can they be approached. There are three of these passages, and three of these ranges of cells, one above the other; but in size, furniture and appearance, they are all precisely alike. Prior to the recorder's report being made, all the prisoners under sentence of death are removed from the day-room at five o'clock in the afternoon, and locked up in these cells, where they are allowed a candle until ten o'clock; and here they remain until seven next morning. When the warrant for a prisoner's execution arrives, he is removed to the cells and confined in one of them until he leaves it for the scaffold. He is at liberty to walk in the yard; but, both in his walks and in his cell, he is constantly attended by a turnkey who never leaves him on any pretence.

We entered the first cell. It was a stone dungeon, eight feet long by six wide, with a bench at the upper end, under which were a common rug, a bible, and prayer-book. An iron candlestick was fixed into the wall at the side; and a small high window in the back admitted as much air and light as could struggle in between a double row of heavy, crossed iron bars. It contained no other furniture of any description.

Conceive the situation of a man, spending his last night on earth in this cell. Buoyed up with some vague and undefined hope of reprieve, he knew not why – indulging in some wild and visionary idea of escaping, he knew not how – hour after hour of the three preceding days allowed him for preparation, has fled with a speed which no man living would deem possible, for none but this

The condemned cell, Newgate, 1862. The blankets are folded with regulation neatness, by an unknown convict detailed to the task.

dying man can know. He has wearied his friends with entreaties, exhausted the attendants with importunities, neglected in his feverish restlessness the timely warnings of his spiritual consoler; and, now that the illusion is at last dispelled, now that eternity is before him and guilt behind, now that his fears of death amount almost to madness, and an overwhelming sense of his helpless, hopeless state rushes upon him, he is lost and stupefied, and has neither thoughts to turn to, nor power to call upon, the Almighty Being, from whom alone he can seek mercy and forgiveness, and before whom his repentance can alone avail.

Hours have glided by, and still he sits upon the same stone bench with folded arms, heedless alike of the fast decreasing time before him, and the urgent entreaties of the good man at his side. The feeble light is wasting gradually, and the deathlike stillness of the street without, broken only by the rumbling of some passing vehicle which echoes mournfully through the empty yards, warns him that the night is waning fast away. The deep bell of St. Paul's strikes – one! He heard it; it has roused him. Seven hours left! He paces the narrow limits of his cell with rapid strides, cold drops of terror starting on his forehead, and every muscle of his frame quivering with agony. Seven hours! He suffers himself to be led to his seat, mechanically takes the bible which is placed in his hand, and tries to read and listen. No: his thoughts will wander. The book is torn and soiled by use – and like the book he read his lessons in, at school, just forty years ago! He has never bestowed a thought upon it, perhaps, since he left it as a child: and yet the place, the time, the room – nay, the very boys he played with, crowd as vividly before him as if they were scenes of yesterday; and some forgotten phrase, some childish word, rings in his ears like the echo of one uttered but a minute since. The voice of the clergyman recalls him to himself. He is reading from the sacred book its solemn promises of pardon for repentance, and its awful denunciation of obdurate men. He falls upon his knees and clasps his hands to pray. Hush! what sound was that? He starts upon his feet. It cannot be two yet. Hark! Two quarters have struck; – the third – the fourth. It is! Six hours left. Tell him not of repentance! Six hours' repentance for eight times six years of guilt and sin! He buries his face in his hands, and throws himself on the bench.

Worn with watching and excitement, he sleeps, and the same unsettled state of mind pursues him in his dreams. An insupportable load is taken from his breast; he is walking with his wife in a pleasant field, with the bright sky above them, and a fresh and boundless prospect on every side – how different from the stone walls of Newgate! She is looking – not as she did when he saw her for the last time in that dreadful place, but as she used when he loved her – long, long ago, before misery and ill-treatment had altered her looks, and vice had changed his nature, and she is leaning upon his arm, and looking up into his face with tenderness and affection – and he does *not* strike her now, nor rudely shake her from him. And oh! how glad he is to tell her all he had

Fagin in the condemned cell: Cruikshank's finished engraving.

forgotten in that last hurried interview, and to fall on his knees before her and fervently beseech her pardon for all the unkindness and cruelty that wasted her form and broke her heart! The scene suddenly changes. He is on his trial again: there are the judge and jury, and prosecutors, and witnesses, just as they were before. How full the court is – what a sea of heads – with a gallows, too, and a scaffold – and how all those people stare at *him*! Verdict, "Guilty". No matter; he will escape.

The night is dark and cold, the gates have been left open, and in an instant he is in the street, flying from the scene of his imprisonment like the wind. The streets are cleared, the open fields are gained and the broad, wide country lies before him. Onwards he dashes in the midst of darkness, over hedge and ditch, through mud and pool, bounding from spot to spot with a speed and lightness, astonishing even to himself. At length he pauses; he must be safe from pursuit now; he will stretch himself on that bank and sleep till sunrise.

A period of unconsciousness succeeds. He wakes, cold and wretched. The dull, grey light of morning is stealing into the cell, and falls upon the form of the attendant turnkey. Confused by his dreams, he starts from his uneasy bed in momentary uncertainty. It is but momentary. Every object in the narrow cell is too frightfully real to admit of doubt or mistake. He is the condemned felon again, guilty and despairing; and in two hours more will be dead.

Cruikshank's preliminary drawing of Fagin in the condemned cell – supposed to have been made by imagining himself in Fagin's position and then drawing himself in a mirror.

From **Oliver Twist** *chapter 52*

HE sat down on a stone bench opposite the door, which served for a seat and bedstead; and casting his blood-shot eyes upon the ground, tried to collect his thoughts. After a while, he began to remember a few disjointed fragments of what the judge had said, though it had seemed to him, at the time, that he could not hear a word. These gradually fell into their proper places, and by degrees suggested more: so that in a little time he had the whole, almost as it was delivered. To be hanged by the neck, till he was dead – that was the end. To be hanged by the neck till he was dead.

As it came on very dark, he began to think of all the men he had known who had died upon the scaffold; some of them through his means. They rose up, in such quick succession, that he could hardly count them. He had seen some of them die – and had joked too, because they died with prayers upon their lips. With what a rattling noise the drop went down; and how suddenly they changed, from strong and vigorous men to dangling heaps of clothes!

Some of them might have inhabited that very cell – sat upon that very spot. It was very dark; why didn't they bring a light? The cell had been built for many years. Scores of men must have passed their last hours there. It was like sitting in a vault strewn with dead bodies – the cap, the noose, the pinioned arms, the faces that he knew, even beneath that hideous veil. – Light, light!

At length, when his hands were raw with beating against the heavy door and walls, two men appeared: one bearing a candle, which he thrust into an iron candlestick fixed against the wall: the other dragging in a mattress on which to pass the night; for the prisoner was to be left alone no more.

Then came night – dark, dismal, silent night. Other watchers are glad to hear the church-clocks strike, for they tell of life and coming day. To the Jew they brought despair. The boom of every iron bell came laden with the one, deep, hollow sound – Death. What availed the noise and bustle of cheerful morning, which penetrated even there, to him? It was another form of knell, with mockery added to the warning. . . .

He cowered down upon his stone bed, and thought of the past. He had been wounded with some missiles from the crowd on the day of his capture, and his head was bandaged with a linen cloth. His red hair hung down upon his bloodless face; his beard was torn, and twisted into knots; his eyes shone with a terrible light; his unwashed flesh crackled with the fever that burnt him up. Eight – nine – ten. If it was not a trick to frighten him, and those were the real hours treading on each other's heels, where would he be, when they came round again! Eleven! Another struck, before the voice of the previous hour had ceased to vibrate. At eight, he would be the only mourner in his own funeral train; at eleven –

Those dreadful walls of Newgate, which have hidden so much misery and such unspeakable anguish, not only from the eyes, but, too often, and too long, from the thoughts, of men, never held so dread a spectacle as that. The few who lingered as they passed, and wondered what the man was doing who was to be hanged tomorrow, would have slept but ill that night, if they could have seen him.

PET PRISONERS

Household Words 27 April 1850

IN this article, which forms part of a continuing and often agonised nineteenth-century discussion about the treatment of criminals, and which in its own right caused controversy, Dickens demonstrates a much tougher and harder side to his nature than the one to which most of us are accustomed. It is almost certainly true that, because he achieved considerable fame as a novelist so early in his career, his reputation for many readers rests largely upon such earlier works as *Pickwick Papers, Oliver Twist, Nicholas Nickleby* and *The Old Curiosity Shop,* where the author appears before us as a warm, tender-hearted, even jolly person. In later years – *Bleak House,* say, or *Our Mutual Friend* – there is much less fun and a sharper edge; but by the time they had been published the jollier image was well established, and even today it has not been seriously modified for many readers, despite the undoubted evidence of the later works.

When he wrote "A Visit to Newgate", Dickens was a young man and the prison itself was one of the old-style penal institutions, barely touched by any far-reaching reforms. Prisoners were allowed a great deal of association with each other, and this remained the system for much of Dickens's life and in all his writings about Newgate. Major reforms were, however, carried out in other prisons, and were the source of much controversy between the advocates of rival theories – the "separate system" and the "silent system".

Pentonville Prison was opened in December 1842 and used the separate system, under which about five hundred male prisoners were housed in separate cells. There was ample room because the prison was purpose-built. Its first inmates – many of them first offenders – were convicts for transportation, with sentences of not less than fifteen years. Aged between eighteen and thirty-five, they were chosen on the grounds of physical fitness and readiness to respond to the prison's reformatory programme. The idea was that they should spend eighteen months there, in solitary confinement, being taught trades which would stand them in good stead in Van Dieman's Land, and also being given moral and religious training. The concept of the scheme was both benevolent and optimistic, although Henry Mayhew described the eighteen months in Pentonville before transportation as "a kind of penal purgatory where men are submitted to the chastisement of separate confinement". Captain Fulford, Superintendent of Stafford Gaol, argued strongly for what he called a "modified" separate system.

It is a matter for regret that, although he was unsympathetic, Dickens did not write about Pentonville. Neither, for that matter, did he write much about the silent system, although we know from some of his letters that he was an ardent supporter. Two London prisons went over to it in the 1830s, and Dickens became a close friend and admirer of their governors, Captain G. L. Chesterton of the Middlesex House of Correction, Coldbath Fields (governor from 1829 to 1854), and Lieutenant A. F. Tracy R.N. of the Westminster Bridewell in Tothill Fields (governor from 1834 to 1855). It was his intention to write an account of Coldbath Fields for *Sketches by Boz,* but he never did so, although he did refer to a visit to the prison.

When Chesterton arrived at Coldbath Fields he found a corrupt prison abounding in all kinds of abuses. Many of the warders were dishonest and made large sums of money out of their prisoners; every kind of contraband entered the prison and was hidden away within its walls; and on one notable afternoon, when touring the prison, Chesterton entered an attic and found prisoners, through the connivance of jailers, entertaining prostitutes. It was several years before he was able to stamp out corruption, but he was eventually successful thanks to the cooperation of some inmates and to the appointment of a chief prison officer from the army. In 1834 he announced to the prisoners that all communication between them by word, sign or gesture was henceforth prohibited. For the remaining twenty years of his governorship this rule was rigorously and ruthlessly enforced, with no infringement ever overlooked. There were few single cells in the gaol, and with prisoners sleeping in dormitories it meant that they had to be watched day and night.

The system was much criticised, often by those who pointed to the expense involved in constant supervision, but Dickens was in favour of it. The severity of his attitude to convicted criminals springs from the fact that he did not believe that very many of them were reclaimable from a life of crime, and he supported Chesterton's reforms not because he believed that the silent system would work wonders among convicts, but because it would minimise the possibility of corruption between prisoners through social contact. He saw it as the best of a series of alternative approaches, and he is quick to point out in "Pet Prisoners", as a criticism of the separate system, that convicted criminals were better treated than paupers – a fact which played a part in shaping his hard line against convicts.

Charles Dickens's view that prisoners were beyond redemption is reflected in the development of most of the major characters in his fiction. Despite his superb characterisation, in few of them can any fundamental change in outlook be discerned. There are, it is true, some exceptions; but for the most part Dickens had a deterministic view of his characters. This is particularly true of his villains – Quilp in *The Old Curiosity Shop* dies horribly and quite unrepentantly, and so do Fagin and Bill Sikes in *Oliver Twist,* although Nancy, in the same novel, is sympathetically treated. She had never known a better life than the one she had led in thieves' kitchens and the gutter, but she does repent – and from the best of motives rather ambivalently betrays her former accomplices. In the same novel, Charley Bates, too, is so appalled at the murder of Nancy that he turns to an honest life as a farm labourer, and eventually becomes a grazier in Northamptonshire.

The clue to this change in Charley Bates and, to a lesser extent, in Nancy, is in their youth. Dickens did believe wholeheartedly in the power of education to prevent crime. Through its agency the young of both sexes might be reclaimed from a lawless life and, even more important, those who were in moral danger on the brink of such an existence might be prevented from taking the final step.

Because of this, Dickens's harsh attitude to crime and the punishment of offenders does not necessarily invalidate the claims made for the quality of sympathy in his journalism. True, he was unforgiving to adult criminals, and thus we can understand Compeyson's death in *Great Expectations,* and even perhaps the death of Magwitch in the same novel (although he did go a long way, as Pip's benefactor, towards redeeming himself); but there was always sympathy for the young. Did not Pip, admittedly under duress, steal food from Mrs. Gargery's cupboard and a file from the blacksmith? Dickens believed that young people, even those subject from a very early age to the temptations of poverty and bad surroundings, could be helped, and with the right kind of encouragement and education were capable of change in a way that adults were not. This is apparent in his attitude to education and, in particular, his untiring advocacy of the Ragged School movement.

PET PRISONERS

THE system of separate confinement first experimented on in England at the model prison, Pentonville, London, and now spreading through the country, appears to us to require a little calm consideration and reflection on the part of the public. We purpose, in this paper, to suggest what we consider some grave objections to this system.

We shall do this temperately, and without considering it necessary to regard every one from whom we differ as a scoundrel, actuated by base motives, to whom the most unprincipled conduct may be recklessly attributed. Our faith in most questions where the good men are represented to be all *pro*, and the bad men to be all *con,* is very small. There is a hot class of riders of hobby-horses in the field, in this century, who think they do nothing unless they make a steeple-chase of their object, throw a vast quantity of mud about, and spurn every sort of decent restraint and reasonable consideration under their horses' heels. This question has not escaped such championship. It has its steeple-chase riders, who hold the dangerous principle that the end justifies any means, and to whom no means, truth and fair-dealing usually excepted, come amiss.

Considering the separate system of imprisonment, here, solely in reference to England, we discard, for the purpose of this discussion, the objection founded on its extreme severity, which would immediately arise if we were considering it with any reference to the State of Pennsylvania in America. For whereas in that State it may be inflicted for a dozen years, the idea is quite abandoned at home of extending it, usually, beyond a dozen months, or in any case beyond eighteen months. Besides which, the school and the chapel afford periods of comparative relief here, which are not afforded in America.

Though it has been represented by the steeple-chase riders as a most enormous heresy to contemplate the possibility of any prisoner going mad or idiotic under the prolonged effects of separate confinement; and although any one who should have the temerity to maintain such a doubt in Pennsylvania would have a chance of becoming a profane St. Stephen; Lord Grey, in his very last speech in the House of Lords on the subject, made in the present session of Parliament, in praise of this separate system, said of it: "Wherever it has been fairly tried, one of its great defects has been discovered to be this – that it cannot be continued for a sufficient length of time without danger to the individual, and that human nature cannot bear it beyond a limited period. The evidence of medical authorities proves beyond dispute that, if it is protracted beyond twelve months, the health of the convict, mental and physical, would require the most close and vigilant superintendence. Eighteen months is stated to be the *maximum* time for the continuance of its infliction, and, as a general rule, it is advised that it never be continued for more than twelve months." This being conceded, and it being clear that the prisoner's mind, and all the apprehensions weighing upon it, must be influenced from the first hour of his imprisonment by the greater or less extent of its duration in perspective before him, we are content to regard the system as dissociated in England from the American objection of too great severity.

We shall consider it, first in the relation of the extraordinary contrast it presents, in a country circumstanced as England is, between the physical condition of the convict in prison, and that of the hard-working man outside, or the pauper outside. We shall then enquire, and endeavour to lay before our readers some means of judging, whether its proved or probable efficiency in producing a real, trustworthy, practically repentant state of mind, is such as to justify the presentation of that extraordinary contrast. If, in the end, we indicate the conclusion that the associated silent system is less objectionable, it is not because we consider it in the abstract a good secondary punishment, but because it is a severe one, capable of judicious administration, much less expensive, not presenting the objectionable contrast so strongly, and not calculated to pet and pamper the mind of the prisoner and swell his sense of his own importance. We are not acquainted with any system of secondary punishment that we think reformatory, except the mark system of Captain Maconochie, formerly governor of Norfolk Island, which proceeds upon the principle of obliging the convict to some exercise of self-denial and resolution in every act of his prison life, and which would condemn him to a sentence of so much labour and good conduct instead of so much time. There are details in Captain Maconochie's scheme on which we have our doubts (rigid silence we consider indispensable); but,

Prisoners exercising in a yard at Pentonville, 1856. Prisoners are numbered, masked, and kept by knots on the rope at a strict distance of fifteen feet, to prevent communication or even recognition. Mayhew writes of "the repulsive and spectral appearance of the brown masked men at Pentonville".

73

in the main, we regard it as embodying sound and wise principles. We infer from the writings of Archbishop Whateley that those principles have presented themselves to his profound and acute mind in a similar light.

We will first contrast the dietary of the Model Prison at Pentonville, with the dietary of what we take to be the nearest workhouse, namely, that of Saint Pancras. In the prison, every man receives twenty-eight ounces of meat weekly. In the workhouse, every able-bodied adult receives eighteen. In the prison, every man receives one hundred and forty ounces of bread weekly. In the workhouse, every able-bodied adult receives ninety-six. In the prison, every man receives one hundred and twelve ounces of potatoes weekly. In the workhouse, every able-bodied adult receives thirty-six. In the prison, every man receives five pints and a quarter of liquid cocoa weekly (made of flaked cocoa or cocoa-nibs), with fourteen ounces of milk and forty-two drams of molasses; also seven pints of gruel weekly, sweetened with forty-two drams of molasses. In the workhouse, every able-bodied adult receives fourteen pints and a half of milk-porridge weekly, and no cocoa, and no gruel. In the prison, every man receives three pints and a half of soup weekly. In the workhouse, every able-bodied adult male receives four pints and a half, and a pint of Irish stew. This, with seven pints of table-beer weekly, and six ounces of cheese, is all the man in the workhouse has to set off against the immensely superior advantages of the prisoner in all the other respects we have stated. His lodging is very inferior to the prisoner's, the costly nature of whose accommodation we shall presently show.

Let us reflect upon this contrast in another aspect. We beg the reader to glance once more at the Model Prison dietary, and consider its frightful disproportion to the dietary of the free labourer in any of the rural parts of England. What shall we take his wages at? Will twelve shillings a week do? It cannot be called a low average, at all events. Twelve shillings a week make thirty-one pounds four a year. The cost, in 1848, for the victualling and management of every prisoner in the Model Prison was within a little of thirty-six pounds. Consequently, that free labourer, with young children to support, with cottage-rent to pay, and clothes to buy, and no advantage of purchasing his food in large amounts by contract, has, for the whole subsistence of himself and family, between four and five pounds a year *less* than the cost of feeding and overlooking one man in the Model Prison. Surely to his enlightened mind, and sometimes low morality, this must be an extraordinary good reason for keeping out of it!

But we will not confine ourselves to the contrast between the labourer's scanty fare and the prisoner's "flaked cocoa or cocoa-nibs", and daily dinner of soup, meat and potatoes. We will rise a little higher in the scale. Let us see what advertisers in the *Times* newspaper can board the middle classes at, and get a profit out of, too.

Male convict no. 19 at Pentonville. Behind the anonymity of the mask, his stance suggests that he is not as cowed as the system might wish. From a photograph by Herbert Watkins, 1856.

74

A LADY, residing in a cottage, with a large garden, in a pleasant and healthful locality, would be happy to receive one or two LADIES to BOARD with her. Two ladies occupying the same apartment may be accommodated for 12s a week each. The cottage is within a quarter of an hour's walk of a good market town, 10 minutes of a South-Western Railway Station, and an hour's distance from town.

These two ladies could not be so cheaply boarded in the Model Prison.

BOARD and RESIDENCE, at £70 per annum, for a married couple, or in proportion for a single gentleman or lady, with a respectable family. Rooms large and airy, in an eligible dwelling, at Islington, about 20 minutes' walk from the Bank. Dinner hour six o'clock. There are one or two vacancies to complete a small, cheerful and agreeable circle.

Still cheaper than the Model Prison!

BOARD and RESIDENCE – A lady, keeping a select school, in a town about 30 miles from London, would be happy to meet with a LADY to BOARD and RESIDE with her. She would have her own bed-room and a sitting-room. Any lady wishing for accomplishments would find this desirable. Terms £30 per annum. References will be expected and given.

Again, some six pounds a year less than the Model Prison! And if we were to pursue the contrast through the newspaper file for a month, or through the advertising pages of two or three numbers of Bradshaw's Railway Guide, we might probably fill the present number of this publication with similar examples, many of them including a decent education into the bargain.

This Model Prison had cost at the close of 1847, under the heads of "building" and "repairs" alone, the insignificant sum of ninety-three thousand pounds – within seven thousand pounds of the amount of the last Government grant for the Education of the whole people, and enough to pay for the emigration to Australia of four thousand, six hundred and fifty poor persons at twenty pounds per head. Upon the work done by five hundred prisoners in the Model Prison, in the year 1848 (we collate these figures from the Reports, and from Mr. Hepworth Dixon's useful work on the London Prisons), there was no profit, but an actual loss of upwards of eight hundred pounds. The cost of instruction, and the time occupied in instruction, when the labour is necessarily unskilled and unproductive, may be pleaded in explanation of this astonishing fact. We are ready to allow all due weight to such considerations, but we put it to our readers whether the whole system is right or wrong; whether the money ought or ought not rather to be spent instructing the unskilled and neglected outside the prison walls. It will be urged that it is expended in preparing the convict for the exile to which he is doomed. We submit to our readers, who are the jury in this case, that all this should be done outside the prison, first; that the first persons to be prepared for emigration are the miserable children who are consigned to the tender mercies of a Drouet, or who disgrace our streets; and that in this beginning at the wrong end, a spectacle of monstrous inconsistency is presented, shocking to the mind. Where is our Model House of Youthful Industry, where is our Model Ragged

This impassive female convict from Millbank Prison gives nothing away. She may be as submissive as she looks; she may be one of the "obscene and impudent" women complained of by Miss Cosgrove, the chief matron: "when they're bad, they're bad indeed!" Her hands suggest a life of harsh toil. From a photograph by Herbert Watkins, 1856.

school, costing for building and repairs, from ninety to a hundred thousand pounds, and for its annual maintenance upwards of twenty thousand pounds a year? Would it be a Christian act to build that, first? To breed our skilful labour there? To take the hewers of wood and drawers of water in a strange country from the convict ranks, until those men by earnest working, zeal, and perseverance, proved themselves, and raised themselves? Here are two sets of people in a densely populated land, always in the balance before the general eye. Is Crime for ever to carry it against Poverty, and to have a manifest advantage? There are the scales before all men. Whirlwinds of dust scattered in men's eyes – and there is plenty flying about – cannot blind them to the real state of the balance.

We now come to enquire into the condition of mind produced by the seclusion (limited in duration as Lord Grey limits it) which is purchased at this great cost in money, and this greater cost in stupendous injustice. That it is a consummation much to be desired, that a respectable man, lapsing into crime, should expiate his offence without incurring the liability of being afterwards recognised by hardened offenders who were his fellow-prisoners, we most readily admit. But, that this object, howsoever desirable and benevolent, is in itself sufficient to outweigh such objections as we have set forth, we cannot for a moment concede. Nor have we any sufficient guarantee that even this solitary point is gained. Under how many apparently insuperable difficulties, men immured in solitary cells will by some means obtain a knowledge of other men immured in other solitary cells, most of us know from all the accounts and anecdotes we have read of secret prisons and secret prisoners from our school-time upwards. That there is a fascination in the desire to know something of the hidden presence beyond the blank wall of the cell; that the listening ear is often laid against that wall; that there is an overpowering temptation to respond to the muffled knock, or any other signal which sharpened ingenuity pondering day after day on one idea can devise, is in that constitution of human nature which impels mankind to communication with one another, and makes solitude a false condition against which nature strives. That such communication within the Model Prison is not only probable, but indisputably proved to be possible by its actual discovery, we have no hesitation in stating as a fact. Some pains have been taken to hush the matter, but the truth is, that when the Prisoners at Pentonville ceased to be selected Prisoners, especially picked out and chosen for the purposes of that experiment, an extensive conspiracy was found out among them, involving, it is needless to say, extensive communication. Small pieces of paper with writing upon them had been crushed into balls, and shot into the apertures of cell doors by prisoners passing along the passages; false responses had been made during Divine Service in the chapel, in which responses they addressed one another; and armed men were secretly dispersed by the Governor in various parts of the building, to prevent

A female convict at Millbank Prison, 1856. She is wearing a coarse canvas dress strapped over her prison uniform as a punishment for tearing her clothes. Miss Cosgrove, the matron, said that the women under punishment generally sang: "They make up songs themselves all about the officers of the prison. Oh! they'll have every one in their verses – the directors, the governor, and all of us."

the general rising, which was anticipated as the consequence of this plot. Undiscovered communication, under this system, we assumed to be frequent.

The state of mind into which a man is brought who is the lonely inhabitant of his own small world, and who is only visited by certain regular visitors, all addressing themselves to him individually and personally, as the object of their particular solicitude – we believe in most cases to have very little promise in it, and very little of solid foundation. A strange absorbing selfishness – a spiritual egotism and vanity, real or assumed – is the first result. It is most remarkable to observe, in the cases of murderers who become this kind of object of interest, when they are at last consigned to the condemned cell, how the rule is (of course there are exceptions) that the murdered person disappears from the stage of their thoughts, except as a part of their own important story; and how they occupy the whole scene. *I* did this, *I* feel that, *I* confide in the mercy of Heaven being extended to *me*; this is the autograph of *me*, the unfortunate and unhappy; in my childhood I was so and so; in my youth I did such a thing, to which I attribute my downfall – not this thing of basely and barbarously defacing the image of my Creator, and sending an immortal soul into eternity without a moment's warning, but something else of a venial kind that many unpunished people do. I don't want the forgiveness of this foully murdered person's bereaved wife, husband, brother, sister, child, friend; I don't ask for it, I don't care for it. I make no enquiry of the clergyman concerning the salvation of that murdered person's soul; *mine* is the matter; and I am almost happy that I came here, as to the gate of Paradise. "I never liked him," said the repentant Mr. Manning, false of heart to the last, calling a crowbar by a milder name to lessen the cowardly horror of it, "and I beat in his skull with the ripping

Manning: Dickens saw Manning and his wife publicly hanged for murder in 1849, and wrote two appalled letters to *The Times* protesting against such spectacles

chisel." I am going to bliss, exclaims the same authority, in effect. Where my victim went to is not my business at all. Now, God forbid that we, unworthily believing in the Redeemer, should shut out hope, or even humble trustfulness, from any criminal at the dread pass; but it is not in us to call this state of mind repentance.

The present question is with a state of mind analogous to this (as we conceive) but with a far stronger tendency to hypocrisy; the dread of death not being present, and there being every possible inducement, either to feign contrition, or to set up an unreliable semblance of it. If I, John Styles, the prisoner, don't do my work, and outwardly conform to the rules of the prison, I am a mere fool. There is nothing here to tempt me to do anything else, and everything to tempt me to do that. The capital dietary (and every meal is a great event in this lonely life) depends upon it; the alternative is a pound of bread a day. I should be weary of myself without occupation. I should be much more dull if I didn't hold these dialogues with the gentlemen who are so anxious about me. I shouldn't be half the object of interest I am, if I didn't make the professions I do. Therefore, I, John Styles, go in for what is popular here, and I may mean it, or I may not.

There will always, under any decent system, be certain prisoners, betrayed into crime by a variety of circumstances, who will do well in exile, and offend against the laws no more. Upon this class, we think the associated silent system would have quite as good an influence as this expensive and anomalous one; and we cannot accept them as evidence of the efficiency of separate confinement. Assuming John Styles to mean what he professes, for the time being, we desire to track the workings of his mind, and to try to test the value of his professions. Where shall we find an account of John Styles, proceeding from no objector to this

A drawing by Phiz (Hablot Knight Browne), showing David Copperfield meeting the "pet prisoners" Uriah Heep and Mr. Littimer. Prison chaplains greatly resented Dickens's criticism of them, and responded in kind. The Rev. J. Field's Prison Discipline: the Advantages of the Separate System of Imprisonment, as established in the new county gaol of Reading *(1846) included a sharp attack on the tone and veracity of Dickens's account in* American Notes *of the separate system as practised in Philadelphia; the chaplain of the Woolwich Hulks refused to allow* Household Words *in the prison library. Dickens later wrote that after publishing the present article he was "severely mauled at the hands of certain Reverend Ordinaries".*

system, but from a staunch supporter of it? We will take it from a work called "Prison Discipline, and the advantages of the separate system of imprisonment", written by the Reverend Mr. Field, chaplain of the new County Gaol at Reading; pointing out to Mr. Field, in passing, that the question is not justly, as he would sometimes make it, a question between this system and the profligate abuses and customs of the old unreformed gaols, but between it and the improved gaols of this time, which are not constructed on his favourite principles.

Now, here is John Styles, twenty years of age, in prison for a felony. He has been there five months, and he writes to his sister,

> Don't fret my dear sister, about my being here. I cannot help fretting when I think about my usage to my father and mother: when I think about it, it makes me quite ill. I hope God will forgive me; I pray for it night and day from my heart. Instead of fretting about imprisonment, I ought to thank God for it, for before I came here, I was living quite a careless life; neither was God in all my thoughts; all I thought about was ways that led me towards destruction. Give my respects to my wretched companions, and I hope they will alter their wicked course, for they don't know for a day nor an hour but what they may be cut off. I have seen my folly, and I hope they may see their folly; but I shouldn't if I had not been in trouble. It is good for me that I have been in trouble. Go to church, my sister, every Sunday, and don't give your mind to going to playhouses and theatres, for that is no good to you. There are a great many temptations.

Observe! John Styles, who has committed the felony, has been "living quite a careless life". That is his worst opinion of it, whereas his companions who did not commit the felony are "wretched companions". John saw *his* "folly", and sees *their* "wicked course". It is playhouses and theatres, which many unfelonious people go to, that prey upon John's mind – not felony. John is shut up in that pulpit to lecture his companions and his sister about the wickedness of the unfelonious world. Always supposing him to be sincere, is there no exaggeration of himself in this? Go to church where I can go, and don't go to theatres where I can't! Is there any tinge of the fox and the grapes in it? Is this the kind of penitence that will wear outside? Put the case that he had written, of his own mind, "My dear sister, I feel that I have disgraced you and all who should be dear to me, and if it please God that I live to be free, I will try hard to repair that, and to be a credit to you. My dear sister, when I committed this felony, I stole something – and these pining five months have not put it back – and I will work my fingers to the bone to make restitution, and oh! my dear sister, seek out my late companions, and tell Tom Jones, that poor boy, who was younger and littler than me, that I am grieved I ever led him so wrong, and I am suffering for it now!" Would that be better? Would it be more like solid truth?

But no. This is not the pattern penitence. There would seem to be a pattern penitence, of a particular form, shape, limits, and dimensions, like the cells. While Mr. Field is correcting his proof-sheets for the press, another letter is brought to him, and in that letter too, that man, also a felon, speaks of his "past folly", and lectures his mother about labouring under "strong delusions

The whipping-post, Surrey House of Correction, Wandsworth, 1862. The separate system, the silent system and the mark system were all part of a movement to reform the old brutalities of prison life; but in prison, as in the army, flogging was still frequent.

of the devil". Does this overweening readiness to lecture other people suggest the suspicion of any parrot-like imitation of Mr. Field, who lectures him, and any presumptuous confounding of their relative positions?

We venture altogether to protest against the citation, in support of this system, of assumed repentance which has stood no test or trial in the working world. We consider that it proves nothing, and is worth nothing, except as a discouraging sign of that spiritual egotism and presumption of which we have already spoken. It is not peculiar to the separate system at Reading; Miss Martineau, who was on the whole decidedly favourable to the separate prison at Philadelphia, observed it there. "The cases I became acquainted with", says she, "were not all hopeful. Some of the convicts were so stupid as not to be relied upon, more or less. Others canted so detestably, and were (always in connexion with their cant) so certain that they should never sin more, that I have every expectation that they will find themselves in prison again some day. One fellow, a sailor, notorious for having taken more lives than probably any man in the United States, was quite confident that he should be perfectly virtuous henceforth. He should never touch anything stronger than tea, or lift his hand against money or life. I told him I thought he could not be sure of this till he was within sight of money and the smell of strong liquors; and that he was more confident than I should like to be. He shook his shock of red hair at me, and glared with his one ferocious eye, as he said he knew all about it. He had been the worst of men, and Christ had had mercy on his poor soul." (Observe again, as in the general case we have put, that he is not at all troubled about the souls of the people whom he had killed).

Let us submit to our readers another instance from Mr. Field, of the wholesome state of mind produced by the separate system.

Terence Nulty, the chief warder at Pentonville, from a photograph by Herbert Watkins, 1856. He wears a campaign medal.

> The 25th of March, in the last year, was the day appointed for a general fast, on account of the threatened famine. The following note is in my journal of that day. "During the evening I visited many prisoners, and found with much satisfaction that a large proportion of them had observed the day in a manner becoming their own situation, and the purpose for which it had been set apart. I think it right to record the following remarkable proof of the effect of discipline. . . . They were all supplied with their usual rations. I went first this evening to the cells of the prisoners recently committed for trial (Ward A.1.), and amongst these (upwards of twenty) I found that but three had abstained from any portion of their food. I then visited twenty-one convicted prisoners who had spent some considerable time in the gaol (Ward C.1.), and amongst them I found that some had altogether abstained from food, and of the whole number two-thirds had partially abstained."

We will take it for granted that this was not because they had more than they could eat, though we know that with such a dietary even that sometimes happens, especially in the case of persons long confined.

> The remark of one prisoner whom I questioned concerning his abstinence was, I believe, sincere, and was very pleasing. "Sir, I have not felt able to eat to-day, whilst I have thought of those poor starving people; but I hope that I have prayed a good deal that God will give *them* something to eat."

If this were not pattern penitence, and the thought of those poor starving people had honestly originated with that man, and were really on his mind, we want to know why he was not uneasy, every day, in the contemplation of his soup, meat, bread, potatoes, cocoa-nibs, milk, molasses, and gruel, and its contrast to the fare of "those poor starving people" who, in some form or other, were taxed to pay for it?

We do not deem it necessary to comment on the authorities quoted by Mr. Field to show what a fine thing the separate system is for the health of the body; how it never affects the mind except for good; how it is the true preventive of pulmonary disease; and so on. The deduction we must draw from such things is that Providence was quite mistaken in making us gregarious, and that we had better all shut ourselves up directly. Neither will we refer to that "talented criminal", Dr. Dodd, whose exceedingly indifferent verses applied to a system now extinct, in reference to our penitentiaries for convicted prisoners. Neither, after what we have quoted from Lord Grey, need we refer to the likewise quoted report of the American authorities, who are perfectly sure that no extent of confinement in the Philadelphia prison has ever affected the intellectual powers of any prisoner. Mr. Croker cogently observes, in "The Good-Natured Man", that either his hat must be on his head, or it must be off. By a parity of reasoning, we conclude that both Lord Grey and the American authories cannot possibly be right – unless indeed the notoriously settled habits of the American people, and the absence of any approach to restlessness in the national character, render them unusually good subjects for protracted seclusion, and an exception from the rest of mankind.

In using the term "pattern penitence" we beg it to be understood that we do not apply it to Mr. Field, or to any other chaplain, but to the system; which appears to us to make these doubtful converts all alike. Although Mr. Field has not shown any remarkable courtesy in the instance we have set forth in a note, it is our wish to show all courtesy to him, and to his office, and to his sincerity in the discharge of its duties. In our desire to represent him with fairness and impartiality, we will not take leave of him without the following quotation from his book:

> Scarcely sufficient time has yet expired since the present system was introduced, for me to report much concerning discharged criminals. Out of a class so degraded – the very dregs of the community – it can be no wonder that some, of whose improvement I cherished the hope, should have relapsed. Disappointed in a few cases I have been, yet by no means discouraged, since I can with pleasure refer to many whose conduct is affording proof of reformation. Gratifying indeed have been some accounts received from liberated offenders themselves, as well as from clergymen of parishes to which they have returned. I have also myself visited the homes of some of our former prisoners, and have been cheered by the testimony given, and the evident signs of improved character which I have there observed. Although I do not venture at present to describe the particular cases of prisoners, concerning whose reformation I feel much

Dr. Dodd: author of *Thoughts in Prison* (1777, reissued in 1846), quoted by Field

Mr. Croker: Thomas Crofton Croker (1798–1854), miscellaneous writer

One of the five principal matrons at the Female Convict Prison, Brixton, from a photograph by Herbert Watkins, 1856. This formidable woman had risen to one of the few heights of office and power open to women of her day.

confidence, because, as I have stated, the time of trial has hitherto been short; yet I can with pleasure refer to some public documents which prove the happy effects of similar discipline in other establishments.

It should also be stated that the Reverend Mr. Kingsmill, the chaplain of the Model Prison at Pentonville, in his calm and intelligent report made to the Commissioners on the 1st February, 1849, expresses his belief "that the effects produced here upon the character of prisoners, have been encouraging in a high degree."

But we entreat our readers once again to look at that Model Prison dietary (which is essential to the system, though the system is so very healthy of itself); to remember the other enormous expenses of the establishment; to consider the circumstances of this old country, with the inevitable anomalies and contrasts it must present; and to decide, on temperate reflection, whether there are any sufficient reasons for adding this monstrous contrast to the rest. Let us impress upon our readers that the existing question is, not between this system and the old abuses of the old profligate Gaols (with which, thank Heaven, we have nothing to do), but between this system and the associated silent system, where the dietary is much lower, where the annual cost of provision, management, repairs, clothing, etc., does not exceed, on a liberal average, £25 for each prisoner; where many prisoners are, and every prisoner would be (if due accommodation were provided in some over-crowded prisons), locked up alone, for twelve hours out of every twenty-four, and where, while preserved from contamination, he is still one of a society of men, and not an isolated being, filling his whole sphere of view with a diseased dilation of himself. We hear that the associated silent system is objectionable, because of the number of punishments it involves for breaches of the prison discipline; but how can we, in the same breath, be told that the resolutions of prisoners for the misty future are to be trusted, and that, on the least temptation, they are so little to be relied on, as to the solid present? How can I set the pattern penitence against the career that preceded it, when I am told that if I put that man with the other men, and lay a solemn charge upon him not to address them by word or sign, there are such and such great chances that he will want the resolution to obey?

Remember that this separate system, though commended in the English Parliament and spreading in England, has not spread in America, despite of all the steeple-chase riders in the United States. Remember that it has never reached the State most distinguished for its learning, for its moderation, for its remarkable men of European reputation, for the excellence of its public Institutions. Let it be tried here, on a limited scale, if you will, with fair representatives of all classes of prisoners: let Captain Maconochie's system be tried: let anything with a ray of hope in it be tried: but only as a part of some general system for raising up the prostrate portion of the people of this country, and not as an exhibition of such astonishing consideration for crime, in

comparison with want and work. Any prison built, at a great expenditure, for this system, is comparatively useless for any other; and the ratepayers will do well to think of this, before they take it for granted that it is a proved boon to the country which will be enduring.

Under the separate system, the prisoners work at trades. Under the associated silent system, the Magistrates of Middlesex have almost abolished the treadmill. Is it no part of the legitimate consideration of this important point of work, to discover what kind of work the people always filtering through the gaols of large towns – the pickpocket, the sturdy vagrant, the habitual drunkard, and the begging-letter impostor – like least, and to give them that work to do in preference to any other? It is out of fashion with the steeple-chase riders we know; but we would have, for all such characters, a kind of work in gaols, badged and degraded as belonging to gaols only, and never done elsewhere. And we must avow that, in a country circumstanced as England is, with respect to labour and labourers, we have strong doubts of the propriety of bringing the results of prison labour into the over-stocked market. On this subject some public remonstrances have recently been made by tradesmen; and we cannot shut our eyes to the fact that they are well-founded.

Male convicts on the tread-mill and picking oakum at the City House of Correction, Holloway. When relieved from their numbered positions on the tread-mill, the prisoners were set to unravel the tarry ropes for oakum. In an article in Household Words *on 14 May 1853 Dickens reiterated, "I think it right and necessary that there should be in jails some degraded kind of hard and irksome work, belonging only to jails". The point of prisons was punishment, not cure.*

Dickens's footnote to "Pet Prisoners"

As Mr. Field condescends to quote some vapouring about the account given by Mr. Charles Dickens in his *American Notes* of the Solitary Prison at Philadelphia, he may perhaps really wish for some few words of information on the subject. For this purpose, Mr. Charles Dickens has referred to the entry in his Diary, made at the close of that day.

He left his hotel for the Prison at twelve o'clock, being waited on, by appointment, by the gentlemen who showed it to him; and he returned between seven and eight at night; dining in the prison in the course of that time; which, according to his calculation, in despite of the Philadelphia Newspaper, rather exceeds two hours. He found the Prison admirably conducted, extremely clean, and the system administered in a most intelligent, kind, orderly, tender, and careful manner. He did not consider (nor should he, if he were to visit Pentonville to-morrow) that the book in which visitors were expected to record their observation of the place, was intended for the insertion of criticisms on the system, but for honest testimony to the manner of its administration; and to that, he bore, as an impartial visitor, the highest testimony in his power. In returning thanks for his health being drunk, at the dinner within the walls, he said that what he had seen that day was running in his mind; that he could not help reflecting on it; and that it was an awful punishment. If the American officer who rode back with him afterwards should ever see these words, he will perhaps recall his conversation with Mr. Dickens on the road, as to Mr. Dickens having said so, very plainly and strongly. In reference to the ridiculous assertion that Mr. Dickens in his book termed a woman "quite beautiful" who was a Negress, he positively believes that he was shown no Negress in the Prison, but one who was nursing a woman much diseased, and to whom no reference whatever is made in his published account. In describing three young women, "all convicted at the same time of a conspiracy", he may, *possibly*, among many cases, have substituted in his memory for one of them whom he did not see, some other prisoner, confined for some other crime, whom he did see; but he has not the least doubt of having been guilty of the (American) enormity of detecting beauty in a pensive quadroon or mulatto girl, or of having seen exactly what he describes: and he remembers the girl more particularly described in this connexion, perfectly. Can Mr. Field really suppose that Mr. Dickens had any interest or purpose in misrepresenting the system, or that if he could be guilty of such unworthy conduct, or desire to do it anything but justice, he would have volunteered the narrative of a man's having, of his own choice, undergone it for two years?

We will not notice the objection of Mr. Field (who strengthens the truth of Burns to nature, by the testimony of Mr. Pitt!) to the discussion of such a topic as the present in a work of "mere amusement", though we had thought we remembered in that book a word or two about slavery, which, although a very amusing, can scarcely be considered an unmitigatedly comic theme. We are quite content to believe, without seeking to make a convert of the Reverend Mr. Field, that no work need be one of "mere amusement", and that some works to which he would apply that designation have done a little good in advancing principles to which, we hope, and will believe, for the credit of his Christian office, he is not indifferent.

From **David Copperfield** *chapter 61*

ON the appointed day – I think it was the next day, but no matter – Traddles and I repaired to the prison where Mr. Creakle was powerful. It was an immense and solid building, erected at a vast expense. I could not help thinking, as we approached the gate, what an uproar would have been made in the country, if any deluded man had proposed to spend one half the money it had cost, on the erection of an industrial school for the young, or a house of refuge for the deserving old.

In an office that might have been on the ground-floor of the Tower of Babel, it was so massively constructed, we were presented to our schoolmaster; who was one of a group, composed of two or three of the busier sort of magistrates, and some visitors they had brought. He received me, like a man who had formed my mind in bygone years, and had always loved me tenderly. On my introducing Traddles, Mr. Creakle expressed, in like manner, but in an inferior degree, that he had always been Traddles's guide, philosopher, and friend. Our venerable instructor was a great deal older, and not improved in appearance. His face was as fiery as ever; his eyes were as small, and rather deeper set. The scanty, wet-looking grey hair, by which I remembered him, was almost gone; and the thick veins in his bald head were none the more agreeable to look at.

After some conversation among these gentlemen, from which I might have supposed that there was nothing in the world to be legitimately taken into account but the supreme comfort of prisoners, at any expense, and nothing on the wide earth to be done outside prison-doors, we began our inspection. It being then just dinner-time, we went, first into the great kitchen, where every prisoner's dinner was in course of being set out separately (to be handed to him in his cell), with the regularity and precision of clockwork. I said aside, to Traddles, that I wondered whether it occurred to anybody, that there was a striking contrast between these plentiful repasts of choice quality, and the dinners, not to say of paupers, but of soldiers, sailors, labourers, the great bulk of the honest, working community; of whom not one man in five hundred ever dined half so well. But I learned that the "system" required high living; and, in short, to dispose of the system, once for all, I found that on that head and on all others, "the system" put an end to all doubts, and disposed of all anomalies. Nobody appeared to have the least idea that there was any other system, but *the* system, to be considered.

As we were going though some of the magnificent passages, I inquired of Mr. Creakle and his friends what were supposed to be the main advantages of this all-governing and universally over-riding system? I found them to be the perfect isolation of prisoners – so that no one man in confinement there, knew anything about another; and the reduction of prisoners to a wholesome state of mind, leading to sincere contrition and repentance.

Now, it struck me, when we began to visit individuals in their cells, and to traverse the passages in which those cells were, and to have the manner of the going to chapel and so forth, explained to us, that there was a strong probability of the prisoners knowing a good deal about each other, and of their carrying on a pretty complete system of intercourse. This, at the time I write, has been proved, I believe, to be the case; but, as it would have been flat blasphemy against the system to have hinted such a doubt then, I looked out for the penitence as diligently as I could.

And here again, I had great misgivings. I found as prevalent a fashion in the form of the penitence, as I had left outside in the forms of the coats and waistcoats in the windows of the tailors' shops. I found a vast amount of profession, varying very little in character: varying very little (which I thought exceedingly suspicious), even in words. I found a great many foxes, disparaging whole vineyards of inaccessible grapes; but I found very few foxes whom I would have trusted within reach of a bunch. Above all, I found that the most professing men were the greatest objects of interest; and that their conceit, their vanity, their want of excitement, and their love of deception (which many of them possessed to an almost incredible extent, as their histories showed), all prompted to these professions, and were all gratified by them.

However, I heard so repeatedly, in the course of our goings to and fro, of a certain Number Twenty Seven, who was the Favourite, and who really appeared to be a Model Prisoner, that I resolved to suspend my judgement until I should see Twenty Seven. Twenty Eight, I understood, was also a bright particular star; but it was his misfortune to have his glory a little dimmed by the extraordinary lustre of Twenty Seven. I heard so much of Twenty Seven, of his pious admonitions to everybody around him, and of the beautiful letters he constantly wrote to his mother (whom he seemed to consider in a very bad way), that I became quite impatient to see him.

I had to restrain my impatience for some time, on account of Twenty Seven being reserved for a concluding effect. But, at last, we came to the door of his cell; and Mr. Creakle, looking through a little hole in it, reported to us, in a state of the greatest admiration, that he was reading a Hymn Book.

There was such a rush of heads immediately, to see Number Twenty Seven reading his Hymn Book, that the little hole was blocked up, six or seven heads deep. To remedy this inconvenience, and give us an opportunity of conversing with Twenty Seven in all his purity, Mr. Creakle directed the door of the cell to be unlocked, and Twenty Seven to be invited out into the passage. This was done; and whom should Traddles and I then behold, to our amazement, in this converted Number Twenty Seven, but Uriah Heep!

He knew us directly; and said, as he came out – with the old writhe –

"How do you do, Mr. Copperfield? How do you do, Mr. Traddles?"

This recognition caused a general admiration in the party. I rather thought that everyone was struck by his not being proud, and taking notice of us.

"Well, Twenty Seven," said Mr. Creakle, mournfully admiring him. "How do you find yourself today?"

"I am very umble sir!" replied Uriah Heep.

"You are always so, Twenty Seven," said Mr. Creakle.

Here, another gentleman asked, with extreme anxiety: "Are you quite comfortable?"

"Yes, I thank you, sir!" said Uriah Heep, looking in that direction. "Far more comfortable here, than ever I was outside. I see my follies, now, sir. That's what makes me comfortable."

Several gentlemen were much affected; and a third questioner, forcing himself to the front, enquired with extreme feeling: "How do you find the beef?"

"Thank you, sir," replied Uriah, glancing in the new direction of this voice, "it was tougher yesterday than I could wish; but it's my duty to bear. I have committed follies, gentlemen," said Uriah, looking round with a meek smile, "and I ought to bear the consequences without repining."

A murmur, partly of gratification at Twenty Seven's celestial state of mind, and partly of indignation against the Contractor who had given him any cause of complaint (a note of which was immediately made by Mr. Creakle), having subsided, Twenty Seven stood in the midst of us, as if he felt himself the principal object of merit in a highly meritorious museum. That we, the neophytes, might have an excess of light shining upon us all at once, orders were given to let out Twenty Eight.

I had been so much astonished already, that I only felt a kind of resigned wonder when Mr. Littimer walked forth, reading a good book!

"Twenty Eight," said a gentleman in spectacles, who had not yet spoken, "you complained last week, my good fellow, of the cocoa. How has it been since?"

"I thank you, sir," said Mr. Littimer, "it has been better made. If I might take the liberty of saying so, sir, I don't think the milk which is boiled with it is quite genuine; but I am aware, sir, that there is great adulteration of milk, in London, and that the article in a pure state is difficult to be obtained."

It appeared to me that the gentleman in spectacles backed his Twenty Eight against Mr. Creakle's Twenty Seven, for each of them took his own man in hand.

"What is your state of mind, Twenty-Eight?" said the questioner in spectacles.

"I thank you, sir," returned Mr. Littimer; "I see my follies now, sir. I am a good deal troubled when I think of the sins of my former companions, sir; but I trust they may find forgiveness."

"You are quite happy yourself?" said the questioner, nodding encouragement.

"I am much obliged to you, sir," returned Mr. Littimer. "Perfectly so." . . . .

With this, Number Twenty Eight retired, after a glance between him and Uriah; as if they were not altogether unknown to each other, through some medium of communication; and a murmur went round the group, as his door shut upon him, that he was a most respectable man, and a beautiful case.

"Now, Twenty Seven," said Mr. Creakle, entering on a clear stage with *his* man, "is there anything that anyone can do for you? If so, mention it."

"I would umbly ask, sir," returned Uriah, with a jerk of his malevolent head, "for leave to write again to mother."

"It shall certainly be granted," said Mr. Creakle.

"Thank you, sir! I am anxious about mother. I am afraid she ain't safe."

Somebody incautiously asked, what from? But there was a scandalised whisper of "Hush!"

"Immortally safe, sir," returned Uriah, writhing in the direction of the voice. "I should wish mother to be got into my state. I never should have been got into my present state if I hadn't come here. I wish mother had come here. It would be better for everybody, if they got took up, and was brought here."

This sentiment gave unbounded satisfaction – greater satisfaction, I think, than anything that had passed yet.

"Before I come here," said Uriah, stealing a look at us, as if he would have blighted the outer world to which we belonged, if he could, "I was given to follies; but now I am sensible of my follies. There's a deal of sin outside. There's a deal of sin in mother. There's nothing but sin everywhere – except here."

"You are quite changed?" said Mr. Creakle.

"Oh dear, yes, sir!" cried this hopeful penitent.

"You wouldn't relapse, if you were going out?" asked somebody else.

"Oh de-ar no, sir!"

"Well!" said Mr. Creakle, "this is very gratifying."

CRIME AND EDUCATION and
A SLEEP TO STARTLE US

Daily News 4 February 1846; Household Words 13 March 1852

THROUGHOUT his adult life Charles Dickens had a great sympathy for suffering and neglected children, and it has become commonplace to suggest that these strong feelings had their origins in his own unhappy childhood. When he was about twelve years old his father was imprisoned for debt in the Marshalsea, the family was in serious financial straits and he, during those sad early days in London, had to work at the hated blacking warehouse. That this experience bit deeply into his consciousness there is no doubt at all, but it is probably not the only reason for his concern with unwanted and harshly treated children. Later commentators on Dickens have drawn attention to a darker side of his nature, and this too may well have been a factor in shaping his continuing concern for neglected children.

Dickens was one of the earliest and most prominent supporters of the Ragged School movement (later the Ragged School Union), started by philanthropists and well-wishers in 1843. Although he tended to see this voluntary movement as a rather unsatisfactory stop-gap in what was, after all, a national problem, he realised that in the absence of a universal system of elementary education it was better than nothing. His support for ragged schools, which offered poor children not so much an education as an attempt to modify their ignorance, must be seen within the context of a solid body of opinion, ranging across the political spectrum from Radical to Tory, which held that England desperately needed a state system of education. But articulate as its protagonists were, such ideas by no means found universal assent. Both the Church of England and the Nonconformists played a sorry role, engaging in shrill doctrinal squabbles which did much to impede the cause of popular education; individual voices reflected other entrenched attitudes. There were men like Gaffer Hexam in *Our Mutual Friend,* unable to read or write, who resented the fact that his son Charley was going to school because it would mean that his son had an educational advantage over him; there were those like Major Bagstock in *Dombey and Son* who were forthright in their opposition to education for poor children – "Never educate that sort of people, Sir! Damme, Sir, it never does! It always fails"; there was Mr. Dombey's slightly more hopeful view that the purpose of elementary education was simply to teach the poor their place in society; and there was many a Podsnap who objected to centralisation on principle.

Dickens was extremely alert to one of the most urgent and sensitive issues of his day, educational reform. So far as ragged schools were concerned, despite his approval of their work, he had doubts on two counts. First, there were the teachers, some of whom he described as "narrow-minded and odd". Secondly, he was bitterly opposed to the inevitable element of sabbatarianism and evangelism. Exeter Hall, the great evangelical centre, moved him to anger: "It might be laid down as a very good rule of social and political guidance, that whatever Exeter Hall champions, is a thing by no means to be done." This antipathy to evangelism is apparent in a letter that he wrote on 24 September 1843 to Mr. S. R. Starey, treasurer of the Field Lane Ragged School, which is described in these two articles. In it he discussed the possibility of raising funds for a school and asked whether, in the event of money being available, visitors to the school might be asked to confine their questioning of the children to broad matters, because it was important "that no person, however well intentioned, should perplex the minds of these unfortunate creatures with religious mysteries that young people with the best advantages can but imperfectly understand." Starey's reply to this is not recorded.

Evangelists sometimes hit back at Dickens. The instalment of *Bleak House* containing the account of Jo's death was published in May 1853. The Annual Meeting of the Ragged School Union was held in Exeter Hall a few days later, and one speaker protested that in describing Jo's miserable life as a vagrant on the streets and as a crossing-sweeper, Dickens had been less than fair to the work of ragged schools and the way in which such outcasts were helped. To the accompaniment of "Hear, hear" from the audience, he went on to say that what had happened to Jo might have been true fifteen or twenty years ago, but was not true in 1853.

Despite such disagreements, Dickens remained a committed advocate of ragged schools, and when he saw them in action he realised that they were achieving more than might have been thought possible. Intended, as their name suggests, for the poorest and most ragged of children, their teachers were largely untrained men and women who gave freely of their time and leisure to teach slum children in cheap and ramshackle premises. After Lord Shaftesbury became head of the movement in 1845, he attracted a royal patron, support from peers and bishops, and an increase in voluntary donations. As a result, the school in Field Lane, for example, which Dickens had been visiting from its inception in 1843, improved greatly; but the real problem remained a lack of funds from central government. Voluntary endeavours just could not cope with the demands which were being made.

Dickens's interest in educational matters is reflected in the many teachers and schools in his novels. There is a good deal of ambivalence in his attitude to teachers. True, his handling of Miss Peacher in *Our Mutual Friend* is sympathetic, but even so he cannot resist poking fun at her professional certificate. As for her colleague, Bradley Headstone, he is a new kind of teacher, "a highly certificated, stipendiary schoolmaster", who has "acquired mechanically a great store of teacher's knowledge" at one of the new training colleges whose recruits entered the schools for the first time in 1853. Although it is made plain that he has struggled successfully, with few advantages, to better himself by qualifying as a teacher (to that extent he is treated rather differently by Dickens), the strength of his passion for Lizzie Hexam, leading ultimately to murder, is depicted in detail but quite without sympathy. Lizzie's brother Charley, also struggling to make his way in life, becomes a pupil teacher in Headstone's school. This is a "National" school, described as "better" than the "jumble" of the ragged school, but still far from perfect, with both buildings and lessons shaped by "the latest Gospel according to Monotony".

Dickens maintained his interest in education and his support for ragged schools, with all their faults. He saw these institutions as crucial in the prevention of juvenile crime, a problem which would not be wished away. Towards the end of "Crime and Education", he mentions "an advertisement in yesterday's paper, announcing a lecture on the Ragged Schools". The lecture had been given at the Literary and Scientific Institution in Aldersgate Street by the Rev. Robert Ainslie. A brief quotation from it will show why Dickens approved of it so heartily:

> The county of Essex had lately been building a large county prison, at an expense of nearly thirty-five thousand pounds. How much better would it not be to have spent that sum in educating the poor rather than in building a prison for punishing them?

No rhetorical question, this. Dickens could hardly have put it better himself.

CRIME AND EDUCATION

I OFFER no apology for entreating the attention of the readers of the *Daily News* to an effort which has been making for some three years and a half, and which is making now, to introduce among the most miserable and neglected outcasts in London, some knowledge of the commonest principles of morality and religion; to commence their recognition as immortal human creatures, before the Gaol Chaplain becomes their only schoolmaster; to suggest to Society that its duty to this wretched throng, foredoomed to crime and punishment, rightfully begins at some distance from the police office; and that the careless maintenance from year to year, in this the capital city of the world, of a vast hopeless nursery of ignorance, misery, and vice: a breeding place for the hulks and jails: is horrible to contemplate.

This attempt is being made, in certain of the most obscure and squalid parts of the Metropolis; where rooms are opened, at night, for the gratuitous instruction of all comers, children or adults, under the title of RAGGED SCHOOLS. The name implies the purpose. They who are too ragged, wretched, filthy, and forlorn, to enter any other place: who could gain admission into no charity school, and who would be driven from any church door; are invited to come in here, and find some people not depraved, willing to teach them something, and show them some sympathy, and stretch a hand out, which is not the iron hand of Law, for their correction.

Before I describe a visit of my own to a Ragged School, and urge the readers of this letter for God's sake to visit one themselves, and think of it (which is my main object), let me say, that I know the prisons of London well. That I have visited the largest of them, more times than I could count; and that the children in them are enough to break the heart and hope of any man. I have never taken a foreigner or a stranger of any kind, to one of these establishments, but I have seen him so moved at sight of the child offenders, and so affected by the contemplation of their utter renouncement and desolation outside the prison walls, that he has been as little able to disguise his emotion, as if some great grief had suddenly burst upon him. Mr. Chesterton and Lieutenant Tracey (than whom more intelligent and humane Governors of Prisons it would be hard, if not impossible, to find) know, perfectly well, that these children pass and repass through the prisons all their lives; that they are never taught; that the first distinctions between right and wrong are, from their cradles, perfectly confounded and perverted in their minds; that they come of untaught parents, and will give birth to another untaught generation; that in exact proportion to their natural abilities, is the extent and scope of their depravity; and that there is no escape or chance for them in any ordinary revolution of human affairs. Happily, there are schools in these prisons now. If any readers doubt how ignorant the children are, let them visit those schools,

A ragged school,
photographed around 1865.

"We are a'reading, read,
*   read, reading –*
We are a'reading in the
*   Ragged School;*
We are reading in a Book
*   far brighter than the sun,*
Which promises a crown
*   when our earthly race is*
*   run!*
We are a'reading, read,
*   read, reading –*
We are a'reading in the
*   Ragged School."*
Ragged School Rhymes
(1851)

and see them at their tasks, and hear how much they knew when they were sent there. If they would know the produce of this seed, let them see a class of men and boys together, at their books (as I have seen them in the House of Correction for this county of Middlesex), and mark how painfully the full grown felons toil at the very shape and form of letters; their ignorance being so confirmed and solid. The contrast of this labour in the men, with the less blunted quickness of the boys; the latent shame and sense of degradation struggling through their dull attempts at infant lessons; and the universal eagerness to learn, impress me, in this passing retrospect, more painfully than I can tell.

For the instruction, and as a first step in the reformation, of such unhappy beings, the Ragged Schools were founded. I was first attracted to the subject, and indeed was first made conscious of their existence, about two years ago, or more, by seeing an advertisement in the papers dated from West Street, Saffron Hill, stating "That a room has been opened and supported in that wretched neighbourhood for upwards of twelve months, where religious instruction had been imparted to the poor", and

explaining in a few words what was meant by Ragged Schools as a
generic term, including, then, four or five similar places of
instruction. I wrote to the masters of this particular school to
make some further enquiries, and went myself soon afterwards.

It was a hot summer night; and the air of Field Lane and Saffron
Hill was not improved by such weather, nor were the people in
those streets very sober or honest company. Being unacquainted
with the exact locality of the school, I was fain to make some
inquiries about it. These were very jocosely received in general;
but everybody knew where it was, and gave the right direction to
it. The prevailing idea among the loungers (the greater part of
them the very sweepings of the streets and station houses) seemed
to be, that the teachers were quixotic, and the school upon the
whole "a lark". But there was certainly a kind of rough respect for
the intention, and (as I have said) nobody denied the school or its
whereabout, or refused assistance in directing to it.

It consisted at that time of either two or three – I forget which –
miserable rooms, upstairs in a miserable house. In the best of
these, the pupils in the female school were being taught to read
and write; and though there were among the number, many
wretched creatures steeped in degradation to the lips, they were
tolerably quiet, and listened with apparent earnestness and
patience to their instructors. The appearance of this room was sad

and melancholy, of course – how could it be otherwise! – but, on the whole, encouraging.

The close, low, chamber at the back, in which the boys were crowded, was so foul and stifling as to be, at first, almost insupportable. But its moral aspect was so far worse than its physical, that this was soon forgotten. Huddled together on a bench about the room, and shown out by some flaring candles stuck against the walls, were a crowd of boys, varying from mere infants to young men; sellers of fruit, herbs, lucifer-matches, flints; sleepers under the dry arches of bridges; young thieves and beggars – with nothing natural to youth about them: with nothing frank, ingenuous, or pleasant in their faces; low-browed, vicious, cunning, wicked; abandoned of all help but this; speeding downward to destruction; and UNUTTERABLY IGNORANT.

This, Reader, was one room as full as it could hold; but these were only grains in sample of a Multitude that are perpetually sifting though these schools; in sample of a Multitude who had within them once, and perhaps have now, the elements of men as good as you or I, and maybe infinitely better; in sample of a Multitude among whose doomed and sinful ranks (oh, think of this, and think of them!) the child of any man upon this earth, however lofty his degree, must, as by Destiny and Fate, be found, if, at its birth, it were consigned to such an infancy and nurture, as these fallen creatures had!

This was the Class I saw at the Ragged School. They could not be trusted with books; they could only be instructed orally; they were difficult of reduction to anything like attention, obedience, or decent behaviour; their benighted ignorance in reference to the Deity, or to any social duty (how could they guess at any social duty, being so discarded by all social teachers but the gaoler and the hangman!) was terrible to see. Yet, even here, and among these, something had been done already. The Ragged School was of recent date and very poor; but it had inculcated some association with the name of the Almighty, which was not an oath, and had taught them to look forward in a hymn (they sang it) to another life, which would correct the miseries and woes of this.

A street boy, drawn by A. Henning, 1847.

The new exposition I found in this Ragged School, of the frightful neglect by the State of those whom it punishes so constantly, and whom it might, as easily and less expensively, instruct and save; together with the sight I had seen there, in the heart of London; haunted me, and finally impelled me to an endeavour to bring these Institutions under the notice of the Government; with some faint hope that the vastness of the question would supersede the Theology of the schools, and that the Bench of Bishops might adjust the latter question, after some small grant had been conceded. I made the attempt; and have heard no more of the subject, from that hour.

The perusal of an advertisement in yesterday's paper, announcing a lecture on the Ragged Schools last night, has led me into

these remarks. I might easily have given them another form; but I address this letter to you, in the hope that some few readers in whom I have awakened an interest, as a writer of fiction, may be, by that means, attracted to the subject, who might otherwise, unintentionally, pass it over.

I have no desire to praise the system pursued in the Ragged Schools; which is necessarily very imperfect, if indeed there be one. So far as I have any means of judging of what is taught there, I should individually object to it, as not being sufficiently secular, and as presenting too many religious mysteries and difficulties, to minds not sufficiently prepared for their reception. But I should very imperfectly discharge in myself the duty I wish to urge and impress on others, if I allowed any such doubt of mine to interfere with my appreciation of the efforts of these teachers, or my true wish to promote them by any slight means in my power. Irritating topics, of all kinds, are equally far removed from my purpose and intention. But I adjure those excellent persons who aid, munificently, in the building of New Churches, to think of these Ragged Schools; to reflect whether some portion of their rich endowments might not be spared for such a purpose; to contemplate, calmly, the necessity of beginning at the beginning; to consider for themselves where the Christian Religion most needs and most suggests immediate help and illustration; and not to decide on any theory or hearsay, but to go themselves into the Prisons and the Ragged Schools, and form their own conclusions. They will be shocked, pained, and repelled, by much that they learn there; but nothing they can learn, will be one-thousandth part so shocking, painful, and repulsive, as the continuance, for one year more, of these things as they have been for too many years already.

Anticipating that some of the more prominent facts connected with the history of the Ragged Schools, may become known to the readers of the *Daily News* through your account of the lecture in question, I abstain (though in possession of some such information) from pursuing the question further, at this time. But if I should see occasion, I will take leave to return to it.

A SLEEP TO STARTLE US

At the top of Farringdon Street in the City of London, once adorned by the Fleet Prison and by a diabolical jumble of nuisances in the middle of the road called Fleet Market, is a broad new thoroughfare in a state of transition. A few years hence, and we of the present generation will find it not an easy task to recall, in the thriving street which will arise upon this spot, the wooden barriers and hoardings – the passages that lead to nothing – the glimpses of obscene Field Lane and Saffron Hill – the mounds of earth, old bricks, and oyster-shells – the arched foundations of unbuilt houses – the backs of miserable tenements with patched windows – the odds and ends of fever-stricken courts and alleys – which are the present features of the place. Not less perplexing do I find it now, to reckon how many years have passed since I traversed these byeways one night before they were laid bare, to find out the first Ragged School.

If I say it is ten years ago, I leave a handsome margin. The discovery was then newly made, that to talk soundingly in Parliament, and cheer for Church and State, or to consecrate and confirm without end, or to perorate to any extent in a thousand market places about all the ordinary topics of patriotic songs and sentiments, was merely to embellish England on a great scale with whited sepulchres, while there was, in every corner of the land where its people were closely accumulated, profound ignorance and perfect barbarism. It was also newly discovered, that out of these noxious sinks where they were born to perish, and where the general ruin was hatching day and night, the people *would not come* to be improved. The gulf between them and all wholesome humanity had swollen to such a depth and breadth, that they were separated from it as by impassable seas or deserts; and so they lived, and so they died: an always-increasing band of outlaws in body and soul, against whom it were to suppose the reversal of all laws, human and divine, to believe that Society could at last prevail.

In this condition of things, a few unaccredited messengers of Christianity, whom no Bishop had ever heard of, and no Goverment-office Porter had ever seen, resolved to go to the miserable wretches who had lost the way to them; and to set up places of instruction in their own degraded haunts. I found my first Ragged School, in an obscure place called West Street, Saffron Hill, pitifully struggling for life, under every disadvantage. It had no means, it had no suitable rooms, it derived no power or protection from being recognised by any authority, it attracted within its wretched walls a fluctuating swarm of faces – young in years but youthful in nothing else – that scowled Hope out of countenance. It was held in a low-roofed den, in a sickening atmosphere, in the midst of taint and dirt and pestilence: with all the deadly sins let loose, howling and shrieking at the doors. Zeal

"The Vagabond Boy". A street arab of the 1860s.

95

did not supply the place of method and training; the teachers knew little of their office; the pupils, with an evil sharpness, found them out, got the better of them, derided them, made blasphemous answers to scriptural questions, sang, fought, danced, robbed each other; seemed possessed by legions of devils. The place was stormed and carried over and over again; the lights were blown out, the books strewn in the gutters, and the female scholars carried off triumphantly to their old wickedness. With no strength in it but its purpose, the school stood it all out and made its way. Some two years since, I found it, one of many such, in a large convenient loft in this transition part of Farringdon Street – quiet and orderly, full, lighted with gas, well whitewashed, numerously attended, and thoroughly established.

The number of houseless creatures who resorted to it, and who were necessarily turned out when it closed, to hide where they could in heaps of moral and physical pollution, filled the managers with pity. To relieve some of the more constant and deserving scholars, they rented a wretched house, where a few common beds – a dozen or dozen-and-a-half perhaps – were made upon the floors. This was the Ragged School Dormitory; and when I found the School in Farringdon Street, I found the Dormitory in a court hard by, which in the time of the Cholera had acquired a dismal fame. The Dormitory was, in all respects, save as a small beginning, a very discouraging Institution. The air was bad; the dark and ruinous building, with its small close rooms, was quite unsuited to the purpose; and a general supervision of the scattered sleepers was impossible. I had great doubts at the time whether, excepting that they found a crazy shelter for their heads, they were better there than in the streets.

Having heard, in the course of last month, that this Dormitory (there are others elsewhere) had grown as the School had grown, I went the other night to make another visit to it. I found the School in the same place, still advancing. It was now an Industrial School too; and besides the men and boys who were learning – some, aptly enough; some, with painful difficulty; some, sluggishly and wearily; some, not at all – to read and write and cipher; there were two groups, one of shoemakers, and one (in a gallery) of tailors, working with great industry and satisfaction. Each was taught and superintended by a regular workman engaged for the purpose, who delivered out the necessary means and implements. All were employed in mending, either their own dilapidated clothes or shoes, or the dilapidated clothes or shoes of some of the other pupils. They were of all ages, from young boys to old men. They were quiet, and intent upon their work. Some of them were almost as unused to it as I should have shown myself to be if I had tried my hand, but all were deeply interested and profoundly anxious to do it somehow or other. They presented a very remarkable instance of the general desire there is, after all, even in the vagabond breast, to know something useful. One shock-headed man when he had mended his own scrap of a coat, drew it

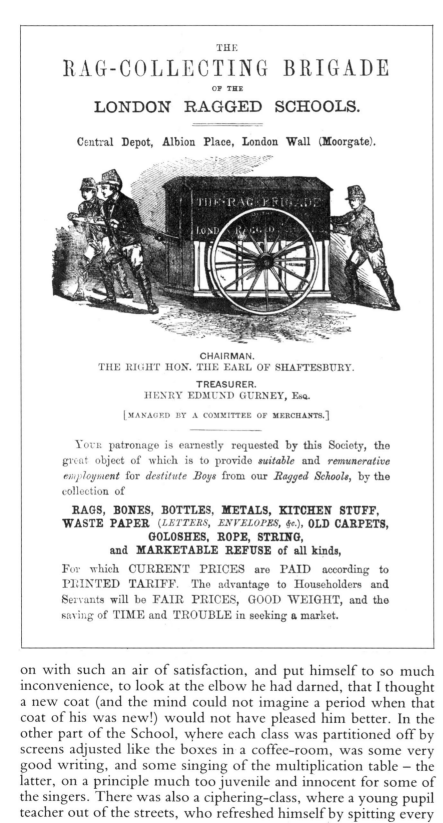

Anthony Ashley Cooper, seventh Earl of Shaftesbury, was Chairman of the Ragged School Union 1845–85. In May 1885 he told old scholars that he would rather be president of the ragged schools than of the Royal Academy. The story of the ragged schools is well told in C. J. Montague's Sixty Years in Waifdom *(1904).*

on with such an air of satisfaction, and put himself to so much inconvenience, to look at the elbow he had darned, that I thought a new coat (and the mind could not imagine a period when that coat of his was new!) would not have pleased him better. In the other part of the School, where each class was partitioned off by screens adjusted like the boxes in a coffee-room, was some very good writing, and some singing of the multiplication table – the latter, on a principle much too juvenile and innocent for some of the singers. There was also a ciphering-class, where a young pupil teacher out of the streets, who refreshed himself by spitting every

The schoolroom of the Brook Street Ragged, Industrial, Sabbath and Free-Day Schools, in Henry Street, Hampstead, in 1853. The school first met in a loft above a blacksmith's forge in 1843, and soon became so crowded that larger premises were built.

half-minute, had written a legible sum in compound addition, on a broken slate, and was walking backward and forward before it, as he worked it, for the instruction of his class, in this way:

Now then! Look here, all on you! Seven and five, how many?

SHARP BOY (in no particular clothes). Twelve!

PUPIL TEACHER. Twelve – and eight?

DULL YOUNG MAN (with water on the brain). Forty-five!

SHARP BOY. Twenty!

PUPIL TEACHER. Twenty. You're right. And nine?

DULL YOUNG MAN (after great consideration). Twenty-nine!

PUPIL TEACHER. Twenty-nine it is. And nine?

RECKLESS GUESSER. Seventy-four!

PUPIL TEACHER (drawing nine strokes). How can that be? Here's nine on 'em! Look! Twenty-nine, and one's thirty, and one's thirty-one, and one's thirty-two, and one's thirty-three, and one's thirty-four, and one's thirty-five, and one's thirty-six, and one's thirty-seven, and one's what?

RECKLESS GUESSER. Four-and-two-pence farden!

DULL YOUNG MAN (who has been absorbed in the demonstration). Thirty–eight!

PUPIL TEACHER (restraining sharp boy's ardour). Of course it is! Thirty-eight pence. There they are! (writing 38 in slate-corner). Now what do you make of thirty-eight pence? Thirty-eight pence, how much? (Dull young man slowly considers and gives it up, under a week). How much, you? (to sleepy boy, who stares and says nothing). How much, *you?*

SHARP BOY. Three-and-twopence!

PUPIL TEACHER. Three-and-twopence. How do I put down three-and-twopence?

SHARP BOY. You puts down the two, and you carries the three.

PUPIL TEACHER. Very good. Where do I carry the three?

RECKLESS GUESSER. T'other side the slate!

SHARP BOY. You carries him to the next column on the left hand, and adds him on!

PUPIL TEACHER. And adds him on! and eight and three's eleven, and eight's nineteen, and seven's what?

– And so on.

The best and most spirited teacher was a young man himself reclaimed through the agency of this School from the lowest depths of misery and debasement, whom the Committee were about to send out to Australia. He appeared quite to deserve the interest they took in him, and his appearance and manner were a strong testimony to the merits of the establishment.

All this was not the Dormitory, but it was the preparation for it. No man or boy is admitted to the Dormitory, unless he is a regular attendant at the school, and unless he has been in the school two hours before the time of opening the Dormitory. If there be reason to suppose that he can get any work to do and will not do it, he is admitted no more, and his place is assigned to some other candidate for the nightly refuge; of whom there are always plenty. There is very little to tempt the idle and profligate. A scanty supper and a scanty breakfast, each of six ounces of bread and nothing else (this quantity is less than the present penny-loaf), would scarcely be regarded by Mr. Chadwick himself as a festive or uproarious entertainment.

Mr. Chadwick: Edwin Chadwick (1800–90), sanitary reformer, stern secretary of the Poor Law Commission, 1834–46

I found the Dormitory below the School: with its bare walls and rafters, and bare floor, the building looked rather like an extensive coach-house, well lighted with gas. A wooden gallery had been recently erected on three sides of it; and, abutting from the centre of the wall on the fourth side, was a kind of glazed meat-safe, accessible by a ladder; in which the presiding officer is posted every night, and all night. In the centre of the room, which was very cool, and perfectly sweet, stood a small fixed stove; on two sides, there were windows; on all sides, simple means of admitting fresh air, and releasing foul air. The ventilation of the place, devised by Doctor Arnott, and particularly the expedient for relieving the sleepers in the galleries from receiving the breath of the sleepers below, is a wonder of simplicity, cheapness, efficiency, and practical good sense. If it had cost five or ten thousand pounds, it would have been famous.

Dr. Arnott: Arnott's ventilation valves were at this time being widely installed in the chimneys of institutions such as workhouses, as a protection against cholera

The whole floor of the building, with the exception of a few narrow pathways, was partitioned off into wooden troughs, or shallow boxes without lids – not unlike the fittings in the shop of a dealer in corn and flour, and seeds. The galleries were parcelled out in same way. Some of these berths were very short – for boys; some, longer – for men. The largest were of very contracted limits; all were composed of the bare boards; each was furnished

99

only with one coarse rug, rolled up. In the brick pathways were iron gratings communicating with trapped drains, enabling the entire surface of these sleeping-places to be soused and flooded with water every morning. The floor of the galleries was cased with zinc, and fitted with gutters and escape-pipes, for the same reason. A supply of water both for drinking and for washing, and some tin vessels for either purpose, were at hand. A little shed, used by one of the industrial classes, for the chopping up of fire-wood, did not occupy the whole of the spare space in that corner; and the remainder was devoted to some excellent baths, available also as washing troughs, in order that those who have any rags of linen may clean them once a week. In aid of this object, a drying-closet, charged with hot-air, was about to be erected in the wood-chopping shed. All these appliances were constructed in the simplest manner, with the commonest means, in the narrowest space, at the lowest cost; but were perfectly adapted to their respective purposes.

I had scarcely made the round of the Dormitory, and looked at all these things, when a moving of feet overhead announced that the School was breaking up for the night. It was succeeded by profound silence, and then by a hymn, sung in a subdued tone, and in very good time and tune, by the learners we had lately seen. Separated from their miserable bodies, the effect of their voices, united in this strain, was infinitely solemn. It was as if their souls were singing – as if the outward differences that parted us had fallen away, and the time was come when all the perverted good that was in them, or that ever might have been in them, arose imploringly to Heaven.

The baker who had brought the bread, and who leaned against a pillar while the singing was in progress, meditating in his way, whatever his way was, now shouldered his basket and retired. The two half-starved attendants (rewarded with a double portion for their pains) heaped the six-ounce loaves into other baskets, and made ready to distribute them. The night-officer arrived, mounted to his meat-safe, unlocked it, hung up his hat, and prepared to spend the evening. I found him to be a very respectable-looking person in black, with a wife and family; engaged in an office all day, and passing his spare time here, from half-past nine every night to six every morning, for a pound a week. He had carried the post against two hundred competitors.

The door was now opened, and the men and boys who were to pass that night in the Dormitory, in number one hundred and sixty-seven (including a man for whom there was no trough, but who was allowed to rest in the seat by the stove, once occupied by the night-officer before the meat-safe was), came in. They passed to their different sleeping-places, quietly and in good order. Every one sat down in his own crib, where he became presented in a curiously foreshortened manner; and those who had shoes took them off, and placed them in the adjoining path. There were, in the assembly, thieves, cadgers, trampers, vagrants, common

A crossing-sweeper of the 1850s; a boy such as Jo in Bleak House.

100

outcasts of all sorts. In casual wards and many other Refuges, they would have been very difficult to deal with; but they were restrained here by the law of kindness, and had long since arrived at the knowledge that those who gave them that shelter could have no possible inducement save to do them good. Neighbours spoke little together – they were almost as uncompanionable as mad people – but everybody took his small loaf when the baskets went round, with a thankfulness more or less cheerful, and immediately ate it up.

There was some excitement in consequence of one man being missing: "the lame old man". Everybody had seen the lame old man upstairs asleep, but he had unaccountably disappeared. What he had been doing with himself was a mystery, but, when the enquiry was at its height, he came shuffling and tumbling in, with his palsied head hanging on his breast – an emaciated drunkard, once a compositor, dying of starvation and decay. He was so near death, that he could not be kept there, lest he should die in the night; and, while it was under deliberation what to do with him, and while his dull lips tried to shape out answers to what was said to him, he was held up by two men. Beside this wreck, but all unconnected with it and with the whole world, was an orphan boy with burning cheeks and great gaunt eager eyes, who was in pressing peril of death too, and who had no possession under the broad sky but a bottle of physic and a scrap of writing. He brought both from the house-surgeon of a Hospital that was too full to admit him, and stood, giddily staggering in one of the little pathways, while the Chief Samaritan read, in hasty characters underlined, how momentous his necessities were. He held the

The workroom of the Brook Street Schools. This section of the school was designed to provide "food and a trade" for boys who would otherwise be driven to petty crime to survive.

101

bottle of physic in his claw of a hand, and stood, apparently unconscious of it, staggering, and staring with his bright glazed eyes; a creature, surely, as forlorn and desolate as Mother Earth can have supported on her breast that night. He was gently taken away, along with the dying man, to the workhouse; and he passed into the darkness with his physic-bottle as if he were going into his grave.

The bread eaten to the last crumb; and some drinking of water and washing in water having taken place, with very little stir or noise indeed, preparations were made for passing the night. Some took off their rags of smock frocks; some, their rags of coats or jackets, and spread them out within their narrow bounds for beds: designing to lie upon them, and use their rugs as a covering. Some sat up, pondering, on the edges of their troughs; others, who were very tired, rested their unkempt heads upon their hands and their elbows on their knees, and dozed. When there were no more who desired to drink or wash, and all were in their places, the night officer, standing below the meat-safe, read a short evening service, including perhaps as inappropriate a prayer as could possibly be read (as though the Lord's Prayer stood in need of it by way of Rider), and a portion of a chapter from the New Testament. Then they all sang the Evening Hymn, and then they all lay down to sleep.

It was an awful thing, looking round upon those one hundred and sixty-seven representatives of many thousands, to reflect that a Government, unable, with the least regard to truth, to plead ignorance of the existence of such a place, should proceed as if the sleepers never were to wake again. I do not hesitate to say – why should I, for I know it to be true! – that an annual sum of money, contemptible in amount as compared with any charges upon any list, freely granted in behalf of these Schools, and shackled with no preposterous Red Tape conditions, would relieve the prisons, diminish county rates, clear loads of shame and guilt out of the streets, recruit the army and navy, waft to new countries fleets full of useful labour, for which their inhabitants would be thankful and beholden to us. It is no depreciation of the devoted people whom I found presiding here, to add, that with such assistance as a trained knowledge of the business of instruction, and a sound system adjusted to the peculiar difficulties and conditions of this sphere of action, their usefulness could be increased fifty-fold in a few months.

My Lords and Gentlemen, can you, at the present time, consider this at last, and agree to do some little easy thing! Dearly beloved brethren elsewhere, do you know that between Gorham controversies, and Pusey controversies, and Newman controversies, and twenty other edifying controversies, a certain large class of minds in the community is gradually being driven out of all religion? Would it be well, do you think, to come out of the controversies for a little while, and be simply Apostolic thus low down!

An evangelical Sunday school teacher and pupil, 1840.

Gorham, Pusey, Newman controversies: doctrinal and theological arguments

From **Our Mutual Friend** *book 2 chapter 1*

THE school at which young Charley Hexam had first learned from a book – the streets being, for pupils of his degree, the great Preparatory Establishment in which very much that is never unlearned is learned without and before book – was a miserable loft in an unsavoury yard. Its atmosphere was oppressive and disagree-able; it was crowded, noisy, and confusing; half the pupils dropped asleep, or fell into a state of waking stupefaction; the other half kept them in either condition by maintaining a monotonous droning noise, as if they were performing, out of time and tune, on a ruder sort of bagpipe. The teachers, animated solely by good intentions, had no idea of execution, and a lamentable jumble was the upshot of their kind endeavours.

It was a school for all ages, and for both sexes. The latter were kept apart, and the former were partitioned off into square assortments. But all the place was pervaded by a grimly ludicrous pretence that every pupil was childish and innocent. This pretence, much favoured by the lady-visitors, led to the ghastliest absurdities. Young women old in the vices of the commonest and worst life, were expected to profess themselves enthralled by the good child's book, the Adventures of Little Margery, who resided in the village cottage by the mill; severely reproved and morally squashed the miller, when she was five and he was fifty; divided her porridge with singing birds; denied herself a new nankeen bonnet, on the ground that the turnips did not wear nankeen bonnets, neither did the sheep who ate them; who plaited straw and delivered the dreariest orations to all comers, at all sorts of unseasonable times. So, unwieldy young dredgers and hulking mudlarks were referred to the experiences of Thomas Twopence, who, having resolved not to rob (under circumstances of uncommon atrocity) his particular friend and benefactor, of eighteenpence, presently came into supernatural possession of three and sixpence, and lived a shining light ever afterwards. (Note, that the benefactor came to no good.) Several swaggering sinners had written their own biographies in the same strain; it always appearing from the lessons of those very boastful persons, that you were to do good, not because it *was* good, but because you were to make a good thing of it. Contrariwise, the adult pupils were taught to read (if they could learn) out of the New Testament; and by dint of stumbling over the syllables and keeping their bewildered eyes on the particular syllables coming round to their turn, were as absolutely ignorant of the sublime history, as if they had never seen or heard of it. An exceedingly and confoundingly perplexing jumble of a school, in fact, where black spirits and grey, red spirits and white, jumbled jumbled jumbled jumbled, jumbled every night. And particularly every Sunday night. For then, an inclined plane of unfortunate infants would be handed over to the prosiest and worst of all the teachers with good intentions, whom nobody older would endure. Who, taking his stand on the floor before them as chief executioner, would be attended by a conventional volunteer boy as executioner's assistant. . . .

Even in this temple of good intentions, an exceptionally sharp boy exceptionally determined to learn, could learn something, and, having learned it, could impart it much better than the teachers; as being more knowing than they, and not at the disadvantage in which they stood towards the shrewder pupils. In this way it had come about that Charley Hexam had risen in the jumble, taught in the jumble, and been received from the jumble into a better school.

A WALK IN A WORKHOUSE

Household Words 25 May 1850

THE common name for the workhouse in street ballads is eloquent of the popular opinion of them: the workhouse was not, as officialdom might prefer, the "Union" but the "*Bastille*". Fear of ending up there dominated many lives. This fear may sometimes have been ill-founded and obstinate, but it was real. Leaving aside the question of harsh treatment, poor diet, debasing work, the workhouse affronted people's sense of dignity and self-respect, their sense of being part of a community. The separation of husbands and wives was simply the bitterest element.

Dickens visited workhouses often, as he did ragged schools, prisons and other institutions for improving or reproving the poor. The particular visit described here was made on Sunday 5 May 1850 with the founder of the Pharmaceutical Society, Jacob Bell. The vivid immediacy of the article owes much to the speed with which Dickens set down his impressions. It was written the very next day, and Dickens was able to send Bell a proof on the following Sunday. He wrote, "I have thought a great deal about that woman, the Wardswoman in the Itch Ward, who was crying about the dead child. If anything useful can be done for her, I should like to do it."

Partly for Bell's sake, Dickens concealed the name of the "large metropolitan workhouse" he describes. It was probably the St. Marylebone workhouse, which, on 6 February 1849, had 1,715 inmates (437 men, 804 women, 203 boys aged 7 to 15, 152 girls aged 7 to 15 and 119 infants under 7) plus a further 345 in the infirmary, including 79 lunatics. But the identity of the specific workhouse scarcely matters, for Dickens as always uses the individual scenes he witnessed to make a broad point about workhouses as a whole. It is a beautifully modulated piece of writing, which brings to fierce life the dry statistics of the report to the Board of Health on the metropolitan workhouses published in the same year.

Dickens returned to the theme of "A Walk in a Workhouse" in a later and lighter essay, "Wapping Workhouse", included in *The Uncommercial Traveller*. Here, too, he journeys first into "the Foul wards", then into a "loft devoted to the idiotic and imbecile", then into the nursery, then to visit "the Refractories" picking oakum (that is, untwisting old rope to reduce it to fibre), then into the wards of the aged and infirm. In four searing articles in John Forster's *Examiner* in 1849, Dickens recorded the scandal of Bartholomew Drouet's baby-farm at Tooting – a private outpost of the workhouse system – at which many children died of cholera and neglect. The servant girl Guster in *Bleak House* is a victim of Drouet's. Guster, "although she was farmed or contracted for, during her growing time, by an amiable benefactor of his species resident at Tooting, and cannot fail to have developed under the most favourable circumstances, 'has fits' – which the parish can't account for." Oliver Twist spends his early years at a similar establishment, run by Mrs. Mann.

Oliver Twist contains a great deal of pointed criticism of workhouses just before and just after the Poor Law Amendment Act of 1834, which, brought in to curb abuses, in many ways only tightened a noose around the neck of the needy. The crucial change in 1834 was the denial of "outdoor relief" to the able-bodied, forcing the needy either to suffer alone or to enter the strict regime of the workhouse. In *Little Dorrit*, Old Nandy's fading years are limited and circumscribed by workhouse rules; *Our Mutual Friend* portrays vividly in the story of Mrs. Higden the continuing revulsion of the poor against the measures supposedly provided for their benefit.

In all these cases, Dickens argues indignantly against the shabby treatment accorded to the inmates, and the iniquity of the whole Poor Law system. In *Our Mutual Friend,* as here, he reverts to his frequent complaint that paupers are treated worse than criminals. In Mrs. Higden's restless flight from the workhouse,

> Now, she would light upon the shameful spectacle of some desolate creature – or some wretched ragged groups of either sex, or of both sexes, with children among them, huddled together like the smaller vermin for a little warmth – lingering and lingering on a doorstep, while the appointed evader of the public trust did his dirty office of trying to weary them out and so get rid of them. Now, she would light upon some poor decent person, like herself, going afoot on a pilgrimage of many weary miles to see some worn-out relative or friend who had been charitably clutched off to a great blank barren Union House, as far from old home as the County Jail (the remoteness of which is always its worst punishment for small rural offenders), and in its dietary, and in its lodging, and in its tending of the sick, a much more penal establishment.

Dickens's portrayal of Mrs. Higden was challenged, and he responded in his postscript with a plain statement of his view of the Poor Law in 1865: "I believe there has been in England, since the days of the Stuarts, no law so often infamously administered, no law so often openly violated, no law habitually so ill-supervised." He referred specifically to the *Lancet* commission of the same year, which exposed shocking conditions in London's workhouse infirmaries. It had found, for instance, a wardful of syphilitic women sharing a single towel. Inadequate hygiene and callous medical care were the rule, not the exception.

It may be thought that such conditions as these would not be suffered to persist. In fact, although there were various notional and part-effective reforms of the system that had led to such horrors, there was very little real improvement throughout the nineteenth century. In 1892, George Lansbury found on his first visit to Poplar Workhouse "sick and aged, mentally deficient, lunatics, babies and children, able-bodied and tramps all herded together in one huge range of buildings. Officers, both men and women, looked upon these people as a nuisance, and treated them accordingly". The Royal Commission on the Aged Poor in 1893-94 numbered the Prince of Wales among the commissioners, a sign that times were changing. Nevertheless, the shadow of the workhouse loomed over the urban and rural poor well into the present century.

Dickens passionately resented the shameful treatment of the elderly, the ill and the imbecile in the workhouses, but he is perhaps most vehement about the morally crippling effect on the young. He saw workhouses as breeding grounds of vice and crime, with the girls neglected and the boys "positively kept like wolves".

Most of all, the workhouses were a standing reminder that society had not changed – perhaps could never change – since the days of Nicholas Nickleby:

> when he thought how regularly things went on from day to day in the same unvarying round – how youth and beauty died, and ugly griping age lived tottering on – how crafty avarice grew rich, and manly honest hearts were poor and sad – how few they were who tenanted the stately houses, and how many those who lay in noisome pens, or rose each day and laid them down at night, and lived and died, father and son, mother and child, race upon race, and generation upon generation, without a home to shelter them or the energies of one single man directed to their aid – how in seeking, not a luxurious and splendid life, but the bare means of a most wretched and inadequate subsistence, there were women and children in that one town, divided into classes, numbered and estimated as regularly as the noble families and folks of great degree, and reared from infancy to drive most criminal and dreadful trades – how ignorance was punished and never taught . . . how much injustice, and misery, and wrong there was, and yet how the world rolled on from year to year, alike careless and indifferent, and no man seeking to remedy or redress it.

A WALK IN A WORKHOUSE

A few Sundays ago, I formed one of the congregation assembled in the chapel of a large metropolitan Workhouse. With the exception of the clergyman and clerk, and a very few officials, there were none but paupers present. The children sat in the galleries; the women in the body of the chapel, and in one of the side aisles; the men in the remaining aisle. The service was decorously performed, though the sermon might have been much better adapted to the comprehension and to the circumstances of the hearers. The usual supplications were offered, with more than the usual significancy in such a place, for the fatherless children and widows, for all sick persons and young children, for all that were desolate and oppressed, for the comforting and helping of the weak-hearted, for the raising-up of them that had fallen; for all that were in danger, necessity, and tribulation. The prayers of the congregation were desired "for several persons in the various wards, dangerously ill"; and others who were recovering returned their thanks to Heaven.

Among this congregation, were some evil-looking young women, and beetle-browed young men; but not many – perhaps that kind of characters kept away. Generally, the faces (those of the children excepted) were depressed and subdued, and wanted colour. Aged people were there, in every variety. Mumbling, blear-eyed, spectacled, stupid, deaf, lame; vacantly winking in the gleams of sun that now and then crept in through the open doors, from the paved yard; shading their listening ears, or blinking eyes, with their withered hands; poring over their books, leering at nothing, going to sleep, crouching and drooping in corners. There were weird old women, all skeleton within, all bonnet and cloak without, continually wiping their eyes with dirty dusters of pocket-handkerchiefs; and there were ugly old crones, both male and female, with a ghastly kind of contentment upon them which was not at all comforting to see. Upon the whole, it was the dragon, Pauperism, in a very weak and impotent condition; toothless, fangless, drawing his breath heavily enough, and hardly worth chaining up.

When the service was over, I walked with the humane and conscientious gentleman whose duty it was to take that walk, that Sunday morning, through the little world of poverty enclosed within the workhouse walls. It was inhabited by a population of some fifteen hundred or two thousand paupers, ranging from the infant newly born or not yet come into the pauper world, to the old man dying on his bed.

In a room opening from a squalid yard, where a number of listless women were lounging to and fro, trying to get warm in the ineffectual sunshine of the tardy May morning – in the "Itch Ward", not to compromise the truth – a woman such as Hogarth has often drawn was hurriedly getting on her gown, before

the Itch: scabies

106

a dusty fire. She was the nurse, or wardswoman, of that insalubrious department – herself a pauper – flabby, raw-boned, untidy – unpromising and coarse of aspect as need be. But, on being spoken to about the patients whom she had in charge, she turned round, with her shabby gown half on, half off, and fell a crying with all her might. Not for show, not querulously, not in any mawkish sentiment, but in the deep grief and affliction of her heart; turning away her dishevelled head: sobbing most bitterly, wringing her hands, and letting fall abundance of great tears, that choked her utterance. What was the matter with the nurse of the itch-ward? Oh, "the dropped child" was dead! Oh, the child that was found in the street, and she had brought up ever since, had died an hour ago, and see where the little creature lay, beneath this cloth! The dear, the pretty dear!

The dropped child seemed too small and poor a thing for Death to be in earnest with, but Death had taken it; and already its diminutive form was neatly washed, composed, and stretched as if in sleep upon a box. I thought I heard a voice from Heaven saying, It shall be well for thee, O nurse of the itch-ward, when some less gentle pauper does those offices to thy cold form, that such as the dropped child are the angels who behold my Father's face!

In another room, were several ugly old women crouching, witch-like, round a hearth, and chattering and nodding, after the manner of the monkeys. "All well here? And enough to eat?" A general chattering and chuckling; at last an answer from a volunteer. "Oh yes gentleman! Bless you gentleman! Lord bless the parish of St. So-and-So! It feed the hungry, Sir, and give drink to the thirsty, and it warm them which is cold, so it do, and good luck to the parish of St. So-and-So, and thankee gentleman!" Elsewhere, a party of pauper nurses were at dinner. "How do *you*

The City Union Workhouse, Bow Road, 1851, from the designs of the architect, Richard Tress. The magnificent facade expresses mid-century civic pride. According to the Illustrated Exhibitor, *"the City of London Union is evidently a magnificent structure, at once elegant and substantial".*

107

Part of a letter from Charles Cochrane, Chairman of the Poor Man's Guardian Society, a body set up to press for workhouse reform.

get on?" "Oh pretty well Sir! We works hard, and we lives hard – like the sodgers!"

In another room, a kind of purgatory or place of transition, six or eight noisy madwomen were gathered together, under the superintendence of one sane attendant. Among them was a girl of two or three and twenty, very prettily dressed, of most respectable appearance, and good manners, who had been brought in from the house where she had lived as domestic servant (having, I suppose, no friends), on account of being subject to epileptic fits, and requiring to be removed under the influence of a very bad one. She was by no means of the same stuff, or the same breeding, or the same experience, or in the same state of mind, as those by whom she was surrounded; and she pathetically complained, that the daily association and the nightly noise made her worse, and was driving her mad – which was perfectly evident. The case was noted for enquiry and redress, but she said she had already been there for some weeks.

If this girl had stolen her mistress's watch, I do not hesitate to say she would, in all probability, have been infinitely better off. Bearing in mind, in the present brief description of this walk, not only the facts already stated in this Journal, in reference to the Model Prison at Pentonville, but the general treatment of convicted prisoners under the associated silent system too, it must be once more distinctly set before the reader, that we have come to this absurd, this dangerous, this monstrous pass, that the dishonest felon is, in respect of cleanliness, order, diet, and accommodation, better provided for, and taken care of, than the honest pauper.

And this conveys no special imputation on the workhouse of the parish of St. So-and-So, where, on the contrary, I saw many things to commend. It was very agreeable, recollecting that most infamous and atrocious enormity committed at Tooting – an enormity which, a hundred years hence, will still be vividly remembered in the bye-ways of English life, and which has done more to engender a gloomy discontent and suspicion among many thousands of the people than all the Chartist leaders could have done in all their lives – to find the pauper children in this workhouse looking robust and well, and apparently the objects of very great care. In the Infant School – a large, light, airy room at the top of the building – the little creatures, being at dinner, and eating their potatoes heartily, were not cowed by the presence of strange visitors, but stretched out their small hands to be shaken, with a very pleasant confidence. And it was comfortable to see two mangy pauper rocking-horses rampant in a corner. In the girls' school, where the dinner was also in progress, everything bore a cheerful and healthy aspect. The meal was over, in the boys' school, by the time of our arrival there, and the room was not yet quite re-arranged; but the boys were roaming unrestrained about a large and airy yard, as any other school-boys might have done. Some of them had been drawing large ships upon the schoolroom wall; and if they had a mast with shrouds and stays set up for practice (as they have in the Middlesex House of Correction), it would be so much the better. At present, if a boy should feel a strong impulse upon him to learn the art of going aloft, he could only gratify it, I presume, as the men and women paupers gratify their aspirations after better board and lodging, by smashing as many workhouse windows as possible, and being promoted to prison.

In one place, the Newgate of the workhouse, a company of boys and youths were locked up in a yard alone; their day-room being a kind of kennel where the casual poor used formerly to be littered down at night. Divers of them had been there some long time. "Are they never going away?" was the natural enquiry. "Most of them are crippled, in some form or other," said the

"In the workhouse school-room, choky and small,
That looks out on the workhouse wall,
Sit the pauper children, drearily,
Under the pauper mistress' rule,
Mumbling, and stumbling, and stuttering wearily,
Over the tasks of the workhouse school;
While the sun-light smites uncheerily
Sodden faces, blank of thinking,
Eyes that cannot keep from blinking,
Little bodies, sore and sinking,
That scarce hold up on bench and stool."
Punch, 1851

Wardsman, "and not fit for anything." They slunk about, like dispirited wolves or hyaenas; and made a pounce at their food when it was served out, much as those animals do. The big-headed idiot shuffling his feet along the pavement, in the sunlight outside, was a more agreeable object everyway.

Groves of babies in arms; groves of mothers and other sick women in bed; groves of lunatics; jungles of men in stone-paved downstairs day-rooms, waiting for their dinners; longer and longer groves of old people, in upstairs Infirmary wards, wearing out life, God knows how – this was the scenery through which the walk lay, for two hours. In some of these latter chambers, there were pictures stuck against the wall, and a neat display of crockery and pewter on a kind of sideboard; now and then it was a treat to see a plant or two; in almost every ward, there was a cat.

In all of these Long Walks of aged and infirm, some old people were bed-ridden, and had been for a long time; some were sitting on their beds half-naked; some dying in their beds; some out of bed, and sitting at a table near the fire. A sullen or lethargic indifference to what was asked, a blunted sensibility to everything but warmth and food, a moody absence of complaint as being of no use, a dogged silence and resentful desire to be left alone again, I thought were generally apparent. On our walking into the midst of one of these dreary perspectives of old men, nearly the following little dialogue took place, the nurse not being immediately at hand:

"All well here?"

No answer. An old man in a Scotch cap sitting among others on a form at the table, eating out of a tin porringer, pushes back his cap a little to look at us, claps it down on his forehead again with the palm of his hand, and goes on eating.

"All well here?" (repeated.)

No answer. Another old man sitting on his bed, paralytically peeling a boiled potato, lifts his head, and stares.

"Enough to eat?"

No answer. Another old man, in bed, turns himself and coughs.

"How are *you* to day?" To the last old man.

That old man says nothing; but another old man, a tall old man of a very good address, speaking with perfect correctness, comes forward from somewhere, and volunteers an answer. The reply almost always proceeds from a volunteer, and not from the person looked at or spoken to.

"We are very old, Sir," in a mild, distinct voice. "We can't expect to be well, most of us."

"Are you comfortable?"

"I have no complaint to make, Sir." With a half shake of his head, a half shrug of his shoulders, and a kind of apologetic smile.

"Enough to eat?"

"Why, Sir, I have but a poor appetite," with the same air as before; "and yet I get through my allowance very easily."

"But," showing a porringer with a Sunday dinner in it; "here is

a portion of mutton, and three potatoes. You can't starve on that?"

"Oh dear no, Sir," with the same apologetic air. "Not starve."

"What do you want?"

"We have very little bread, Sir. It's an exceedingly small quantity of bread."

The nurse, who is now rubbing her hands at the questioner's elbow, interferes with, "It ain't much raly, Sir. You see they've only six ounces a day, and when they've took their breakfast, there *can* only be a little left for night, Sir."

Another old man, hitherto invisible, rises out of his bedclothes, as out of a grave, and looks on.

"You have tea at night?" The questioner is still addressing the well-spoken old man.

"Yes, Sir, we have tea at night."

"And you save what bread you can from the morning, to eat with it?"

"Yes, Sir — if we can save any."

"And you want more to eat with it?"

"Yes, Sir." With a very anxious face.

The questioner, in the kindness of his heart, appears a little discomposed, and changes the subject.

"What has become of the old man who used to lie in that bed in the corner?"

The nurse don't remember what old man is referred to. There has been such a many old men. The well-spoken old man is doubtful. The spectral old man who has come to life in bed says, "Billy Stevens." Another old man who has previously had his head in the fireplace pipes out, "Charley Walters."

Something like a feeble interest is awakened. I suppose Charley Walters had conversation in him.

Mothers and infants in the workhouse, an etching by Phiz, 1858. In "Wapping Workhouse", published in All the Year Round *on 18 February 1860, Dickens wrote: "There were many babies here, and more than one handsome young mother. There were ugly young mothers also, and sullen young mothers, and callous young mothers. But the babies had not appropriated to themselves any bad expression yet".*

"He's dead!" says the piping old man.

Another old man, with one eye screwed up, hastily displaces the piping old man, and says:

"Yes! Charley Walters died in that bed, and – and –"

"Billy Stevens," persists the spectral old man.

"No, no! and Johnny Rogers died in that bed, and – and – they're both on 'em dead – and Sam'l Bowyer," this seems very extraordinary to him, "he went out!"

With this he subsides, and all the old men (having had quite enough of it) subside, and the spectral old man goes into his grave again, and takes the shade of Billy Stevens with him.

As we turn to go out at the door, another previously invisible old man, a hoarse old man in a flannel gown, is standing there, as if he had just come up through the floor.

"I beg your pardon, Sir, could I take the liberty of saying a word?"

"Yes; what is it?"

"I am greatly better in my health, Sir; but what I want, to get me quite round," with his hand on his throat, "is a little fresh air, Sir. It has always done my complaint so much good, Sir. The regular leave for going out, comes round so seldom, that if the gentlemen, next Friday, would give me leave to go out walking, now and then – for only an hour or so, Sir! –"

Who could wonder, looking through those weary vistas of bed and infirmity, that it should do him good to meet with some other scenes, and assure himself that there was something else on earth? Who could help wondering why the old men lived on as they did; what grasp they had on life; what crumbs of interest or occupation they could pick up from its bare board; whether Charley Walters had ever described to them the days when he kept company with some old pauper woman in the bud, or Billy Stevens ever told them of the time when he was a dweller in the far-off foreign land called Home!

The morsel of burnt child, lying in another room, so patiently, in bed, wrapped in lint, and looking steadfastly at us with his bright quiet eyes when we spoke to him kindly, looked as if the knowledge of these things, and of all the tender things there are to think about, might have been in his mind – as if he thought, with us, that there was a fellow-feeling in the pauper nurses which appeared to make them more kind to their charges than the race of common nurses in the hospitals – as if he mused upon the Future of some older children lying around him in the same place, and thought it best, perhaps, all things considered, that he should die – as if he knew, without fear, of those many coffins, made and unmade, piled up in the store below – and of his unknown friend, "the dropped child", calm upon the box-lid covered with a cloth. But there was something wistful and appealing, too, in his tiny face, as if, in the midst of all the hard necessities and incongruities he pondered on, he pleaded, in behalf of the helpless and the aged poor, for a little more liberty – and a little more bread.

"The Late Act with a
Vengeance": a savage
depiction of the Poor Law
in action, from George
Augustus Sala's short-lived
journal Banter,
23 December 1867. The
beadle recalls Mr. Meagles
in Little Dorrit, who says:
"If there is anything that is
not to be tolerated on any
terms, anything that is a
type of Jack-in-office
insolence and absurdity,
anything that represents in
coats, waistcoats, and big
sticks our English holding
on by nonsense after every
one has found it out, it is a
beadle."

113

From **Little Dorrit** *book 1 chapter 31*

ANYBODY may pass, any day, in the thronged thoroughfares of the metropolis, some meagre, wrinkled, yellow old man (who might be supposed to have dropped from the stars, if there were any star in the Heavens dull enough to be suspected of casting off so feeble a spark), creeping along with a scared air, as though bewildered and a little frightened by the noise and bustle. This old man is always a little old man. If he were ever a big old man, he has shrunk into a little old man; if he were always a little old man, he has dwindled into a less old man. His coat is a colour, and cut, that never was the mode anywhere, at any period. Clearly, it was not made for him, or for any individual mortal. Some wholesale contractor measured Fate for five thousand coats of such quality, and Fate has lent this old coat to this old man, as one of a long unfinished line of many old men. It has always large dull metal buttons, similar to no other buttons. This old man wears a hat, a thumbed and napless and yet an obdurate hat, which has never adapted itself to the shape of his poor head. His coarse shirt and his coarse neck-cloth have no more individuality than his coat and hat; they have the same character of not being his – of not being anybody's. Yet this old man wears these clothes with a certain unaccustomed air of being dressed and elaborated for the public ways; as though he passed the greater part of his time in a nightcap and gown. And so, like the country mouse in the second year of a famine, come to see the town mouse, and timidly threading his way to the town mouse's lodging through a city of cats, this old man passes in the streets.

Sometimes, on holidays towards evening, he will be seen to walk with a slightly increased infirmity, and his old eyes will glimmer with a moist and marshy light. Then the little old man is drunk. A very small measure will overset him; he may be bowled off his unsteady legs with a half-pint pot. Some pitying acquaintance – chance acquaintance very often – has warmed up his weakness with a treat of beer, and the consequence will be the lapse of a longer time than usual before he shall pass again. For the little old man is going home to the Workhouse; and on his good behaviour they do not let him out often (though methinks they might, considering the few years he has before him to go out in, under the sun); and on his bad behaviour they shut him up closer than ever in a grove of two score and nineteen more old men, every one of whom smells of all the others. . . .

But no poverty in him, and no coat on him that never was the mode, and no Old Men's Ward for his dwelling-place, could quench his daughter's admiration. Mrs. Plornish was as proud of her father's talents as she could possibly have been if they had made him Lord Chancellor. She had as firm a belief in the sweetness and propriety of his manners as she could possibly have had if he had been Lord Chamberlain. The poor little old man knew some pale and vapid little songs, long out of date, about Chloe, and Phyllis, and Strephon being wounded by the son of Venus; and for Mrs. Plornish there was no such music at the Opera as the small internal flutterings and chirpings wherein he would discharge himself of these ditties, like a weak, little, broken barrel-organ, ground by a baby. On his "days out", those flecks of light in his flat vista of pollard old men, it was at once Mrs. Plornish's delight and sorrow, when he was strong with meat, and had taken his full halfpenny-worth of porter, to say, "Sing us a song, Father." Then he would give them Chloe, and if he were in pretty good spirits, Phyllis also – Strephon he had hardly been up to since he went into retirement – and then would Mrs. Plornish declare she did believe there never was such a singer as Father, and wipe her eyes.

From **Our Mutual Friend** *book 1 chapter 16*

"AND Master – or Mister – Sloppy?" said the Secretary, in doubt whether he was man, boy, or what.

"A love-child," returned Betty Higden, dropping her voice; "parents never known; found in the street. He was brought up in the –" with a shiver of repugnance, "– the House."

"The Poor-house?" said the Secretary.

Mrs. Higden set that resolute old face of hers, and darkly nodded yes.

"You dislike the mention of it."

"Dislike the mention of it?" answered the old woman. "Kill me sooner than take me there. Throw this pretty child under cart-horses' feet and a loaded waggon, sooner than take him there. Come to us and find us all a-dying, and set a light to us all where we lie, and let us all blaze away with the house into a heap of cinders, sooner than move a corpse of us there!"

A surprising spirit in this lonely woman after so many years of hard working, and hard living, my Lords and Gentlemen and Honourable Boards! What is it that we call it in our grandiose speeches? British independence, rather perverted? Is that, or something like it, the ring of the cant?

"Do I never read in the newspapers," said the dame, fondling the child – "God help me and the like of me! – how the worn-out people that do come down to that, get driven from post to pillar and pillar to post, a-purpose to tire them out! Do I never read how they are put off, put off, put off – how they are grudged, grudged, grudged, the shelter, or the doctor, or the drop of physic, or the bit of bread? Do I never read how they grow heartsick of it and give it up, after having let themselves drop so low, and how they after all die out for want of help? Then I say, I hope I can die as well as another, and I'll die without that disgrace."

Absolutely impossible my Lords and Gentlemen and Honourable Boards, by any stretch of legislative wisdom to set these perverse people right in their logic?

"Johnny, my pretty," continued old Betty, caressing the child, and rather mourning over it than speaking to it, "your old Granny Betty is nigher fourscore year than threescore and ten. She never begged nor had a penny of the Union money in all her life. She paid scot and she paid lot when she had money to pay; she worked when she could, and she starved when she must. You pray that your Granny may have strength enough left her at the last (she's strong for an old one, Johnny), to get up from her bed and run and hide herself, and swown to death in a hole, sooner than fall into the hands of those Cruel Jacks we read of, that dodge and drive, and worry and weary, and scorn and shame, the decent poor."

A NIGHTLY SCENE IN LONDON

Household Words 26 January 1856

IN this, one of the most moving and most angry of his shorter pieces, Dickens describes what he and the writer Albert Smith witnessed outside a workhouse in November 1855. Because he mentions the neighbourhood, we are able to pinpoint with unusual precision the exact spot where this encounter with London vagrants took place. The Whitechapel Workhouse was in Bakers Row, Thomas Street, now renamed Vallance Road after Sir William Vallance, Secretary to the Board of Guardians which was responsible for running the institution from 1868 to 1902. Over this period Sir William acquired an unenviable reputation for lack of charity. He was knighted, so hostile rumour said, because he stuck rigidly and ruthlessly to the rule book and kept parish expenditure on the poor to a minimum, acting in a manner untempered by any feelings of humanity towards his less fortunate fellow beings. The site of Whitechapel Workhouse is now a recreation ground.

Although the *Pictorial Handbook of London* of 1854 described the nearby City of London Union Workhouse in almost lyrical terms, such places were not popular with their inmates. Dickens, in *Oliver Twist,* had some harsh things to say about parish workhouses and those who ran them. Besides offering a permanent refuge to local paupers and outdoor relief for starving families, these institutions also had a casual or vagrant ward where the human flotsam and jetsam of the streets could be accommodated overnight, given a minimal amount of food – bread, gruel – in return, as a rule, for a few hours' labour. The problem of vagrancy in nineteenth-century London – and, indeed, elsewhere – was considerable; despite these casual wards, large numbers of men, women and children slept rough in the streets throughout the year. Although it was a crime, they begged for money in public thoroughfares. One of the most appalling depictions of Victorian values is the painting by Sir Luke Fildes (a Dickens illustrator) entitled "Applicants for Admission to a Casual Ward, 1874". It conveys vividly the sense of degradation and misery which characterised most of the poor who were driven to seek refuge overnight in a casual ward. On the wet evening that Dickens describes, he would have met people like this, crouched against the wall of the workhouse. Who could such people have been? What had brought them to such straits?

Here we can turn to Henry Mayhew, whose section on Vagrants in Volume 3 of *London Labour and the London Poor* adds a great deal more humanity to the subject than the rather bare statistics in official publications. After a discussion of the causes of vagrancy, which he sees partly as unemployment and the general uncertainty in the labour market, but mostly as the result of "the non-inculcation of a habit of industry", Mayhew also asserted – unusually for him, because he did not often make judgements of this kind – that many young people were being corrupted by sensational fiction in which highwaymen like Dick Turpin and Jack Sheppard were portrayed as heroes. In Dickens's time, the impulse to Christian charitable endeavour, which expressed itself in a duty to help society's casualties, struggled with a desire to punish those who could, but would not, help themselves. People could not be left to starve, homeless, in the streets; but at the same time the recipients of charity should never be made so comfortable that their will to work was further sapped. Clearly there was ambivalence about both the purpose and the scope of the

116

nineteenth-century philanthropic endeavour. On the one hand, Dickens's anger on behalf of vagrants might be justified; on the other, the rigid approach of such a man as Sir William Vallance might have better effect.

Mayhew, unlike some of his contemporaries, did distinguish quite specifically between honest people down on their luck and what were called "degraded, vicious beggars". As always, he set about his investigations with thoroughness: "Previous to entering upon my enquiry into the subject," he wrote, "I consulted with a gentleman who had long paid considerable attention to the question, and who was, moreover, in a position peculiarly fitted for gaining the greatest experience, and arriving at the correctest notions upon the matter." Through this informant Mayhew was referred to Mr. Knapp, Master of the Wandsworth and Clapham Union, for whom he came to have a high regard. Before his promotion Mr. Knapp had been Relieving Officer, and was therefore particularly well qualified to talk about vagrants and casual wards. Knapp told Mayhew that he believed a casual ward was necessary in every workhouse because there was always a migratory population of labourers looking for employment and destitute women travelling to their husbands or friends. Such people, however, formed only a small proportion of those who sought relief. The majority were Irish families, young men, prostitutes and professional beggars, and of these, the young formed about half the total, their ages ranging from twelve to twenty.

A number of the vagrants Mayhew came across were encouraged to tell him the story of their lives, and he reproduces several of these statements. They are depressing accounts of leaving home and hoping to find work in London, of unemployment, and sometimes of sheer bad luck. An ex-cotton worker of Chorlton-upon-Medlock in Lancashire describes how he lost his job in the mill when it became cheaper to employ young girls as machine minders than to pay male operatives. Subsequently he became a soldier, and was discharged when his regiment was disbanded some years later in Dublin. Making his way to Manchester, he "slept in unions . . . and had oatmeal porridge for breakfast, work at grinding logwood in the mill from six to twelve and then turn out". Elsewhere he would receive "a pint of coffee and half-a-pound of bread in the morning and no work". Like so many others, he came to London, and was sent to prison for begging. Another vagrant was a girl of eighteen who told Mayhew that she had been imprisoned in Tunbridge Wells for begging. Yet another was a convict returned from transportation.

Such, then, were the unfortunates who would be driven to seek a night's shelter in the casual ward. Dickens provides a horrifying account of some who did not get a place, and it was left to another journalist, about ten years later, to describe in detail what happened to those who did. James Greenwood, nicknamed "The Amateur Casual", disguised himself as a tramp and presented himself at the Lambeth Workhouse. He wanted to learn "by actual experience how casual paupers are lodged and fed, and what the 'casual' is like, and what the porter who admits him, and the master who rules over him; and how the night passes with the outcasts we have all seen crowding about the workhouse doors on a cold and rainy evening." Greenwood's article, published in the *Pall Mall Gazette* and soon afterwards reprinted as a pamphlet, paints a grim picture of the realities of life in a casual ward. Charles Dickens had used the epithet "infamous" to describe what he saw outside: it may well apply equally to what Greenwood tells of what went on inside.

A NIGHTLY SCENE IN LONDON

ON the fifth of last November, I, the Conductor of this journal, accompanied by a friend well-known to the public, accidentally strayed into Whitechapel. It was a miserable evening; very dark, very muddy, and raining hard.

There are many woeful sights in that part of London, and it has been well-known to me in most of its aspects for many years. We had forgotten the mud and rain in slowly walking along and looking about us, when we found ourselves, at eight o'clock, before the Workhouse.

Crouched against the wall of the Workhouse, in the dark street, on the muddy pavement-stones, with the rain raining upon them, were five bundles of rags. They were motionless, and had no resemblance to the human form. Five great beehives, covered with rags – five dead bodies taken out of graves, tied neck and heels, and covered with rags – would have looked like those five bundles upon which the rain rained down in the public street.

"What is this!" said my companion. "What *is* this!"

"Some miserable people shut out of the Casual Ward, I think," said I.

We had stopped before the five ragged mounds, and were quite rooted to the spot by their horrible appearance. Five awful Sphinxes by the wayside, crying to every passer-by, "Stop and guess! What is to be the end of a state of society that leaves us here!"

As we stood looking at them, a decent working-man, having the appearance of a stone-mason, touched me on the shoulder.

"This is an awful sight, sir," said he, "in a Christian country!"

"God knows it is, my friend," said I.

"I have often seen it much worse than this, as I have been going home from my work. I have counted fifteen, twenty, five-and-twenty, many a time. It's a shocking thing to see."

"A shocking thing, indeed," said I and my companion together. The man lingered near us a little while, wished us good-night, and went on.

We should have felt it brutal in us who had a better chance of being heard than the working-man, to leave the thing as it was, so we knocked at the Workhouse Gate. I undertook to be spokesman. The moment the gate was opened by an old pauper, I went in, followed close by my companion. I lost no time in passing the old porter, for I saw in his watery eye a disposition to shut us out.

"Be so good as to give that card to the master of the Workhouse, and say I shall be glad to speak to him for a moment."

We were in a kind of covered gateway, and the old porter went across it with the card. Before he had got to a door on our left, a man in a cloak and hat bounced out of it very sharply, as if he were

Vagrants in the casual ward of a London workhouse, 1850s.

in the nightly habit of being bullied and of returning the compliment.

"Now, gentlemen," said he in a loud voice, "what do you want here?"

"First," said I, "will you do me the favour to look at that card in your hand. Perhaps you may know my name."

"Yes," says he, looking at it. "I know this name."

"Good. I only want to ask you a plain question in a civil manner, and there is not the least occasion for either of us to be angry. It would be very foolish in me to blame you, and I don't blame you. I may find fault with the system you administer, but pray understand that I know you are here to do a duty pointed out to you, and that I have no doubt you do it. Now, I hope you won't object to tell me what I want to know."

"No," said he, quite mollified, and very reasonable, "not at all. What is it?"

"Do you know that there are five wretched creatures outside?"

"I haven't seen them, but I dare say there are."

"Do you doubt that there are?"

"No, not at all. There might be many more."

"Are they men? Or women?"

"Women, I suppose. Very likely one or two of them were there last night, and the night before last."

"There all night, do you mean?"

"Very likely."

My companion and I looked at one another, and the master of the Workhouse added quickly, "Why, Lord bless my soul, what am I to do? What can I do? The place is full. The place is always full – every night. I must give the preference to women with children, mustn't I? You wouldn't have me not do that?"

"Surely not," said I. "It is a very humane principle, and quite right; and I am glad to hear of it. Don't forget that I don't blame *you*."

Detail from "Houseless and Hungry" by Luke Fildes, from The Graphic, *1869. Fildes later reworked this picture as his poignant oil painting "Applicants for Admission to a Casual Ward". Fildes was the last illustrator to work with Dickens, on the unfinished* Mystery of Edwin Drood.

"Well!" said he. And subdued himself again.

"What I want to ask you," I went on, "is whether you know anything against those five miserable beings outside?"

"Don't know anything about them," said he, with a wave of his arm.

"I ask, for this reason: that we mean to give them a trifle to get a lodging – if they are not shelterless because they are thieves for instance. You don't know them to be thieves?"

"I don't know anything about them," he repeated emphatically.

"That is to say, they are shut out, solely because the Ward is full?"

"Because the Ward is full."

"And if they got in, they would only have a roof for the night and a bit of bread in the morning, I suppose?"

"That's all. You'll use your own discretion about what you give them. Only understand that I don't know anything about them beyond what I have told you."

"Just so. I wanted to know no more. You have answered my question civilly and readily, and I am much obliged to you. I have nothing to say against you, but quite the contrary. Good night!"

"Good night, gentlemen!" And out we came again.

We went to the ragged bundle nearest to the Workhouse-door, and I touched it. No movement replying, I gently shook it. The rags began to be slowly stirred within, and by little and little a head was unshrouded. The head of a young woman of three or

The Asylum for the Houseless Poor, Cripplegate, 1850s: these outcasts are loitering until the doors open. According to Augustus Mayhew in his realistic novel Paved with Gold (1858), *the asylum was opened only "when the thermometer reaches freezing-point". Inside, it offered nothing but "dry bread and warm shelter".*

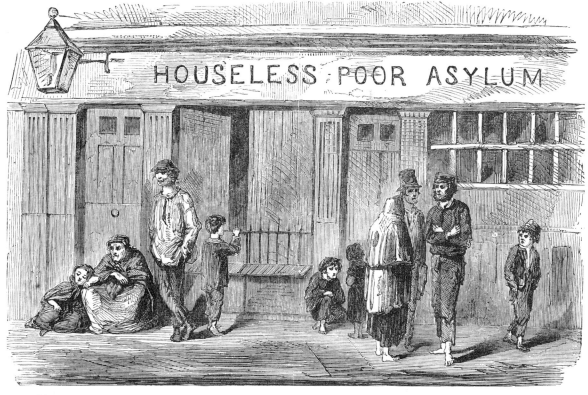

four and twenty, as I should judge; gaunt with want, and foul with dirt; but not naturally ugly.

"Tell us," said I, stooping down. "Why are you lying here?"

"Because I can't get into the Workhouse."

She spoke in a faint dull way, and had no curiosity or interest left. She looked dreamily at the black sky and the falling rain, but never looked at me or my companion.

"Were you here last night?"

"Yes. All last night. And the night afore too."

"Do you know any of these others?"

"I know her next but one. She was here last night, and she told me she come out of Essex. I don't know no more of her."

"You were here all last night, but you have not been here all day?"

"No. Not all day."

"Where have you been all day?"

"About the streets."

"What have you had to eat?"

"Nothing."

"Come!" said I. "Think a little. You are tired and have been asleep, and don't quite consider what you are saying to us. You have had something to eat to-day. Come! Think of it!"

"No I haven't. Nothing but such bits as I could pick up about the market. *Why, look at me!*"

She bared her neck, and I covered it up again.

"If you had a shilling to get some supper and a lodging, should you know where to get it?"

"Yes. I could do that."

"For God's sake get it then!"

I put the money into her hand, and she feebly rose up and went away. She never thanked me, never looked at me – melted away into the miserable night, in the strangest manner I ever saw. I have seen many strange things, but not one that has left a deeper impression on my memory than the dull impassive way in which that worn-out heap of misery took that piece of money, and was lost.

One by one I spoke to all the five. In every one, interest and curiosity were as extinct as in the first. They were all dull and languid. No one made any sort of profession or complaint; no one cared to look at me; no one thanked me. When I came to the third, I suppose she saw that my companion and I glanced, with a new horror upon us, at the two last, who had dropped against each other in their sleep, and were lying like broken images. She said, she believed they were young sisters. These were the only words that were originated among the five.

And now let me close this terrible account with a redeeming and beautiful trait of the poorest of the poor. When we came out of the Workhouse, we had gone across the road to a public house, finding ourselves without silver, to get change for a sovereign. I held the money in my hand while I was speaking to the five

A vagrant, "on tramp".

A maidservant confronting a menacing vagrant on the area steps. Offered food rather than money, he is peevishly asking, "Do you mean to say as you've brought a poor covey down the airey steps a purpose to give him a cold sandwich without mustard?" Cartoon from Banter, *1868.*

apparitions. Our being so engaged, attracted the attention of many people of the very poor sort usual to that place; as we leaned over the mounds of rags, they eagerly leaned over us to see and hear; what I had in my hand, and what I said, and what I did, must have been plain to nearly all the concourse. When the last of the five had got up and faded away, the spectators opened to let us pass; and not one of them, by word, or look, or gesture, begged of us. Many of the observant faces were quick enough to know that it would have been a relief to us to have got rid of the rest of the money with any hope of doing good with it. But there was a feeling among them all, that their necessities were not to be placed by the side of such a spectacle; and they opened a way for us in profound silence, and let us go.

My companion wrote to me, next day, that the five ragged bundles had been upon his bed all night. I debated how to add our testimony to that of many other persons who from time to time are impelled to write to the newspapers, by having come upon some shameful and shocking sight of this description. I resolved to write in these pages an exact account of what we had seen, but to wait until after Christmas, in order that there might be no heat or haste. I know that the unreasonable disciples of a reasonable school, demented disciples who push arithmetic and political economy beyond all bounds of sense (not to speak of such a weakness as humanity), and hold them to be all-sufficient for every case, can easily prove that such things ought to be, and that no man has any business to mind them. Without disparaging those indispensable sciences in their sanity, I utterly renounce and abominate them in their insanity; and I address people with a respect for the spirit of the New Testament, who do mind such things, and who think them infamous in our streets.

disciples: of the economist T. R. Malthus (1766–1834), who regarded vice and misery as necessary checks on population growth

From **Bleak House** *chapter 46*

ON the banks of the stagnant channel of mud which is the main street of Tom-all-Alone's, nothing is to be seen but the crazy houses, shut up and silent. No waking creature save himself appears, except in one direction, where he sees the solitary figure of a woman sitting on a door-step. He walks that way. Approaching, he observes that she has journeyed a long distance, and is footsore and travel-stained. She sits on the door-step in the manner of one who is waiting, with her elbow on her knee and her head upon her hand. Beside her is a canvas bag, or bundle, she has carried. She is dozing probably, for she gives no heed to his steps as he comes toward her.

The broken footway is so narrow, that when Allan Woodcourt comes to where the woman sits, he has to turn into the road to pass her. Looking down at her face, his eye meets hers, and he stops.

"What is the matter?"

"Nothing, sir."

"Can't you make them hear? Do you want to be let in?"

"I'm waiting till they get up at another house – a lodging-house – not here," the woman patiently returns. "I'm waiting here because there will be sun here presently to warm me."

"I am afraid you are tired. I am sorry to see you sitting in the street."

"Thank you sir. It don't matter."

A habit in him of speaking to the poor, and of avoiding patronage or con-descension, or childishness (which is the favourite device, many people deeming it quite a subtlety to talk to them like little spelling books), has put him on good terms with the woman easily.

"Let me look at your forehead," he says, bending down. "I am a doctor. Don't be afraid. I wouldn't hurt you for the world."

He knows that by touching her with his skilful and accustomed hand, he can soothe her yet more readily. She makes a slight objection, saying, "It's nothing"; but he has scarcely laid his fingers on the wounded place when she lifts it up to the light.

"Aye! A bad bruise, and the skin sadly broken. This must be very sore."

"It do ache a little, sir," returns the woman, with a started tear upon her cheek.

"Let me try to make it more comfortable. My handkerchief won't hurt you."

"O dear no, sir, I'm sure of that!"

He cleanses the injured place and dries it; and having carefully examined it, and gently pressed it with the palm of his hand, takes a small case from his pocket, dresses it, and binds it up. While he is thus employed, he says, after laughing at his establishing a surgery in the street:

"And so your husband is a brickmaker?"

"How do you know that, sir?" asked the woman, astonished.

"Why, I suppose so, from the colour of the clay upon your bag and on your dress. And I know brickmakers go about working at piecework in different places. And I am sorry to say I have known them cruel to their wives too."

The woman hastily lifts up her eyes as if she would deny that her injury is referable to such a cause. But feeling the hand upon her forehead, and seeing his busy and composed face, she quietly drops them again.

"Where is he now?" asks the surgeon.

"He got into trouble last night, sir; but he'll look for me at the lodging-house."

HOME FOR HOMELESS WOMEN

Household Words 23 April 1853

THIS essay shows Dickens seemingly at his most impartial and uninvolved. There is no extravagant emotional commitment to a cause; simply a judicious, quietly effective statement of facts. It brought him a flood of correspondence from people wanting to visit or to support the home which it describes, all of which Dickens politely turned aside. The truth behind this camouflage of objectivity is that it was Dickens himself who had set up the home, and it was Dickens himself who administered it, on behalf of its backer, the philanthropist Angela Burdett-Coutts. Neither of them wanted their involvement publicised. Dickens promised her while writing the article, "it shall not leave my hands until it is perfectly discreet".

Dickens had met the banking heiress Angela Burdett, as she was then, in 1835. Their friendship was immediate and lasting, and their common interest in social problems – Dickens solicited her support, for instance, for the ragged schools – led to Dickens becoming her unofficial almoner. She wrote to Dickens, "What is the use of my means but to try and do some good with them?"

In the 1840s Angela Burdett-Coutts became troubled by the sight of young girls forced by poverty and ignorance into prostitution, and then into a closed cycle of misery: street–prison–street–prison–street. Over the years there had been numbers of attempts to provide a way out of this trap, for instance the Magdalen Hospital, mentioned towards the end of "Home for Homeless Women". The problem with these was that whatever encouragement they gave the girls and women in them, they made no real provision for the future. After a year at the Magdalen, girls were turned back on to the street to make room for others.

The distinctive feature of the home established by Miss Coutts and Dickens, Urania Cottage in Shepherd's Bush, was that it prepared the girls for emigration, and a new life. This solution to the twin problems of social stigma and the pulling power of known ways and old companions appealed strongly to Dickens.

The planning for Urania Cottage fired Dickens's imagination, and overseeing its development absorbed him. His first letter to Miss Coutts on the subject, on 26 May 1846, is long, detailed and enthusiastic. He wrote an "Appeal to Fallen Women" for circulation, and enlisted the help of the prison governors Chesterton and Tracey, who both sat on the home's management committee, and who supplied most of the girls – petty criminals as well as prostitutes.

It cannot be overstressed that nearly every significant feature of the regime at Urania Cottage – from the night's grace for thought before a girl was allowed to leave of her own accord, to the encouragement of good behaviour by the use of a modification of the mark system devised by the former governor of the penal colony in Norfolk Island, Captain Alexander Maconochie, and set out by him in his *Crime and Punishment* (1846) – is attributable to Dickens's influence.

Dickens attached great importance to the word "home"; he wanted the girls to be "*tempted* to virtue". Doleful penitence was counter-productive; he wrote to Miss Coutts, "it is very essential in dealing with this class of persons to have a system of training established, which, while it is steady and firm, is cheerful and hopeful".

But Dickens was no pliable do-gooder. He can seem, to modern eyes, implacably stern. In his essay "The Ruffian" in *The Uncommercial Traveller,* he describes having a girl arrested for using bad language in the street, and insisting on her punishment despite the reluctance and incredulity of both police and magistrate. Asked, "do you really wish this girl to be sent to prison?", "I grimly answered, staring: 'If I didn't, why should I take the trouble to come here?'"

Dickens did not despise the girls at Urania Cottage; nor was he easily taken in by them. There were, of course, failures: for instance Jemima Hiscock, who "forced open the door of the little beer-cellar with knives, and drank until she was dead drunk; when she used the most horrible language and made a very repulsive exhibition of herself", and Sesina Bollard, of whom Dickens wearily recorded, "I think she would corrupt a Nunnery in a fortnight". Others, such as Louisa Cooper, fulfilled all hopes, and were gratefully launched on a new life. Dickens's letters to Miss Coutts are full of lively accounts of goings-on at the home, and show him taking a firm and active role in the admission of new girls and the discipline of unruly ones.

Prostitution and female destitution were so prevalent that there was an unending stream of suitable candidates for the home. Mayhew estimates a low figure of 80,000 professional prostitutes in London, supplemented by an incalculable number of "Dollymops": nursemaids, maidservants, shopgirls, milliners, who augmented their income in the same way. The difficulty Victorians had in treating the problem sensibly may be seen in the highly-charged tone of Mayhew's section on prostitutes. It is melodramatic and artificially moralistic; the sense of the uninterrupted voice, so freshly present elsewhere, is entirely missing. Dickens's fictional representation of prostitutes – Nancy in *Oliver Twist,* Lilian in *The Chimes,* Alice Marwood in *Dombey,* Martha and Emily in *David Copperfield* – scarcely makes use of the real understanding he showed in his dealings with the girls at Urania Cottage. That knowledge is better shown in his portrait of the foundling servant-girl Tattycoram in *Little Dorrit,* full of "passion and protest" even at her employers' kindness.

The standard Victorian idea of a "fallen woman" was that she was "ruined". Dickens shares this perception in his depiction of Martha Endell, though he also shows that for those such as Emily, and the girls at Urania Cottage, emigration offers a way out. In reality, as William Acton, one of the most forthright of contemporary writers on the subject, noted, prostitutes were not irredeemable social outcasts. For many, prostitution was a temporary resort rather than a life's work.

Successful prostitutes could better themselves. The diarist Arthur Munby knew a maid-of-all-work called Sarah Tanner who became a prostitute in 1855 because she "wanted to see life and be independent". She stayed on the game for three years, and then bought herself a coffee-house by Waterloo Bridge and settled down in respectable comfort. It was their independence, and their anger, which the girls had to resign when they entered Urania Cottage.

But, of course, life for most of the city's teeming prostitutes was humiliating and miserable. Prostitution was more likely to lead to a London park than to a successful coffee-house. There, as Mayhew records, the diseased and the degraded plied a desperate trade; there, as Munby found in July 1864, human wreckage huddled together like the damned:

> One girl lay in her rags at my feet, her face hidden between her outstretched arms. I spoke to her: but it was at least a minute before she heeded. When she did lift her dirty sodden face, she seemed halfmazed: answered, that she was about twenty; a shawlfringemaker; out of work; no father nor mother; no home; comes here to lie down, every day; wouldn't come if she had anywhere else to go, of course not.

Urania Cottage offered, at least for some, at least for a time, somewhere else to go.

HOME FOR HOMELESS WOMEN

FIVE years and a half ago, certain ladies, grieved to think that numbers of their own sex were wandering about the streets in degradation, passing through and through the prisons all their lives or hopelessly perishing in other ways, resolved to try the experiment on a limited scale of a Home for the reclamation and emigration of women. As it was clear to them that there could be little or no hope in this country for the greater part of those who might become the objects of their charity, they determined to receive into their Home only those who distinctly accepted this condition: that they came there to be ultimately sent abroad (whither was at the discretion of the ladies); and that they also came there to remain for such length of time as might, according to the circumstances of each individual case, be considered necessary as a term of probation, and for instruction in the means of obtaining an honest livelihood. The object of the Home was twofold. First, to replace young women, who had already lost their characters and lapsed into guilt, in a situation of hope. Secondly, to save other young women who were in danger of falling into the like condition, and give them an opportunity of flying from crime when they and it stood face to face.

The projectors of this establishment, in undertaking it, were sustained by nothing but the high object of making some unhappy women a blessing to themselves and others instead of a curse, and raising up among the solitudes of a new world some virtuous homes, much needed there, from the sorrow and ruin of the old. They had no romantic visions or extravagant expectations. They were prepared for many failures and disappointments, and to consider their enterprise rewarded, if they in time succeeded with one third or one half of the cases they received.

As the experience of this small Institution, even under the many disadvantages of a beginning, may be useful and interesting, this paper will contain an exact account of its progress and results.

It was (and is) established in a detached house with a garden. The house was never designed for any such purpose, and is only adapted to it, in being retired and not immediately overlooked. It is capable of containing thirteen inmates besides two Superintendents. Excluding from consideration ten young women now in the house, there have been received in all, since November 1847, fifty-six inmates. They have belonged to no particular class, but have been starving needlewomen of good character, poor needlewomen who have robbed their furnished lodgings, violent girls committed to prison for disturbances in ill-conducted workhouses, poor girls from Ragged Schools, destitute girls who have applied at police offices for relief, young women from the streets; young women of the same class taken from the prisons after undergoing punishment there as disorderly characters, or for shoplifting, or for thefts from the person; domestic servants who have been seduced, and two young women held to bail for attempting suicide. No class has been favoured more than another; and misfortune and distress are a sufficient introduction. It is not usual to receive women of more than five or six-and-twenty; the average age in the fifty-six cases would probably be about twenty. In some instances there have been great personal attractions; in others, the girls have been very homely and plain. The reception has been wholly irrespective of such sources of interest. Nearly all have been extremely ignorant.

Of these fifty-six cases, seven went away by their own desire during their probation; ten were sent away for misconduct in the Home; seven ran away; three emigrated and relapsed on the

A street-walker, 1871. Arthur Munby met such a girl – "elegant & well-dressed" – on 17 August 1860: "In Oxford Street a fashionable prostitute accosted me who once before had begged me to go home with her; & she now explained her importunity by saying 'All my gentlemen have left town, and I really am so hard up – I shall have to give up my lodgings!' 'Then why not go out of town too?' 'I've nowhere to go!' . . . She was a farmer's daughter from near Chesterfield; & came to town, nominally to be a draper's assistant, but ready to become of her own accord what she is. N.B. After nine months, her family still think she is at the shop." Derek Hudson, Munby: Man of Two Worlds (1972).

passage out; thirty (of whom seven are now married), on their arrival in Australia or elsewhere, entered into good service, acquired a good character, and have done so well ever since as to establish a strong prepossession in favour of others sent out from the same quarter. It will be seen from these figures that the failures are generally discovered in the Home itself, and that the amount of misconduct after the training and emigration is remarkably small. And it is to be taken into consideration that many cases are admitted into the Home, of which there is, in the outset, very little hope, but which it is not deemed right to exclude from the experiment.

The Home is managed by two Superintendents. The second in order acts under the first, who has from day to day the supreme direction of the family. On the cheerfulness, quickness, good-temper, firmness, and vigilance of these ladies, and on their never bickering, the successful working of the establishment in a great degree depends. Their position is one of high trust and responsibility, and requires not only an always accumulating experience, but an accurate observation of every character about them. The ladies who established the Home hold little confidential communication with the inmates, thinking the system better administered when it is undisturbed by individuals. A committee, composed of a few gentlemen of experience, meets once a month to audit the accounts, receive the principal Superintendent's reports, investigate any unusual occurrence, and see all the inmates separately. None but the committee are present as they enter one by one, in order that they may be under no restraint in anything they wish to say. A complaint from any of them is exceedingly uncommon. The history of every inmate, taken down from her own mouth – usually after she has been some little time in the Home – is preserved in a book. She is shown that what she relates of herself she relates in confidence, and does not even communicate to the Superintendents. She is particularly admonished by no means to communicate her history to any of the other inmates: all of whom have in their turns received a similar admonition. And she is encouraged to tell the truth, by having it explained to her that nothing in her story but falsehood can possibly affect her position in the Home after she has been once admitted.

The work of the Home is thus divided. They rise, both in summer and winter, at six o'clock. Morning prayers and scripture reading take place at a quarter before eight. Breakfast is had immediately afterwards. Dinner at one. Tea at six. Evening prayers are said at half-past eight. The hour of going to bed is nine. Supposing the Home to be full, ten are employed upon the household work; two in the bed-rooms; two in the general living room; two in the Superintendents' rooms; two in the kitchen (who cook); two in the scullery; three at needlework. Straw-plaiting has been occasionally taught besides. On washing-days, five are employed in the laundry, three of whom are taken from the needlework, and two are told off from the household work.

A maid-of-all-work cleaning the front step, 1847. For a record of the drudgery of such a life, see The Diaries of Hannah Cullwick *(1984).*

The nature and order of each girl's work is changed every week, so that she may become practically acquainted with the whole routine of household duties. They take it in turns to bake the bread which is eaten in the house. In every room, every Monday morning, there is hung up, framed and glazed, the names of the girls who are in charge there for the week and who are, consequently, responsible for its neat condition and the proper execution of the work belonging to it. This is found to inspire them with a greater pride in good housewifery, and a greater sense of shame in the reverse.

The book-education is of a very plain kind, as they have generally much to learn in the commonest domestic duties, and are often singularly inexpert in acquiring them. They read and write, and cipher. School is held every morning at half-past ten (Saturday excepted) for two hours. The Superintendents are the teachers. The times for recreation are half an hour between school-time and dinner, and an hour after dinner; half an hour before tea, and an hour after tea. In the winter, these intervals are usually employed in light fancy work, the making of little presents for their friends, etc. In the fine summer weather they are passed in the garden, where they take exercise, and have their little flower-beds. In the afternoon and evening, they sit all together at needle-work, and some one reads aloud. The books are carefully chosen, but are always interesting.

Angela Burdett-Coutts (1814–1906). There are two modern biographies of her: Edna Healey, Lady Unknown *(1978) and Diana Orton,* Made of Gold *(1980).*

Saturday is devoted to an extraordinary cleaning up and polishing of the whole establishment, and to the distribution of clean clothes; every inmate arranging and preparing her own. Each girl also takes a bath on Saturday.

On Sundays they go to church in the neighbourhood, some to morning service, some to afternoon service, some to both. They are invariably accompanied by one of the Superintendents. Wearing no uniform and not being dressed alike, they attract little notice out of doors. Their attire is that of respectable plain servants. On Sunday evenings they receive religious instruction from the principal Superintendent. They also receive regular religious instruction from a clergyman on one day in every week, and on two days in every alternate week. They are constantly employed, and always overlooked.

They are allowed to be visited under the following restrictions: if by their parents, once in a month; if by other relatives or friends, once in three months. The principal Superintendent is present at all such interviews, and hears the conversation. It is not often found that the girls and their friends have much to say to one another; any display of feeling on these occasions is rare. It is generally observed that the inmates seem rather relieved than otherwise when the interviews are over.

They can write to relatives, or old teachers, or persons known to have been kind to them, once a month on application to the committee. It seldom happens that a girl who has any person in the world to correspond with fails to take advantage of this

opportunity. All letters dispatched from the Home are read and posted by the principal Superintendent. All letters received are likewise read by the Superintendent; but she does not open them. Every such letter is opened by the girl to whom it is addressed, who reads it first, in the Superintendent's presence. It never happens that they wish to reserve the contents; they are always anxious to impart them to her immediately. This seems to be one of their chief pleasures in receiving letters.

They make and mend their own clothes, but do not keep them. In many cases they are not for some time to be trusted with such a charge; in other cases, when temper is awakened, the possession of a shawl and bonnet would often lead to an abrupt departure which the unfortunate creature would ever afterwards regret. To distinguish between these cases and others of a more promising nature would be to make invidious distinctions, than which nothing could be more prejudicial to the Home, as the objects of its care are invariably sensitive and jealous. For these various reasons their clothes are kept under lock and key in a wardrobe room. They have a great pride in the state of their clothes, and the neatness of their persons. Those who have no such pride on their admission are sure to acquire it.

Formerly, when a girl accepted for admission had clothes of her own to wear, she was allowed to be admitted in them, and they were put by for her; though within the Institution she always wore the clothing it provides. It was found, however, that a girl with a hankering after old companions rather relied on these reserved clothes, and that she put them on with an air, if she went away or were dismissed. They now invariably come, therefore, in clothes belonging to the Home, and bring no other clothing with them. A suit of the commonest apparel has been provided for the next inmate who may leave during her probation, or be sent away; and it is thought that the sight of a girl departing so disgraced, will have a good effect on those who remain. Cases of dismissal or departure are becoming more rare, however, as the Home increases in experience, and no occasion for making the experiment has yet arisen.

When the Home had been opened for some time, it was resolved to adopt a modification of Captain Maconochie's mark system: so arranging the mark table as to render it difficult for a girl to lose marks under any one of its heads, without also losing under nearly all the others. The mark table is divided into the nine following heads: Truthfulness, Industry, Temper, Propriety of Conduct and Conversation, Temperance, Order, Punctuality, Economy, Cleanliness. The word Temperance is not used in the modern slang acceptation, but in its enlarged meaning as defined by Johnson, from the English of Spenser: "Moderation, patience, calmness, sedateness, moderation of passion." A separate account for every day is kept with every girl as to each of these items. If her conduct be without objection, she is marked in each column, three – excepting the truthfulness and temperance columns in which, saving under extraordinary circumstances, she is only marked two, the temptation to err in those particulars being considered low under the circumstances of the life she leads in the Home. If she be particularly deserving under any of the other heads, she is marked the highest number – four. If her deserts be low, she is marked only one, or not marked at all. If her conduct under any head have been, during the day, particularly objectionable, she receives a bad mark (marked in red ink, to distinguish it at a glance from the others) which destroys forty good marks. The value of the good marks is six shillings and sixpence per thousand; the earnings of each girl are withheld until she emigrates, in order to form a little fund for her first subsistence on her disembarkation. The inmates are found, without an exception, to value their marks highly. A bad mark is very infrequent, and occasions great distress in the recipient and great excitement in the community. In case of dismissal or premature departure from the Home, all the previous gain in marks is forfeited. If a girl be ill through no fault of her own, she is marked, during her illness, according to her average marking. But, if she be ill through her own act (as in a recent case, where a girl set herself on fire, through carelessness and a violation of the rules of the house) she is credited with no marks until she is again in a condition to earn them. The usual earnings in a year are about equal to the average wages of the commoner class of domestic servant.

They are usually brought to the Home by the principal Superintendent in a coach. From wheresoever they come, they generally weep on the road, and are silent and depressed. The average term of probation is about a year; longer when the girl is very slow to learn what she is taught. When the time of her emigration arrives, the same lady accompanies her on board ship. They usually go out, three or four together, with a letter of recommendation to some influential person at their destination; sometimes they are placed under the charge of a respectable family of emigrants; sometimes they act as nurses or as servants to individual ladies with children, on board. In these capacities they have given great satisfaction. Their grief at parting from the Superintendent is always strong, and frequently of a heart-rending

A London barmaid glimpsed by Gavarni in the late 1840s.

131

kind. They are also exceedingly affected by their separation from the Home; usually going round and round the garden first, as if they clung to every tree and shrub in it. Nevertheless, individual attachments among them are rare, though strong affections have arisen when they have afterwards encountered in distant solitudes. Some touching circumstances have occurred, where unexpected recognitions of this kind have taken place on Sundays in lonely churches to which the various members of the little congregations have repaired from great distances. Some of the girls now married have chosen old companions thus encountered for their bridesmaids, and in their letters have described their delight very pathetically.

A considerable part of the needlework done in the Home is necessary to its own internal neatness, and the preparation of outfits for the emigrants; especially as many of the inmates know little or nothing of such work, and have it all to learn. But, as they become more dexterous, plain work is taken in, and the proceeds are applied as a fund to defray the cost of outfits. The outfits are always of the simplest kind. Nothing is allowed to be wasted or thrown away in the Home. From the bones, and remnants of food, the girls are taught to make soup for the poor and sick. This at once extends their domestic knowledge, and preserves their sympathy for the distressed.

Some of the experiences, not already mentioned, that have been acquired in the management of the Home are curious, and perhaps deserving of consideration in prisons and other institutions. It has been observed, in taking the histories – especially of the more artful cases – that nothing is so likely to elicit the truth as a perfectly imperturbable face, and an avoidance of any leading question or expression of opinion. Give the narrator the least idea what tone will make her an object of interest, and she will take it directly. Give her none, and she will be driven on the truth, and in most cases will tell it. For similar reasons it is found desirable always to repress stock religious professions and religious phrases; to discourage shows of senti- ment, and to make their lives practical and active. "Don't talk about it – do it!" is the motto of the place. The inmates find everywhere about them the same kind discriminating firmness, and the same determination to have no favourite subjects, or favourite objects, of interest. Girls from Ragged Schools are not generally so impressible as reduced girls who have failed to sup- port themselves by hard work, or as women from the streets – probably because they have suffered less. The poorest of the Ragged School condition, who are odious to approach when first picked up, invariably affect afterwards that their friends are "well off". This psychological curiosity is considered inexplicable. Most of the inmates are depressed at first. At holiday times the more doubtful part of them usually become restless and uncertain; there would also appear to be, usually, a time of considerable restless- ness after six or eight months. In any little difficulty, the general feeling is invariably with the establishment and never with the offender. When a girl is discharged for misconduct, she is generally in deep distress, and goes away miserably. The rest will sometimes intercede for her with tears; but it is found that firmness on this and every point, when a decision is once taken, is the most humane course as having a wholesome influence on the greatest number. For this reason, a mere threat of discharge is never on any account resorted to. Two points of management are extremely important: the first, to refer very sparingly to the past; the second, never to treat the inmates as children. They must never be allowed to suppose it possible that they can get the better of the management. Judicious commendation, when it is deserved, has a very salutary influence. It is also found that a serious and urgent entreaty to a girl, to exercise her self-restraint on some point (generally temper) on which her mark-table shows her to be deficient, often has an excellent effect when it is accompanied with such encouragement as, "You know how changed you are since you have been here; you know we have begun to entertain great hopes of you. For God's sake consider! Do not throw away this great chance of your life, by making yourself and everybody around you unhappy – which will oblige us to send you away – but conquer this. Now, try hard for a month, and pray let us have no fault to find with you at the end of that time." Many will make great and successful efforts to control themselves, after such remonstrance. In all cases, the fewest and plainest words are the best. When new to the place, they are found to break and spoil through great carelessness. Patience, and the strictest attention to order and punctuality, will in most cases overcome these discouragements. Nothing else will. They are often rather disposed to quarrel among themselves, particularly in bad weather when their lives are necessarily monotonous and confined; but, on the whole, allowing for their different breeding, they perhaps quarrel less than the average of passengers in the state cabin on a voyage out to India.

As some of the inmates of the Home have to be saved and guarded from themselves more than from any other people, they can scarcely be defended by too many precautions. These precautions are not obtruded upon them, but are strictly observed. Keys are never left about. The garden gate is always kept locked; but the girls take it in turn to act as porteress, overlooked by the second superintendent. They are proud of this trust. Any inmate missing from her usual place for ten minutes would be looked after. Any suspicious circumstance would be quickly and quietly investigated. As no girl makes her own bed, no girl has the opportunity of safely hiding any secret correspondence, or anything else, in it. Each inmate has a separate bed, but there are several beds in a room. The occupants of each room are always arranged with a reference to their several characters and counteracting influences. A girl declaring that she wishes to leave is not allowed to do so hastily, but is locked in a chamber by herself, to consider of it until next day: when, if she still persist, she is formally discharged. It has never once happened that a girl, however excited, has refused to submit to this restraint.

One of the most remarkable effects of the Home, even in many of the cases where it does not ultimately succeed, is the extraordinary change it produces in the appearance of its inmates. Putting out of the question their look of cleanliness and health (which may be regarded as a physical consequence of their treatment) a refining and humanising alteration is wrought in the expression of the features, and in the whole air of the person, which can scarcely be imagined. Teachers in Ragged Schools have made the observation in reference to young women whom they had previously known well, and for a long time. A very sagacious and observant police magistrate, visiting a girl before her emigration who had been taken from his bar, could detect no likeness in her to the girl he remembered. It is considered doubtful whether, in the majority of the worst cases, the subject would easily be known again at a year's end, among a dozen, by an old companion.

The moral influence of the Home, still applying the remark even to cases of failure, is illustrated in a no less remarkable manner. It has never had any violence done to a chair or a stool. It has never been asked to render any aid to the one lady and her assistant, who are shut up with the thirteen the year round. Bad language is so uncommon that its utterance is an event. The committee have never heard the least approach to it, or seen anything but submission; though it has often been their task to reprove and dismiss women who have been violently agitated, and unquestionably (for the time) incensed against them. Four of the fugitives have robbed the Institution of some clothes. The rest had no reason on earth for running away in preference to asking to be dismissed, but shame in not remaining.

A specimen or two of cases of success may be interesting.

Case number twenty-seven was a girl supposed to be about eighteen, but who had none but supposititious knowledge of her age, and no knowledge at all of her birthday. Both her parents had died in her infancy. She had been brought up in the establishment of that amiable victim of popular prejudice, the late Mr. Drouet, of Tooting. It did not appear that she was naturally stupid, but her intellect had been so dulled by neglect that she was in the Home many months before she could be imbued with a thorough understanding that Christmas Day was so called as the birthday of Jesus Christ. But when she acquired this piece of learning, she was amazingly proud of it. She had been apprenticed to a small artificial flower maker with three others. They were all ill-treated, and all seemed to have run away at different times, this girl last, who absconded with an old man, a hawker, who brought "combs and things" to the door for sale. She took what she called "some old clothes" of her mistress with her, and was apprehended with the old man, and they were tried together. He was acquitted; she

was found guilty. Her sentence was six months' imprisonment, and, on its expiration, she was received into the Home. She was appallingly ignorant, but most anxious to learn, and contended against her blunted faculties with a consciously slow perseverance. She showed a remarkable capacity for copying writing by the eye alone, without having the least idea of its sound, or what it meant. There seemed to be some analogy between her making letters and her making artificial flowers. She remained in the Home, bearing an excellent character, about a year. On her passage out, she made artificial flowers for the ladies on board, earned money, and was much liked. She obtained a comfortable service as soon as she landed, and is happy and respected. This girl had not a friend in the world, and had never known a natural affection, or formed a natural tie, upon the face of this earth.

Case number thirteen was a half-starved girl of eighteen whose father had died soon after her birth, and who had long eked out a miserable subsistence for herself and a sick mother by doing plain needlework. At last her mother died in a workhouse and the needlework "falling off bit by bit", this girl suffered, for nine months, every extremity of dire distress. Being one night without any food or shelter from the weather, she went to the lodging of a woman who had once lived in the same house with herself and her mother, and asked to be allowed to lie down on the stairs. She was refused, and stole a shawl which she sold for a penny. A fortnight afterwards, being still in a starving and houseless state, she went back to the same woman's, and preferred the same request. Again refused she stole a bible from her, which she sold for twopence. The theft was immediately discovered, and she was taken as she lay asleep in the casual ward of a workhouse. These facts were distinctly proved upon her trial. She was sentenced to three months' imprisonment, and was then admitted into the Home. She had never been corrupted. She remained in the Home, bearing an excellent character, a little more than a year; emigrated; conducted herself uniformly well in a good situation; and is now married.

Case number forty-one was a pretty girl of a quiet and good manner, aged nineteen. She came from a watering place where she had lived with her mother until within a couple of years, when her mother married again and she was considered an incumbrance at a very bad home. She became apprenticed to a dressmaker, who, on account of her staying out beyond the prescribed hours one night when she went with some other young people to a Circus, positively refused to admit her or give her any shelter from the streets. The natural consequences of this unjustifiable behaviour followed. She came to the Home on the recommendation of a clergyman to whom she fortunately applied, when in a state of sickness and misery too deplorable to be even suggested to the reader's imagination. She remained in the Home (with an interval of hospital treatment) upwards of a year and a half, when she was sent abroad. Her character is irreproachable, and she is industrious, happy and full of gratitude.

Case number fifty was a very homely, clumsy, ignorant girl, supposed to be about nineteen, but who again had no knowledge of her birthday. She was taken from a Ragged School; her mother had died when she was a little girl; and her father, marrying again, had turned her out of doors, though her mother-in-law had been kind to her. She had been once in prison for breaking some windows near the Mansion House, "having nowheres as you can think of, to go to". She had never gone wrong otherwise, and particularly wished that "to be wrote down". She was in as dirty and unwholesome a condition, on her admission, as she could well be, but was inconsolable at the idea of losing her hair, until the fortunate suggestion was made that it would grow more luxuriantly after shaving. She then consented, with many tears, to that (in her case) indispensable operation. This deserted and unfortunate creature, after a short period of depression began to brighten, uniformly showed a very honest and truthful nature, and after remaining in the Home a year, has recently emigrated; a thoroughly good plain servant, with every susceptibility for forming a faithful and affectionate attachment to her employers.

Case number fifty-eight was a girl of nineteen, all but starved through inability to live by needlework. She had never gone wrong, was gradually brought into a good bodily condition, invariably conducted herself well, and went abroad, rescued and happy.

Case number fifty-one was a little ragged girl of sixteen or seventeen, as she said; but of very juvenile appearance. She was put to the bar at a police office, with two much older women, regular vagrants, for making a disturbance at the workhouse gate on the previous night on being refused relief. She had been a

A maid-of-all-work, drawn by Kenny Meadows in 1840.

professed tramp for six or seven years, knew of no relation, and had had no friends but one old woman, whose very name she did not appear to be sure of. Her father, a scaffold builder, she had "lost" on London Bridge when she was ten or eleven years old. There appeared little doubt that he had purposely abandoned her, but she had no suspicion of it. She had long been hop-picking in the hop season, and wandering about the country at all seasons, and was unaccustomed to shoes, and had seldom slept in a bed. She answered some searching questions without the least reserve, and not at all in her own favour. Her appearance of destitution was in perfect keeping with her story. This girl was received into the Home. Within a year, there was clinging round the principal Superintendent's neck, on board a ship bound for Australia – in a state of grief at parting that moved the bystanders to tears – a pretty little neat modest useful girl, against whom not a moment's complaint had been made, and who had diligently learnt everything that had been set before her.

Case number fifty-four, a good-looking young woman of two-and-twenty, was first seen in prison under remand on a charge of attempting to commit suicide. Her mother had died before she was two years old, and her father had married again; but she spoke in high and affectionate terms both of her father and her mother-in-law. She had been a travelling maid with an elderly lady, and, on her mistress going to Russia, had returned home to her father's. She had stayed out late one night, in company with a "commissioner" whom she had known abroad, was afraid or ashamed to go home, and so went wrong. Falling lower, and becoming poorer, she became at last acquainted with a ticket-taker at a railway station, who tired of the acquaintance. One night when he had made an appointment (as he had often done before) and, on the plea of inability to leave his duties, had put this girl in a cab, that she might be taken safely home (she seemed to have inspired him with that much enduring regard), she pulled up the window, and swallowed two shillings' worth of the essential oil of almonds which she had bought at a chemist's an hour before. The driver happened to look round when she still had the bottle to her lips, immediately made out the whole story, and had the presence of mind to drive her straight to a hospital, where she remained a month before she was cured. She was in that state of depression in the prison, that it was a matter for grave consideration whether it would be safe to take her into the Home, where, if she were bent upon committing suicide, it would be almost impossible to prevent her. After some talk with her, however, it was decided to receive her. She proved one of the best inmates it has ever had, and remained in it seven months before she emigrated. Her father, who had never seen her since the night of her staying out late, came to see her in the Home, and confirmed these particulars. It is doubtful whether any treatment but that pursued in such an institution would have restored this girl.

Case number fourteen was an extremely pretty girl of twenty,

A former maidservant reduced to sweeping a crossing, 1850s, from a photograph.

whose mother was married to a second husband – a drunken man who ill-treated his step-daughter. She had been engaged to be married, but had been deceived, and had run away from home in shame, and had been away three years. Within that period, however, she had twice returned home; the first time for six months; the second time for a few days. She had also been in a London hospital. She had also been in the Magdalen: which institution her father-in-law, with a drunkard's inconsistency, had induced her to leave, to attend her mother's funeral – and then ill-treated her as before. She had been once in prison as a disorderly character, and was received from the prison into the Home. Her health was impaired and her experiences had been of a bad kind in a bad quarter of London, but she was still a girl of remarkably engaging and delicate appearance. She remained in the Home, improving rapidly, thirteen months. She was never complained of, and her general deportment was unusually quiet and modest. She emigrated, and is a good, industrious, happy wife.

This paper can scarcely be better closed than by the following pretty passage from a letter of one of the married young women.

HONNOURED LADIES,

I have again taken the liberty of writing to you to let you know how I am going on since I last wrote Home for I can never forget that name that still comes fresh to my mind, Honnoured Ladies I received your most kind letter on Tuesday the 21st of May my Mistress was kind enough to bring it over to me she told me that she also had a letter from you and that she should write Home and give you a good account of us. Honnoured Ladies I cannot describe the feelings which I felt on receiving your most kind letter, I first read my letter then I cried but it was with tears of joy, to think you was so kind to write to us Honnoured Ladies I have seen Jane and I showed my letter she is going write Home, she is living about 36 miles from where I live and her and her husband are very happy together she has been down to our Town this week and it is the first that we have seen of her since a week after they were married. My Husband is very kind to me and we live very happy and comfortable together we have a nice garden where we grow all that we want we have sown some peas turnips and I helped to do some we have three such nice pigs and we killed one last week he was so fat that he could not see out of his eyes he used to have to sit down to eat and I have got such a nice cat – she peeps over me while I am writing this. My Husband was going out one day, and he heard that cat cry and he fetched her in she was so thin. My tow little birds are gone – one dide and the other flew away now I have got none, get down Cat do. My Husband has built a shed at the side of the house to do any thing for hisself when he coms home from work of a night he tells me that I shall every 9 years com Home if we live so long please God, but I think that he is only making game of me. Honnoured Ladies I can never feel grateful enough for your kindness to me and the kind indulgences which I received at my happy Home, I often wish that I could come Home and see that happy place again once more and all my kind friends which I hope I may one day please God.

No comments or arguments shall be added to swell the length this account has already attained. Our readers will judge for themselves what some of these cases must have soon become, but for the timely interposition of the Home established by the Ladies whose charity is so discreet and so impartial.

A street-seller moved on by the law, Punch, *1850. Henry Mayhew writes: "I did not hear of any girls who had run away from their homes having become street-sellers merely. They more generally fall into a course of prostitution, or sometimes may be ostensibly street-sellers as a means of accosting men, and, perhaps, for an attractive pretence to the depraved, that they are poor, innocent girls, struggling for an honest penny."*

From **David Copperfield** *chapter 51*

"SHE come," said Mr. Peggotty, dropping his voice to an awe-stricken whisper, "to London. She – as had never seen it in her life – alone – without a penny – young – so pretty – come to London. A'most the moment as she lighted heer, all so desolate, she found (as she believed) a friend; a decent woman as spoke to her about the needlework as she had been brought up to do, about finding plenty of it fur her, about a lodging fur the night, and making secret inquiration concerning of me and all at home, tomorrow. When my child," he said aloud, and with an energy of gratitude that shook him from head to foot, "stood upon the brink of more than I can say or think on – Martha, trew to her promise, saved her."

I could not repress a cry of joy.

"Mas'r Davy!" said he, gripping my hand in that strong hand of his, "it was you as first made mention of her to me. I thankee, sir! She was arnest. She had know'd of her bitter knowledge wheer to watch and what to do. She had done it. And the Lord was above all! She come, white and hurried, upon Em'ly in her sleep. She says to her, 'Rise up from worse than death, and come with me!' Them belonging to the house would have stopped her, but they might as soon have stopped the sea. 'Stand away from me,' she says, 'I am a ghost that calls her from beside her open grave!' She told Em'ly she had seen me, and know'd I loved her, and forgive her. She wrapped her, hasty, in her clothes. She took her, faint and trembling, on her arm. She heeded no more what they said, than if she had had no ears. She walked among 'em with my child, minding only her; and brought her safe out, in the dead of the night, from that black pit of ruin!

"She attended on Em'ly," said Mr. Peggotty, who had released my hand, and put his own hand on his heaving chest; "she attended to my Em'ly, lying wearied out, and wandering betwixt whiles, till late next day. Then she went in search of me; then in search of you, Mas'r Davy. She didn't tell Em'ly what she come out fur, lest her 'art should fail, and she should think of hiding of herself. How the cruel lady know'd of her being theer, I can't say. Whether him as I have spoke so much of, chanced to see 'em going theer, or whether (which is most like, to my thinking) he had heerd it from the woman, I don't greatly ask myself. My niece is found.

"All night long," said Mr. Peggotty, "we have been together, Em'ly and me. 'Tis little (considering the time) as she has said, in wureds, through them broken-hearted tears; 'tis less as I have seen of her dear face, as grow'd into a woman's at my hearth. But, all night long, her arms has been about my neck; and her head has laid heer; and we knows full well, as we can put our trust in one another, ever more."

He ceased to speak, and his hand upon the table rested there in perfect repose, with a resolution in it that might have conquered lions. . . .

"You have quite made up your mind," said I to Mr. Peggotty, "as to the future, good friend? I need scarcely ask you."

"Quite, Mas'r Davy," he returned; "and told Em'ly. Theer's mighty countries, fur from heer. Our future life lays over the sea."

"They will emigrate together, aunt," said I.

"Yes!" said Mr. Peggotty, with a hopeful smile. "No one can't reproach my darling in Australia. We will begin a new life over theer!"

ON STRIKE

Household Words 11 February 1854

PRESTON, Lancashire, was in the grip of a bitter dispute between cotton operatives and factory owners when Charles Dickens visited it late in 1853 and a few months later in 1854. It was a town with a strong radical tradition. William Cobbett fought an unsuccessful election there in 1826, and from 1830 to 1832 Henry "Orator" Hunt, a leading radical of the time, was its Member of Parliament. Feelings often ran high in Preston, and after Hunt's visit on Guy Fawkes' Day in 1831 they spilled over into riot. With its many mills and growing working-class population, the town was at the heartland of northern English radicalism.

In 1842 four strikers had been shot dead by troops sent to maintain order during a strike. The hard line maintained by the Preston masters in the face of modest demands from their workforce was well known; as late as 1860 it was being said that "increases in wages are sometimes given elsewhere, in Preston never." The troubles which brought Dickens twice to the town began in 1853, and were part of a general agitation on the part of workers in the cotton industry for an increase in wages, which were hardly above subsistence level, and for a shortening of the working day, which was unconscionably long. By June 1853 the strike had developed into the biggest "turn out" since the strife of 1842.

Its immediate cause was a request by the powerloom weavers to their employers for a restoration of the ten per cent cut in wages enforced in 1847. The factory owners refused to meet the representatives of their workers, and responded to all requests by sacking many of the hands. To support men and women who had lost their jobs, and to strengthen their claims, trade union membership increased and strikes spread to other mills in the town. The response of the Preston Masters' Association was immediate: from September all workers were locked out of the mills, and none would be re-employed unless trade union membership was renounced. Further, prosecutions were brought against the workers' leaders – but these were soon dropped. Funds were raised in London and elsewhere by Trades Committees to assist the workless in Preston, and long after Dickens had left the town strikes were still breaking out all over mid-Lancashire.

They were, in fact, still erupting some weeks after Dickens's *Hard Times* had begun to appear, in parts, in 1854. This novel was Dickens's one response to the problems of an industrial society, and also the one in which London played no part at all. As a response to the struggle between master and worker in a capitalist society it was muted; and the fact that the novel was set out of the great metropolis made Dickens's handling of social themes less sure than it usually was. He was familiar with London streets, prisons, casual wards, slums, alleys and police courts, but when it came to Coketown – a place of "machinery and tall chimneys, out of which interminable serpents of smoke trailed themselves for ever and ever" (a telling contrast to the "cold smokeless factory chimneys" in this article) – his touch was not so deft. He seemed unable to comprehend the reality of the struggle between classes which he had seen for himself in Preston and wrote about in *Hard Times*.

As always, Dickens was unwilling to take sides in economic issues. He is quite specific in "On Strike" about being sympathetic to both parties in dispute, and uses the words "employers and employed, in preference to Capital and Labour". He took this stance partly, no doubt, because he disliked the rigid impersonality of the latter words, and partly because he saw capitalism as a joint enterprise between partners. What is unusual in this article is his view of the Preston workers, not as stereotyped figures – a sullen, faceless crowd crushed by factory routine, poverty and despair – but as having a prevailing tone of resilience, solidarity and self-respect. In *Hard Times* – and in an earlier *Household Words* piece on the strike, not by Dickens – the strikers are seen in a much narrower and less humane perspective. Among most Victorian novelists, this inability to see as real people factory workers living in the mean streets of industrial towns was very common (one exception was Mrs. Gaskell, whose novel *North and South* first appeared as a serial in *Household Words* in 1854). The differences in approach in Dickens's article and in his novel demonstrate that he experienced difficulties in coming to terms with, and portraying for his readers, the new realities of a capitalist society.

Underlying the commonly held view of the working class lay the tacit assumption that its members were somehow less than human and had no culture of their own. But there existed in Victorian England a rich and many-sided popular culture which expressed itself in songs, ballads, poems, festivals and sundry entertainments. Dickens himself was well aware of this culture and his novels abound in references to it. He mentioned, too, ballads being sung around the streets of Preston, and bought street ballads there himself. Because of this familiarity with popular culture, it remains puzzling that he should have treated the inhabitants of Coketown in so dismissive a manner.

It is even more difficult to comprehend Dickens's attitude when we recall his intervention in the matter of Henry Morley's article on "The Manchester Strike", which was published in *Household Words* on 2 February 1856, but not until some changes had, at Dickens's insistence, been made in the text. He wrote to W.H. Wills, his sub-editor, urging him to get Morley to tone down his view of the strikers:

> And O Good God when Morley treats of the suffering wife and children, can he suppose that these mistaken men and women don't feel in the depths of their hearts, and don't honestly and honourably – most devoutly and faithfully believe that for those very children when they shall have children, they are bearing all these miseries now!

What blurred Dickens's vision – though not his human warmth – was the widely held view of his time that militancy and trade union membership were not compatible with the kind of working-class decency exhibited, for example, by the Peggotty family in *David Copperfield*. That such an attitude was a travesty of the situation he had seen and written about in "On Strike" does not seem to have occurred to him. He wrote about a meeting of strikers with rare sympathy and understanding – why, then, did he pander in *Hard Times* to the conventional misconceptions of his day?

There can be no comfortable answer to this question, and it is ironic to note that the first English novel to deal with industrial problems, *Michael Armstrong, the Factory Boy* by Frances Trollope, published in 1840, contains a very sympathetic depiction of working-class life and experience that Dickens, in his fiction at least, could never achieve – even although in most respects the novel was inferior to *Hard Times*. The author, Anthony Trollope's mother, held strong views on what she referred to as "the fearful evils inherent in the factory system", and *Michael Armstrong* occasioned much adverse criticism. There was no authorised reprint in her lifetime, and the industrial scene was not one to which she returned in any of her many subsequent novels.

ON STRIKE

TRAVELLING down to Preston a week from this date, I chanced to sit opposite to a very acute, very determined, very emphatic personage, with a stout railway rug so drawn over his chest that he looked as if he were sitting up in bed with his great-coat, hat, and gloves on, severely contemplating your humble servant from behind a large blue and grey checked counterpane. In calling him emphatic, I do not mean that he was warm; he was coldly and bitingly emphatic as a frosty wind is.

"You are going through to Preston, sir?" says he, as soon as we were clear of the Primrose Hill tunnel.

The receipt of his question was like the receipt of a jerk of the nose; he was so short and sharp.

"Yes."

"This Preston strike is a nice piece of business!" said the gentleman. "A pretty piece of business!"

"It is very much to be deplored," said I, "on all accounts."

"They want to be ground. That's what they want, to bring 'em to their senses," said the gentleman; whom I had already began to call in my own mind Mr. Snapper, and whom I may as well call by that name here as by any other.

I deferentially enquired, who wanted to be ground?

"The hands," said Mr. Snapper. "The hands on strike, and the hands who help 'em."

I remarked that if that was all they wanted, they must be a very unreasonable people, for surely they had had a little grinding, one way and another, already. Mr. Snapper eyed me with sternness, and after opening and shutting his leathern-gloved hands several times outside his counterpane, asked me abruptly, "Was I a delegate?"

I set Mr. Snapper right on that point, and told him I was no delegate.

"I am glad to hear it," said Mr. Snapper. "But a friend to the Strike, I believe?"

"Not at all," said I.

"A friend to the Lock-out?" pursued Mr. Snapper.

"Not in the least," said I.

Mr. Snapper's rising opinion of me fell again, and he gave me to understand that a man *must* either be a friend to the Masters or a friend to the Hands.

"He may be a friend to both," said I.

Mr. Snapper didn't see that; there was no medium in the Political Economy of the subject. I retorted on Mr. Snapper, that Political Economy was a great and useful science in its own way and its own place; but that I did not transplant my definition of it from the Common Prayer Book, and make it a great king above all gods. Mr. Snapper tucked himself up as if to keep me off, folded his arms on the top of his counterpane, leaned back, and looked out of window.

"Pray what would you have, sir," enquired Mr. Snapper, suddenly withdrawing his eyes from the prospect to me, "in the relations between Capital and Labour, *but* Political Economy?"

I always avoid the stereotyped terms in these discussions as much as I can, for I have observed, in my little way, that they often supply the place of sense and moderation. I therefore took my gentleman up with the words employers and employed, in preference to Capital and Labour.

"I believe," said I, "that into the relations between employers and employed, as into all the relations of this life, there must enter something of feeling and sentiment; something of mutual explanation, forbearance, and consideration; something which is not to be found in Mr. McCulloch's dictionary, and is not exactly stateable in figures; otherwise those relations are wrong and rotten at

Mr. McCulloch: the economist J. R. McCulloch, whose solution to poverty was to advise the poor to have fewer children

143

the core and will never bear sound fruit."

Mr. Snapper laughed at me. As I thought I had just as good reason to laugh at Mr. Snapper, I did so, and we were both contented.

"Ah!" said Mr. Snapper, patting his counterpane with a hard touch. "You know very little of the improvident and unreasoning habits of the common people, *I* see."

"Yet I know something of those people, too," was my reply. "In fact, Mr. –," I had so nearly called him Snapper! "in fact, sir, I doubt the existence at this present time of many faults that are merely class faults. In the main, I am disposed to think that whatever faults you may find to exist, in your own neighbourhood for instance, among the hands, you will find tolerably equal in amount among the masters also, and even among the classes above the masters. They will be modified by circumstances, and they will be the less excusable among the better-educated, but they will be pretty fairly distributed. I have a strong expectation that we shall live to see the conventional adjectives now apparently inseparable from the phrases working people and lower orders, gradually fall into complete disuse for this reason."

"Well, but we began with strikes," Mr. Snapper observed impatiently. "The masters have never had any share in strikes."

"Yet I have heard of strikes once upon a time in that same county of Lancashire," said I, "which were not disagreeable to some masters when they wanted a pretext for raising prices."

"Do you mean to say those masters had any hand in getting up those strikes?" asked Mr. Snapper.

"You will perhaps obtain better information among persons engaged in some Manchester branch trades, who have good memories," said I.

Mr Snapper had no doubt, after this, that I thought the hands had a right to combine?

"Surely," said I. "A perfect right to combine in any lawful manner. The fact of their being able to combine and accustomed to combine may, I can easily conceive, be a protection to them. The blame even of this business is not all on one side. I think the associated Lock-out was a grave error. And when you Preston masters –"

"*I* am not a Preston master," interrupted Mr. Snapper.

"When the respectable combined body of Preston masters," said I, "in the beginning of this unhappy difference, laid down the principle that no man should be employed henceforth who belonged to any combination – such as their own – they attempted to carry with a high hand a partial and unfair impossibility, and were obliged to abandon it. This was an unwise proceeding, and the first defeat."

Mr. Snapper had known, all along, that I was no friend to the masters.

"Pardon me," said I, "I am unfeignedly a friend to the masters, and have many friends among them."

"Yet you think these hands in the right?" quoth Mr. Snapper.

"By no means," said I; "I fear they are at present engaged in an unreasonable struggle, wherein they began ill and cannot end well."

Mr. Snapper, evidently regarding me as neither fish, flesh, nor fowl, begged to know after a pause if he might enquire whether I was going to Preston on business?

Indeed I was going there, in my unbusiness-like manner, I confessed, to look at the strike.

"To look at the strike!" echoed Mr. Snapper, fixing his hat on firmly with both hands. "To look at it! Might I ask you now, with what object you are going to look at it?"

"Certainly," said I. "I read, even in liberal pages, the hardest Political Economy – of an extraordinary description too some-times, and certainly not to be found in the books – as the only touchstone of this strike. I see, this very day, in a to-morrow's liberal paper, some astonishing novelties in the politico-econ-omical way, showing how profits and wages have no connexion whatever; coupled with such references to these hands as might be made by a very irascible General to rebels and brigands in arms. Now, if it be the case that some of the highest virtues of the working people still shine through them brighter than ever in their conduct of this mistake of theirs, perhaps the fact may reasonably suggest to me – and to others besides me – that there is some little thing wanting in the relations between them and their employers, which neither political economy nor Drum-head proclamation writing will altogether supply, and which we cannot too soon or too temperately unite in trying to find out."

Mr. Snapper, after again opening and shutting his gloved hands several times, drew the counterpane higher over his chest, and went to bed in disgust. He got up at Rugby, took himself and counterpane into another carriage, and left me to pursue my jour-ney alone.

When I got to Preston, it was four o'clock in the afternoon. The day being Saturday and market-day, a foreigner might have ex-pected, from among so many idle and not over-fed people as the town contained, to find a turbulent, ill-conditioned crowd in the streets. But, except for the cold smokeless factory chimneys, the placards at the street corners, and the groups of working people attentively reading them, nor foreigner nor Englishman could have had the least suspicion that there existed any interruption to the usual labours of the place. The placards thus perused were not remarkable for their logic certainly, and did not make the case particularly clear; but, considering that they emanated from, and were addressed to, people who had been out of employment for three-and-twenty consecutive weeks, at least they had little passion in them, though they had not much reason. Take the worst I could find:

A ragged factory child, 1840.

145

FRIENDS AND FELLOW OPERATIVES,

Accept the grateful thanks of twenty thousand struggling Operatives, for the help you have showered upon Preston since the present contest commenced.

Your kindness and generosity, your patience and long-continued support deserve every praise, and are only equalled by the heroic and determined perseverance of the outraged and insulted factory workers of Preston, who have been struggling for some months, and are, at this inclement season of the year, bravely battling for the rights of themselves and the whole toiling community.

For many years before the strike took place at Preston, the Operatives were the down trodden and insulted serfs of their Employers, who in times of good trade and general prosperity, wrung from their labour a California of gold, which is now being used to crush those who created it, still lower and lower in the scale of civilization. This has been the result of our commercial prosperity! – *more wealth for the rich and more poverty for the Poor!* Because the workpeople of Preston protested against this state of things, – because they combined in a fair and legitimate way for the purpose of getting a reasonable share of the reward of their own labour, the *fair dealing* Employers of Preston, to their eternal shame and disgrace, *locked up* their Mills, and at one fell swoop deprived, as they thought, from twenty to thirty thousand human beings of the means of existence. Cruelty and tyranny always defeat their own object; it was so in this case, and to the honour and credit of the working classes of this country, we have to record, that those whom the rich and wealthy sought to destroy, the poor and industrious have protected from harm. This love of justice and hatred of wrong, is a noble feature in the character and disposition of the working man, and gives us hope that in the future, this world will become what its great architect intended, not a place of sorrow, toil, oppression and wrong, but the dwelling place and the abode of peace, plenty, happiness and love, where avarice and all the evil passions engendered by the present system of fraud and injustice shall not have a place.

The earth was not made for the misery of its people; intellect was not given to man to make himself and fellow creatures unhappy. No, the fruitfulness of the soil and the wonderful inventions – the result of mind – all proclaim that these things were bestowed upon us for our happiness and well-being, and not for the misery and degradation of the human race.

It may serve the manufacturers and all who run away with the lion's share of labour's produce, to say that the *impartial* God intended that there should be a *partial* distribution of his blessings. But we know that it is against nature to believe that those who plant and reap all the grain should not have enough to make a mess of porridge; and we know that those who weave all the cloth should not want a yard to cover their persons, whilst those who never wove an inch have more calico, silks and satins, than would serve the reasonable wants of a dozen working men and their families.

This system of giving everything to the few, and nothing to the many, has lasted long enough, and we call upon the working people of this country to be determined to establish a new and improved system – a system that shall give to all who labour, a fair share of those blessings and comforts which their toil produce; in short, we wish to see that divine precept enforced, which says, "Those who will not work, shall not eat."

The task is before you, working men; if you think the good which would result from its accomplishment is worth struggling for, set to work and cease not, until you have obtained the *good time coming*, not only for the Preston Operatives, but for yourselves as well.

By Order of the Committee.

Murphy's Temperance Hotel, Chapel Walks, Preston, January 24th, 1854.

Mill hands trudging to work. A detail from an illustration by A. Hervieu, 1840.

146

It is a melancholy thing that it should not occur to the Committee to consider what would become of themselves, their friends, and fellow operatives, if those calicoes, silks, and satins, were *not* worn in very large quantities; but I shall not enter into that question. As I had told my friend Snapper, what I wanted to see with my own eyes was how these people acted under a mistaken impression, and what qualities they showed, even at that disadvantage, which ought to be the strength and peace – not the weakness and trouble – of the community. I found, even from this literature, however, that all masters were not indiscriminately unpopular. Witness the following verses from the New Song of the Preston Strike:

There's Henry Hornby, of Blackburn, he is a jolly brick,
He fits the Preston masters nobly, and is very bad to trick;
He pays his hands a good price, and I hope he will never sever,
So we'll sing success to Hornby and Blackburn for ever.

There is another gentleman, I'm sure you'll all lament,
In Blackburn for him they're raising a monument,
You know his name, 'tis of great fame, it was late Eccles of honour,
May Hopwood, and Sparrow, and Hornby live for ever.

So now it is time to finish and end my rhyme,
We warn these Preston Cotton Lords to mind for future time.
With peace and order too I hope we shall be clever,
We sing success to Stockport and Blackburn for ever.

Now, lads, give your minds to it.

The balance sheet of the receipts and expenditure for the twenty-third week of the strike was extensively posted. The income for that week was two thousand one hundred and forty pounds odd. Some of the contributors were poetical. As,

Love to all and peace to the dead,
May the poor now in need never want bread.
Three-and-sixpence

The following poetical remonstrance was appended to the list of contributions from the Gorton district:

Within these walls the lasses fair
Refuse to contribute their share,
Careless of duty – blind to fame,
For shame, ye lasses, oh! for shame!
Come, pay up, lasses, think what's right,
Defend your trade with all your might;
Fer if you don't the world will blame,
And cry, ye lasses, oh, for shame!
Let's hope in future all will pay,
That Preston folks may shortly say –
That by your aid they have obtain'd
The greatest victory ever gained.

Some of the subscribers veiled their names under encouraging sentiments, as Not tired yet, All in a mind, Win the day, Fraternity, and the like. Some took jocose appellations, as A stunning friend, Two to one Preston wins, Nibbling Joe, and The Donkey Driver. Some expressed themselves through their trades, as Cobbler Dick, sixpence, The tailor true, sixpence, Shoemaker, a shilling, The chirping blacksmith, sixpence, and A few of Maskery's most feeling coachmakers, three and threepence. An old balance sheet for the fourteenth week of the Strike was headed with this quotation from Mr. Carlyle. "Adversity is sometimes hard upon a man; but for one man who can stand prosperity, there are a hundred that will stand adversity." The Elton district prefaced its report with these lines:

> Oh! ye who start a noble scheme,
>   For general good designed;
> Ye workers in a cause that tends
>   To benefit your kind!
> Mark out the path ye fain would tread,
>   The game ye mean to play;
> And if it be an honest one,
>   Keep steadfast in your way!
>
> Although you may not gain at once
>   The points ye most desire;
> Be patient – time can wonders work;
>   Plod on, and do not tire:
> Obstructions, too, may crowd your path,
>   In threatening, stern array;
> Yet flinch not! fear not! they may prove
>   Mere shadows in your way.
>
> Then, while there's work for you to do,
>   Stand not despairing by,
> Let "forward" be the move ye make,
>   Let "onward" be your cry;
> And when success has crowned your plans,
>   'Twill all your pains repay,
> To see the good your labour's done –
>   Then droop not on your way.

In this list, "Bear ye one another's burthens," sent one pound fifteen. "We'll stand to our text, see that ye love one another," sent nineteen shillings. "Christopher Hardman's men again, they say they can always spare one shilling out of ten," sent two and sixpence. The following masked threats were the worst feature in any bill I saw:

> If that fiddler at Uncle Tom's Cabin blowing room does not pay Punch will set his legs straight.
> If that drawer at card side and those two slubbers do not pay, Punch will say something about their bustles.
> If that winder at last shift does not pay next week, Punch will tell about her actions.

But, on looking at this bill again, I found that it came from Bury

and related to Bury, and had nothing to do with Preston. The Masters' placards were not torn down or disfigured, but were being read quite as attentively as those on the opposite side.

That evening, the Delegates from the surrounding districts were coming in, according to custom, with their subscription lists for the week just closed. These delegates meet on Sunday as their only day of leisure; when they have made their reports, they go back to their homes and their Monday's work. On Sunday morning, I repaired to the Delegates' meeting.

These assemblages take place in a cockpit, which, in the better times of our fallen land, belonged to the late Lord Derby for the purposes of the intellectual recreation implied in its name. I was directed to the cockpit up a narrow lane, tolerably crowded by the lower sort of working people. Personally, I was quite unknown in the town, but every one made way for me to pass, with great civility, and perfect good humour. Arrived at the cockpit door, and expressing my desire to see and hear, I was handed through the crowd, down into the pit, and up again, until I found myself seated on the topmost circular bench, within one of the secretary's table, and within three of the chairman. Behind the chairman was a great crown on the top of a pole, made of parti-coloured calico, and strongly suggestive of May-day. There was no other symbol or ornament in the place.

A Chartist meeting, 1840s. In the background is a factory chimney. Chartism was one of the earliest working-class political movements, and as such was viewed with suspicion and fear even by those, such as Dickens, who were temperamentally in sympathy with its aims.

It was hotter than any mill or factory I have ever been in; but there was a stove down in the sanded pit, and delegates were seated close to it, and one particular delegate often warmed his hands at it, as if he were chilly. The air was so intensely close and hot, that at first I had but a confused perception of the delegates down in the pit, and the dense crowd of eagerly listening men and women (but not very many of the latter) filling all the benches and choking such narrow standing-room as there was. When the atmosphere cleared a little on better acquaintance, I found the question under discussion to be, Whether the Manchester Delegates in attendance from the Labour Parliament, should be heard?

If the Assembly, in respect of quietness and order, were put in comparison with the House of Commons, the Right Honourable the Speaker himself would decide for Preston. The chairman was a Preston weaver, two or three and fifty years of age, perhaps; a man with a capacious head, rather long dark hair growing at the sides and back, a placid attentive face, keen eyes, a particularly composed manner, a quiet voice, and a persuasive action of his right arm. Now look'ee heer my friends. See what t' question is. T' question is, sholl these heer men be heerd. Then 't cooms to this, what ha' these men got t' tell us? Do they bring mooney? If they bring mooney t'ords t' expenses o' this strike, they're welcome. For, Brass, my friends, is what we want, and what we must ha' (hear hear hear!). Do they coom to us wi' any suggestion for the conduct of this strike? If they do, they're welcome. Let 'em give us their advice and we will hearken to 't. But, if these men coom heer, to tell us what t' Labour Parliament is, or what Ernest Jones's opinions is, or t' bring in politics and differences amoong us when what we want is 'armony, brotherly love, and con-cord; then I say t' you, decide for yoursel' carefully, whether these men ote to be heerd in this place. (Hear hear hear! and No no no!) Chairman sits down, earnestly regarding delegates, and holding both arms of his chair. Looks extremely sensible; his plain coarse working man's shirt collar easily turned down over his loose Belcher neckerchief. Delegate who has moved that Manchester delegates be heard, presses motion – Mr. Chairman, will that delegate tell us, as a man, that these men have anything to say concerning this present strike and lock-out, for we have a deal of business to do, and what concerns this present strike and lock-out is our business and nothing else is. (Hear hear hear!) – Delegate in question will not compromise the fact; these men want to defend the Labour Parliament from certain charges made against them. – Very well, Mr. Chairman. Then I move as an amendment that you do not hear these men now, and that you proceed wi' business – and if you don't I'll look after you, I tell you that. (Cheers and laughter) – Coom lads, prove 't then! – Two or three hands for the delegates; all the rest for the business. Motion lost, amendment carried, Manchester deputation not to be heard.

But now, starts up the delegate from Throstletown, in a dreadful state of mind. Mr. Chairman, I hold in my hand a bill; a bill

Ernest Jones: 1819–69, prominent Chartist lecturer and writer; organiser of the Chartist "Labour Parliament" held in Manchester from 6 to 18 March 1854. Marx wrote, "The mere assembling of such a Parliament marks a new epoch in the history of the world"

that requires and demands explanation from you, sir; an offensive bill; a bill posted in my town of Throstletown without my knowledge, without the knowledge of my fellow delegates who are here beside me; a bill purporting to be posted by the authority of the massed committee sir, and of which my fellow delegates and myself were kept in ignorance. Why are we to be slighted? Why are we to be insulted? Why are we to be meanly stabbed in the dark? Why is this assassin-like course of conduct to be pursued towards us? Why is Throstletown, which has nobly assisted you, the operatives of Preston, in this great struggle, and which has brought its contributions up to the full sevenpence a loom, to be thus degraded, thus aspersed, thus traduced, thus despised, thus outraged in its feelings by un-English and unmanly conduct? Sir, I hand you up that bill, and I require of you, sir, to give me a satisfactory explanation of that bill. And I have that confidence in your known integrity, sir, as to be sure that you will give it, and that you will tell us who is to blame, and that you will make reparation to Throstletown for this scandalous treatment. Then, in hot blood, up starts Gruffshaw (professional speaker) who is somehow responsible for this bill. O my friends, but explanation is required here! O my friends, but it is fit and right that you should have the dark ways of the real traducers and apostates, and the real un-English stabbers, laid bare before you. My friends when this dark conspiracy first began – But here the persuasive right hand of the chairman falls gently on Gruffshaw's shoulder. Gruffshaw stops in full boil. My friends, these are hard words of my friend Gruffshaw, and this is not the business! – No more it is, and once again, sir, I, the delegate who said I would look after you, do move that you proceed to business! – Preston has not the strong relish for personal altercation that Westminster hath. Motion seconded and carried, business passed to, Gruffshaw dumb.

Perhaps the world could not afford a more remarkable contrast than between the deliberate collected manner of these men pro-

*The Preston strike. Wood
engraving, 1853.
"Traveller on the Northern
    Railway!
Look and learn, as on you
    speed;
See the hundred smokeless
    chimneys;
Learn their tale of cheerless
    need."*
The Smokeless Chimney

ceeding with their business, and the clash and hurry of the engines among which their lives are passed. Their astonishing fortitude and perseverance; their high sense of honour among themselves; the extent to which they are impressed with the responsibility that is upon them of setting a careful example, and keeping their order out of any harm and loss of reputation; the noble readiness in them to help one another, of which most medical practitioners and working clergymen can give so many affecting examples; could scarcely ever be plainer to an ordinary observer of human nature than in this cockpit. To hold, for a minute, that the great mass of them were not sincerely actuated by the belief that all these qualities were bound up in what they were doing, and that they were doing right, seemed to me little short of an impossibility. As the different delegates (some in the very dress in which they had left the mill last night) reported the amounts sent from the various places they represented, this strong faith on their parts seemed expressed in every tone and every look that was capable of expressing it. One man was raised to enthusiasm by his pride in bringing so much; another man was ashamed and depressed because he brought so little; this man triumphantly made it known that he could give you, from the store in hand, a hundred pounds in addition next week, if you should want it; and that man pleaded that he hoped his district would do better before long; but I could as soon have doubted the existence of the walls that enclosed us, as the earnestness with which they spoke (many of them referring to the children who were to be born to labour after them) of "this great, this noble, gallant, godlike struggle." Some designing and turbulent spirits among them, no doubt there are; but I left the place with a profound conviction that their mistake is generally an honest one, and that it is sustained by the good that is in them, and not by the evil.

Neither by night nor by day was there any interruption to the peace of the streets. Nor was this an accidental state of things, for the police records of the town are eloquent to the same effect. I traversed the streets very much, and was, as a stranger, the subject of a little curiosity among the idlers; but I met with no rudeness or ill-temper. More than once, when I was looking at the printed balance-sheets to which I have referred, and could not quite comprehend the setting forth of the figures, a bystander of the working class interposed with his explanatory forefinger and helped me out. Although the pressure in the cockpit on Sunday was excessive, and the heat of the room obliged me to make my way out as I best could before the close of the proceedings, none of the people whom I put to inconvenience showed the least impatience; all helped me, and all cheerfully acknowledged my word of apology as I passed. It is very probable, notwithstanding, that they may have supposed from my being there at all – I and my companion were the only persons present, not of their own order – that I was there to carry what I heard and saw to the opposite side; indeed one speaker seemed to intimate as much.

On the Monday at noon, I returned to this cockpit, to see the people paid. It was then about half filled, principally with girls and women. They were all seated, waiting, with nothing to occupy their attention; and were just in that state when the unexpected appearance of a stranger differently dressed from themselves, and with his own individual peculiarities of course, might, without offence, have had something droll in it even to more polite assemblies. But I stood there, looking on, as free from remark as if I had come to be paid with the rest. In the place which the secretary had occupied yesterday, stood a dirty little common table, covered with five-penny piles of halfpence. Before the paying began, I wondered who was going to receive these very small

Back-to-back cottages in Preston, 1844. A cesspool runs between the rows. Low rates and cheap land allowed the Preston masters to build cottages for their hands, and exercise considerable power over their lives. They could rely on the military to suppress disturbances, and on Irish immigrants and agricultural workers from the north to feed the labour market and keep wages down.

sums; but when it did begin, the mystery was soon cleared up. Each of these piles was the change for sixpence, deducting a penny. All who were paid, in filing round the building to prevent confusion, had to pass this table on the way out; and the greater part of the unmarried girls stopped here, to change, each a sixpence, and subscribe her weekly penny in aid of the people on strike who had families. A very large majority of these girls and women were comfortably dressed in all respects, clean, wholesome and pleasant-looking. There was a prevalent neatness and cheerfulness, and an almost ludicrous absence of anything like sullen discontent.

Exactly the same appearances were observable on the same day, at a not numerously attended open air meeting in "Chadwick's Orchard" – which blossoms in nothing but red bricks. Here, the chairman of yesterday presided in a cart, from which speeches were delivered. The proceedings commenced with the following sufficiently general and discursive hymn, given out by a workman from Burnley, and sung in long metre by the whole audience:

> Assembled beneath thy broad blue sky,
> To thee, O God, thy children cry.
> Thy needy creatures on Thee call,
> For thou art great and good to all.
>
> Thy bounty smiles on every side,
> And no good thing hast thou denied;
> But men of wealth and men of power,
> Like locusts, all our gifts devour.
>
> Awake, ye sons of toil! nor sleep
> While millions starve, while millions weep;
> Demand your rights; let tyrants see
> You are resolved that you'll be free.

154

Mr. Hollins's Sovereign Mill was open all this time. It is a very beautiful mill, containing a large amount of valuable machinery, to which some recent ingenious improvements have been added. Four hundred people could find employment in it; there were eighty-five at work, of whom five had "come in" that morning. They looked, among the vast array of motionless power-looms, like a few remaining leaves in a wintry forest. They were protected by the police (very prudently not obtruded on the scenes I have described), and were stared at every day when they came out, by a crowd which had never been large in reference to the numbers on strike, and had diminished to a score or two. One policeman at the door sufficed to keep order then. These eighty-five were people of exceedingly decent appearance, chiefly women, and were evidently not in the least uneasy for themselves. I heard of one girl among them, and only one, who had been hustled and struck in a dark street.

In any aspect in which it can be viewed, this strike and lock-out is a deplorable calamity. In its waste of time, in its waste of a great people's energy, in its waste of wages, in its waste of wealth that seeks to be employed, in its encroachment on the means of many thousands who are labouring from day to day, in the gulf of separation it hourly deepens between those whose interests must be understood to be identical or must be destroyed, it is a great national affliction. But, at this pass, anger is of no use, starving out is of no use – for what will that do, five years hence, but overshadow all the mills in England with the growth of a bitter remembrance? – political economy is a mere skeleton unless it has a little human covering and filling out, a little human bloom upon it, and a little human warmth in it. Gentlemen are found, in great manufacturing towns, ready enough to extol imbecile mediation with dangerous madmen abroad; can none of them be brought to think of authorised mediation and explanation at home? I do not suppose that such a knotted difficulty as this, is to be at all untangled by a morning-party in the Adelphi; but I would entreat both sides now so miserably opposed, to consider whether there are no men in England, above suspicion, to whom they might refer the matters in dispute, with a perfect confidence above all things in the desire of those men to act justly, and in their sincere attachment to their countrymen of every rank and to their country. Masters right, or men right; masters wrong, or men wrong; both right, or both wrong; there is certain ruin to both in the continuance or frequent revival of this breach. And from the ever-widening circle of their decay, what drop in the social ocean shall be free!

From **Hard Times** *book 2 chapter 4*

"Oh my friends, the down-trodden operatives of Coketown! Oh my friends and fellow countrymen, the slaves of an iron-handed and a grinding despotism! Oh my friends and fellow-sufferers, and fellow-workmen, and fellow-men! I tell you that the hour is come, when we must rally round one another as One united power, and crumble into dust the oppressors that too long have battened upon the plunder of our families, upon the sweat of our brows, upon the labour of our hands, upon the strength of our sinews, upon the God-created glorious rights of Humanity, and upon the holy and eternal privileges of Brotherhood!"

"Good!" "Hear, hear, hear!" "Hurrah!" and other cries arose in many voices from various parts of the densely crowded and suffocatingly close Hall, in which the orator, perched on a stage, delivered himself of this and what other froth and fume he had in him. He had declaimed himself into a violent heat, and was as hoarse as he was hot. By dint of roaring at the top of his voice under a flaring gas-light, clenching his fists, knitting his brows, setting his teeth, and pounding with his arms, he had taken so much out of himself by this time, that he was brought to a stop and called for a glass of water.

As he stood there, trying to quench his fiery face with his drink of water, the comparison between the orator and the crowd of attentive faces turned towards him, was extremely to his disadvantage. Judging him by Nature's evidence, he was above the mass in very little but the stage on which he stood. In many great respects, he was essentially below them. He was not so honest, he was not so manly, he was not so good-humoured; he substituted cunning for their simplicity, and passion for their safe solid sense. An ill-made high-shouldered man, with lowering brows, and his features crushed into an habitually sour expression, he contrasted most unfavourably, even in his mongrel dress, with the great body of his hearers in their plain working clothes. Strange as it always is to consider any assembly in the act of submissively resigning itself to the dreariness of some complacent person, lord or commoner, whom three-fourths of it could, by no human means, raise out of the slough of inanity to their own intellectual level, it was particularly strange, and it was even particularly affecting, to see this crowd of earnest faces, whose honesty in the main no competent observer free from bias could doubt, so agitated by such a leader.

Good! Hear, hear! Hurrah! The eagerness, both of attention and intention, exhibited in all the countenances, made them a most impressive sight. There was no carelessness, no languor, no idle curiosity; none of the many shades of indifference to be seen in all other assemblies, visible for one moment there. That every man felt his condition to be, somehow or other, worse than it might be; that every man considered it incumbent on him to join the rest, towards the making of it better; that every man felt his only hope to be in his allying himself to the comrades by whom he was surrounded; and that in this belief, right or wrong (unhappily wrong then), the whole of that crowd were gravely, deeply, faithfully in earnest; must have been as plain to any one who chose to see what was there, as the bare beams of the roof, and the whitened brick walls. Nor could any such spectator fail to know in his own breast, that these men, through their very delusions, showed great qualities, susceptible of being turned to the happiest and best account; and that to pretend (on the strength of sweeping axioms, howsoever cut and dried) that they went astray wholly without cause, and of their own irrational wills, was to pretend that there could be smoke without fire; death without birth, harvest without seed, anything or everything produced from nothing.

FURTHER READING

Dickens's Life:

The authorised biography by Dickens's friend John Forster, *The Life of Charles Dickens* (Chapman & Hall, 1872–4), remains an indispensible source. It has been reprinted in two Everyman volumes (Biblio Distribution Centre, 1976) and in one volume (Folcroft Library Editions, 1977). The standard modern life is Edgar Johnson's magisterial *Charles Dickens: His Tragedy and Triumph* (2 vols, Simon & Schuster, 1952; revised in one vol., Viking, 1977). Supplementary to these is Philip Collins's excellent two-volume selection, *Dickens: Interviews and Recollections* (Barnes & Noble, 1981).

The definitive edition of Dickens's letters is the Oxford University Press "Pilgrim" edition; the first volume appeared in 1965 and the edition is still in progress. Meanwhile, the most complete edition is the three-volume *Letters* edited by Walter Dexter for the Nonesuch Press, London, in 1938. This was a limited edition and is very rare, but a good selection from it has been made by David Paroissien in *Selected Letters* (Twayne, 1985). Two volumes of letters to single correspondents are of key interest: R. C. Lehmann's *Charles Dickens as Editor: Being Letters Written by him to William Henry Wills his Sub-editor* (Sturgis & Walton, 1912; reissued by Kraus Reprints and by Richard West) and *The Heart of Charles Dickens as Revealed in his Letters to Angela Burdett-Coutts* (selected and edited by Edgar Johnson, Duell, Sloan & Pearce, 1952).

Dickens's Journalism:

Dickens made three collections of his journalistic work, *Sketches by Boz* (1836), *Reprinted Pieces* (1858) and *The Uncommercial Traveller* (1861). Each of these has been reprinted many times. In addition, B. W. Matz collected two volumes of *Miscellaneous Papers* for the 1908 "National" edition which have been most recently reissued by Kraus Reprints. Harry Stone's two-volume *Charles Dickens' Uncollected Writings from Household Words, 1850–1859* (Indiana University Press, 1968) is essential for its meticulous picture of Dickens as editor and collaborator. Both *Household Words* and *All the Year Round* in their entirety bear Dickens's impress as well as his name on every page. They are indexed in Anne Lohrli *Household Words: Table of Contents, List of Contributors and their Contributions* (University of Toronto Press, 1973) and Ann Oppenlander *Dickens' All the Year Round: An Index* (Whitston Pub. Co., 1983).

Criticism:

R. C. Churchill *A Bibliography of Dickensian Criticism 1836–1975* (Garland Publishing, 1975) is a useful guide. Of particular interest in this context are Philip Collins *Dickens and Crime* (St. Martin's Press, 1962) and *Dickens and Education* (St. Martin's Press, 1963); Humphry House *The Dickens World* (2nd ed., Oxford University Press, 1942); Norris Pope *Dickens and Charity* (Columbia University Press, 1978); and Michael Slater *Dickens and Women* (Stanford University Press, 1983). Since 1905 *The Dickensian*, published by The Dickens Fellowship in London, has maintained a consistently high standard; there is an index by Frank T. Dunn, *The Dickensian: A Cumulative Analytical Index 1905–1974* (Humanities Press, 1976).

Background

The two volumes of *The Victorian City: Images and Realities* edited by H. J. Dyos and Michael Wolff (Routledge & Kegan Paul, 1973) contain much pertinent material, including a succinct account by Philip Collins of "Dickens and London". Also of particular interest are Gertrude Himmelfarb *The Idea of Poverty: England in the Early Industrial Age* (Alfred Knopf, 1983); Sheila Smith *The Other Nation: The Poor in English Novels of the 1840s and 1850s* (Oxford University Press, 1980); Raymond Williams *The Country and the City* (Oxford University Press, 1975); and Anthony S. Wohl *Endangered Lives: Public Health in Victorian Britain* (Harvard University Press, 1983). The classic *London Labour and the London Poor* by Dickens's contemporary Henry Mayhew has been reprinted in four volumes (Dover Publications, 1968) and in a one-volume selection by Victor Neuburg (Penguin, 1985).

PICTURE CREDITS

BBC Hulton Picture Library: 91
Bodleian Library, John Johnson Collection (Education 10): 92, 97
Dickens House: 6, 8, 9, 17, 28
London Library: 16, 45, 51, 52, 98, 101, 107, 151
Mansell Collection: 127
Museum of Labour History: 129, 149
Museum of London: 58, 60, 108
Punch: 21, 22, 109, 138
Victoria & Albert Museum: 7, 46, 68, 94
Wellcome Institute for the History of Medicine: 154
All other pictures are from the editors' collections

ACKNOWLEDGEMENTS

The publishers would like to thank the staffs of all the institutions listed above, and also of the Bridgeman Art Library, for their assistance in locating pictures.

For help in various ways, the editors would like to thank W. J. Fishman, Barbara Gilbert and Bernard Richards; Emma Bradford, Jane Havell and Elizabeth Loving at the Albion Press; and Dan Franklin at William Collins.

The editors would like to record their indebtedness to many scholars whose work could not always be cited directly in the text, notably those listed in "Further Reading" and the editors of the Penguin editions of Dickens's novels. They were especially thankful for the detailed and authoritative studies of Philip Collins, which have covered so much of the necessary ground so well.

INDEX